*Passage from the Raj*

# PASSAGE FROM THE RAJ

## *Story of a Family*

## *1770-1939*

Nora Naish

Champak Press

Copyright © Nora Naish 2005
First published in 2005 by Champak Press
8 River Road
Chipping Sodbury
Bristol BS37 6HQ

Distributed by Gazelle Book Services Limited
Hightown, White Cross Mills, South Rd, Lancaster
England LA1 4XS

British Library Cataloguing in Publication Data
A catalogue record for this book is available from the British Library

ISBN 0-9548323-0-2

Typeset by Amolibros, Milverton, Somerset
This book production has been managed by Amolibros
Printed and bound by Advance Book Printing, Oxford, England

# Preface

When I began to think of writing a book about my childhood and family growing up under the Raj, I came across Graham Greene's observation that the best source of material for writers was the mine of their own childhood. That encouraged me to start digging into my personal mine. It is not as easy to do as you might think. Falls of rock (hitherto unknown facts, some possibly libellous) may block the shaft; irrelevant bright pebbles (new details suddenly coming to light) may sideline the main work; clouds of dust (uncertainties) may obscure the way. I had, too, to consider the question of truth. What is it? Memory is selective; art even more so. Where in memory does truth exist? I am not the first to ask myself that question. The great naturalist of the human psyche, who shut himself into a cork-lined room impermeable to sounds to protect himself from interruption and distractions while he pondered the problem, tells us in *Time Regained* that what we want to write is already there in memory, but we must delve down deep into consciousness to explore, and will there discover it: 'reality as we have felt it to be...' That truth Proust recorded in his life's work *Remembrance of Things Past.*

My own intellect and talents being so small in comparison with Proust's to go to such extremes of dedication in the cause of Art would have been unproductive; but I did sit down to some long solitary sessions of silent thought about the past.

Childhood memories form a chain of islands. History and Time are the latitude and longitude in which they lie. These are the only frail certainties I have. These disconnected islands in the archipelago of memory slip away from the solid mainland of remembered adult life and disappear into an ocean of oblivion that is infancy.

A series of ferry boats, the whys and wherefores of events, has to be built and boarded for the necessary island hopping; a spool has to be run out to connect one island to the next: the thread of interwoven memory and imagination to lead me through our common collective conscious/unconscious experience until at last the totally unremembered place is reached.

But over this wine dark sea of the unknown past come sailing towards me ships from India carrying my Prinsep ancestors with their cargoes of tea and opium and chintz sold long ago, together with letters, diaries, and paintings of distant places they have seen, revealing to me the people they were, with their sayings all ripened on the family grapevine. From even further away and longer ago scraps of recorded history tell of my Daniell ancestors marching into battles. Their family crest of a rather mangy-looking dog is emblazoned with three words: *Esse quam videre.* It is impossible for me to translate the lucid brevity of the Latin original into our multi-layered, multi-rooted modern English. The best I can offer is: 'Better to be in the thick of things than to look on.'

I have enjoyed a long and busy life; I have studied records made by ancestors who all lived in the thick of things. But to write this book I have had to step back and look on.

What is the past after all but a glance over the shoulder? A pile of papers, the fading image of a face, a hand waving, distant voices and ourselves remembered.

# Acknowledgements

Many people in different ways have helped me to write this book. I would specially like to thank: Yashu Amlani, Maxine Balls, Fr Bruce Bradley S J, Dr Om Prakash Kejariwal, Diana McLeod, Elizabeth Murray, Alice Naish, Robert Naish, Jimmy O'Toole, Bob Ruthven and Alan Woolley for research, H Bhattachariya for his photograph of the tomb of Ramohun Roy, Hilary Johnson and Sarah Molloy for professional editorial comment, and for the loan of family papers and the gift of personal information Linda Collins, Mary Furness, Barbara Gray, Diana MacLeod, Almora Murdoch, Henry Reid and Christina Vuillin. I would also like to thank all those who have helped me with their kindly interest and encouragement.

Permission to quote has been granted by Christopher Hibbert to quote from *The Great Mutiny*; by Dr Om Prakash Kejariwal to quote from *The Prinseps of India: Indian Archives, 1993, Vol XLI;* by Garth Hewitt to quote Richard Powers' *Epitaphs from The Old Lad,* and the Society of Authors, Literary Representative of the Virginia Woolf Estate, to quote from "Sketch of the Past".

# List of illustrations

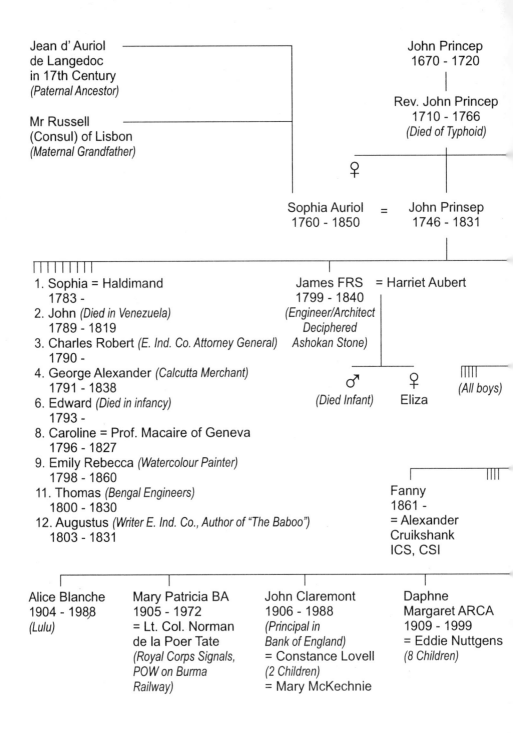

Jean d' Auriol
de Langedoc
in 17th Century
*(Paternal Ancestor)*

Mr Russell
(Consul) of Lisbon
*(Maternal Grandfather)*

John Princep
1670 - 1720

Rev. John Princep
1710 - 1766
*(Died of Typhoid)*

♀

Sophia Auriol  =  John Prinsep
1760 - 1850         1746 - 1831

1. Sophia = Haldimand
   1783 -
2. John *(Died in Venezuela)*
   1789 - 1819
3. Charles Robert *(E. Ind. Co. Attorney General)*
   1790 -
4. George Alexander *(Calcutta Merchant)*
   1791 - 1838
6. Edward *(Died in infancy)*
   1793 -
8. Caroline = Prof. Macaire of Geneva
   1796 - 1827
9. Emily Rebecca *(Watercolour Painter)*
   1798 - 1860
11. Thomas *(Bengal Engineers)*
    1800 - 1830
12. Augustus *(Writer E. Ind. Co., Author of "The Baboo")*
    1803 - 1831

James FRS  = Harriet Aubert
1799 - 1840
*(Engineer/Architect
Deciphered
Ashokan Stone)*

♂
*(Died Infant)*

♀
Eliza

⊓⊓⊓
*(All boys)*

Fanny
1861 -
= Alexander
Cruikshank
ICS, CSI

Alice Blanche
1904 - 1988
*(Lulu)*

Mary Patricia BA
1905 - 1972
= Lt. Col. Norman
de la Poer Tate
*(Royal Corps Signals,
POW on Burma
Railway)*

John Claremont
1906 - 1988
*(Principal in
Bank of England)*
= Constance Lovell
*(2 Children)*
= Mary McKechnie

Daphne
Margaret ARCA
1909 - 1999
= Eddie Nuttgens
*(8 Children)*

*(Surgeon in Tamworth)*

*(Eton Scholar, Scholar of Balliol
Headmaster Tamworth Grammar School)*

♀ ♀  *(Both Died of Typhoid 1766)*

*(Calcutta Merchant 1771 - 1788
Introduced Indigo planting to India
Independent MP Queensborough 1802)*

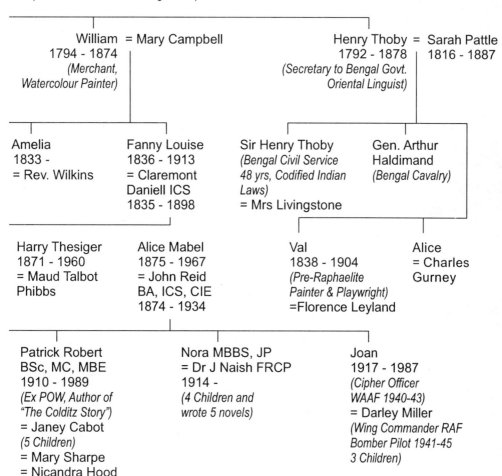

William = Mary Campbell
1794 - 1874
*(Merchant,
Watercolour Painter)*

Henry Thoby = Sarah Pattle
1792 - 1878 | 1816 - 1887
*(Secretary to Bengal Govt.
Oriental Linguist)*

Amelia
1833 -
= Rev. Wilkins

Fanny Louise
1836 - 1913
= Claremont
Daniell ICS
1835 - 1898

Sir Henry Thoby
*(Bengal Civil Service
48 yrs, Codified Indian
Laws)*
= Mrs Livingstone

Gen. Arthur
Haldimand
*(Bengal Cavalry)*

Harry Thesiger
1871 - 1960
= Maud Talbot
Phibbs

Alice Mabel
1875 - 1967
= John Reid
BA, ICS, CIE
1874 - 1934

Val
1838 - 1904
*(Pre-Raphaelite
Painter & Playwright)*
=Florence Leyland

Alice
= Charles
Gurney

Patrick Robert
BSc, MC, MBE
1910 - 1989
*(Ex POW, Author of
"The Colditz Story")*
= Janey Cabot
*(5 Children)*
= Mary Sharpe
= Nicandra Hood

Nora MBBS, JP
= Dr J Naish FRCP
1914 -
*(4 Children and
wrote 5 novels)*

Joan
1917 - 1987
*(Cipher Officer
WAAF 1940-43)*
= Darley Miller
*(Wing Commander RAF
Bomber Pilot 1941-45
3 Children)*

# PART ONE

## *Growing Up Under The Raj*

The bungalow built long ago by the East India Company for its Rice Collector in Patna had verandahs on all sides. The north, being the coolest, was reserved for my parents, the east for the administrative offices and for the colonnaded entrance, arrived at by a flight of wide steps. From here an avenue of very old banyan trees led to ironwork gates beyond which was a dirt road to the Ganges, the great river of holiness and healing, whose brown waters glistening in the hot sun less than half a mile away carried off the sins of those who washed in it, along with alluvial mud, an occasional dead dog, or some half-cremated human body swept away from one of the burning-ghats on it banks. On the south and west and hottest sides of the house the servants worked, cooking, washing and scrubbing, and heating water slowly on charcoal fires for the evening bathtubs. The house servants lived around the edge of the compound, but clerks and secretaries came into work on foot, or bicycle, or rickshaw from the city of Patna.

In 1920, by the time I was six years old, I already understood some of the social divisions and the pecking order in my complex multi-racial multi-religious hierarchical world. At the top my father, a big handsome man with a high forehead and well-shaped nose above a short moustache, sat at an enormous desk of Burmese teak, beside him Babu Chaudhury, his Bengali secretary, who was small and thin, with diffident, apologetic hands. He was often laughed at by my parents on account of the peculiar English in some of his letters:—'I thank you from the bottom of my heart, and from my wife's bottom also...', but possessed a sense of humour and an astringent snicker, which when adroitly used could most effectively dissolve pomposity.

Behind my father, and screened off by a plaster-and-lath partition, sat the *punkah wallah*, who came low in the order of things, crouched as he was cross-legged on the floor, sometimes asleep because of the heat, or perhaps through sheer boredom, and sometimes, when he'd been shouted at, actively pulling the ropes that flapped the fringed folds of cloth hanging from the ceiling, to create a small stir of air in the torpor of noon.

My father never slept during the siesta hour, nor did he escape the oppressive summer by going up north to Simla for its season of trying-to-be-an-English-County in the Himalayas. He relished the work of the Indian Civil Service, its variety and challenges, but he dreaded the demands of its social life. Perhaps the seeds of that agoraphobia that later took possession of his days were sown in Patna. He found most of the people he met at social gatherings, and the conversation exchanged there, trivial and boring, certainly not interesting enough to persuade him to overcome the shyness amounting to awkwardness he always suffered. My mother moved with confidence among these English men and women who all shared similar middle-class roots and could fraternise easily over their whisky *chota-pegs*; but he was a bit of a country boy from Ireland. His roots had grown in a different soil; he stood at the edge of the group and knew that, though he saw himself as more perceptive and cleverer than the rest, he would never be fully accepted in the club. For her part, Mabel, though she loved the bright lights, voices of women a little sharpened by excitement, the sound of three beats to the bar struck up by the regimental band to announce the opening of a waltz, and, above all, simply to dance, knew his feelings, and bowed to his wishes. So she stayed with him in the heat of the plains while he toiled away at something called Administration, and at Rice Collection, which I understood better. I had seen the Gola, a great storage vat built long ago under the supervision of Warren Hastings himself to save rice in times of plenty. It had a spiral staircase climbing its round surface, up which coolies ran with sacks of rice that they tipped into a wide mouth at the top. At ground level there was a wooden door through which rice was to be extracted in times of famine. That was another joke, because the door had been constructed to open inwards, which would prove impossible against the great weight of rice inside. What will they do, I wondered in alarm, when they are dying of hunger and can't get the rice out. Ayesha, my Ayah, who was Moslem, answered briefly, 'Smash it with an axe.'

I looked at the door nervously. 'Is it where Daddy collects his rice?' I asked.

'Long, long time Sahibs collect rice,' she replied. 'Now it is taxes.'

'What's taxess?'

'Rupees and annas.'

Ayesha always answered shortly, and often crossly.

We passed a group of skinny, naked children playing at the roadside, their pot-bellies protruding above matchstick legs.

'Why are their tummies so big?' I asked.

'Because they are hungry.'

'Why can't they have rice from the Gola then?'

She made a clicking noise with her tongue. 'Because they are not hungry enough,' she said.

It was a mystery to me how their tummies were so big when they were empty; but I didn't press Ayah for more information. She was fat, and didn't like taking me and my little sister Dodie for walks, and we were walking. She didn't like moving about in the heat; and it was very hot.

Another reason my father worked so hard was that he was trying to introduce land reforms, as well as implement the franchise in the state of Bihar and Orissa. 'One day,' he told me, 'Indians will govern their own country; and we must show them how to do it.' He sighed, adding, 'I feel like Sisyphus.'

'What's Sissy Fuss?'

'He was a man who had to roll a heavy stone up a steep hill, and every time he got it to the top it rolled down and he had to start all over again.'

'What a silly man!'

Daddy laughed at that. He was a serious man, and seldom laughed. I never saw him during the day, but sometimes in the cool of the evening when he sat on the verandah sipping his whisky *chota-peg* and smoking a cigarette to ward off mosquitoes I was allowed to climb on his knee and talk to him, or read to him from my book with big printed words.

Bearer came to refill his glass. He was a tall Moslem from the north. He wore a long brown coat over white trousers, and a wide red cummerbund round his ample middle. His brown feet were bare and made no sound as he moved gravely round the house. He was the head servant, second in authority only to my mother, and sometimes, when she couldn't hear what he was saying, above even her. Moslems, I knew, didn't think too highly of women.

'Will you rule India one day?' I asked him.

'If the Sahib says so. But not I—' He sighed.

'Why do people sigh when they talk about ruling India?'

'It is difficult. Perhaps it will never be.'

The Hindu servant sitting cross-legged on the floor, polishing my mother's silver rose-bowl in his lap, looked up quickly. 'If the Sahib says so,' he said. And suddenly he laughed, upon which Bearer made a small clicking movement with his fingers, and a tutting sound with his tongue; and the Hindu polisher bent his

6

head, breathed on the silver, rubbing it vigorously, and said no more.

Mummy was second in importance on the compound, because although only a woman she was the *memsahib*. She was small, and moved quickly; she had lots of fair hair piled up on top of her head, and very bright blue eyes. She had elegant slim ankles, 'a dancer's feet', Daddy said. Her voice was forthright and clear, and she laughed often. There was nothing devious about her, no feminine wiles; she didn't like frills and flounces on her clothes, and she never smelt of any perfume more sophisticated than eau de Cologne. She was transparently honest; you could trust my mother. Daddy told me she was brave, although she'd been nervous at first about driving with him in the new car.

'She was brave enough to marry me,' he said.

They exchanged glances over my head and smiled.

'Why did she have to be brave to marry you?' I asked. I found out why only gradually over the years.

My mother who was born in India in 1875 and christened Alice Mabel, was the eighth child of Clarmont Daniell and Fanny Louise, *née* Prinsep. The ancestors of both her parents had travelled back and forth between London and Calcutta since the eighteenth century, the Daniells as East India Company merchants, and later civil servants, the Prinseps as entrepreneurs, merchants, and engineers before being civil servants. The first Prinsep in India was John, son of a clergyman who was also headmaster of Tamworth Grammar School. When John was twenty-five, eager for adventure and determined to make money, he knew India was the place for him. So, ignoring warnings from well-meaning friends about the dangers to life and health, and the temptations to his soul he would face in that tropical climate he sailed on the long route round the Cape in the Rodney in 1770. It was a full century before the opening of the Suez Canal, in the days before steamships ploughed their way across oceans, and before refrigeration was invented. Cows were stabled on board sailing ships, and had to be milked for the passengers' breakfast tea and porridge, and as the weeks went by sheep had to be slaughtered to provide mutton for dinner. So no doubt there was plenty of work to do below decks for a young man travelling steerage as he was. He arrived penniless in Calcutta, but was able to borrow £10 from a fellow passenger to pay for his first meal and accommodation on land.

He had obtained through the patronage of a landed squire of Bicester, in Oxfordshire, who employed his father as tutor to his sons, a place in the East India Company's militia, but had no intention of remaining in that position, and soon bought himself out. He must have been innovative as he'd invented, while working for a linen-draper in London's Cheapside, a method of printing on cotton to produce a cheaper version of the popular Chinese fabric, chintz. He now began printing Indian calico with indigo dye, and obtained a contract to supply the East India Co with 'chintz' for ten years. He was soon involved in all sorts of business schemes: buying and renting plots of land for the planting of indigo, opening a ferry service across the river at Pulta, near his 'chintz' factory.

In 1780 he proposed to Warren Hastings that John Co (colloquial name for the East India Company) should have a proper coinage instead of the rough cut and stamped bits of metal, and even shells previously used, and so secured a grant to copper mines, and was appointed Superintendent of Copper Coinage. At about this time John Co were in deep financial trouble, having run out of money to pay their soldiers, who were deserting as mercenaries to the army of a neighbouring Rajah. Prinsep's fertile brain came up with the idea of meeting the Company's expenses by selling 'grants' on paper of money to be paid with interest at a later date.

The idea was successfully put into practice; it was the first time such Bonds were issued in India.

A painting by Zoffany of a group of *nabobs* (one smoking a hookah) looking relaxed and happy with their ladies in a garden, while a couple of discreet Indian servants stand among trees in the background, shows John Prinsep seated near the charming girl, Sophia Auriol, he is about to marry.[1] He is a handsome fellow, smiling and confident, with no doubts about his place in the world. He left India in 1788 having made a fortune of £40,000, (equivalent to about £1 million today), perhaps sometimes by methods that with moral hindsight we might condemn as not entirely scrupulous; but having made the acquaintance of many Indians, and seen at first hand how the poor lived in Bengal, he channelled the exuberant energy of his youth into more altruistic activity in middle-age. He was still a merchant, but he became interested in politics as well. From his house at 147 Leadenhall Street in the City, in the days when Islington was a village in the country (to which his younger children walked with their nurses to visit a local 'Bun House' and spend their pocket-money pennies on delectable buns), he wrote letters to the *Morning Chronicle*, signing himself Gurreeb Doss, Servant of the Poor, while waiting for his imports of rice and tea to arrive in the port of London. He wrote about the injustices of land tenure in India, and in support of Indian cotton weavers; but chiefly he argued for free trade and the abolition of the East India Company's monopoly. In 1802, when he was fifty-six, he became an Independent MP for Queensborough, and set about fighting in parliament for Indian causes. 'It was on Indian affairs that Prinsep embarrassed the Government', a historian of the House of Commons has noted.[2] The East India Company's monopoly of trade and shipping was not abolished till 1833, the year after his death.

Although his elder sons were sent to public schools (Toby to Harrow where he carved his name on the back of a pew in the chapel), the boys seem to have received much of their education at home from governesses and tutors, among them an expert carpenter, whose lessons were eagerly absorbed, so that when they were little more than children they were making complicated models of ships, castles, and churches in wood. William, his seventh child, was seized by a love of painting early in life when, on visiting a great mansion in the city with his father, he looked upwards and saw on the ceiling a whole world of beautiful gods and goddesses. He was so entranced that he lay on his back to stare at them, and for several days could think of nothing else; and somehow these images of colourful lives got mixed up with his ideas of heaven. He was soon trying to draw them. There must have been a good drawing master in the house, because all the children, including William's sister Emily, learned to draw well; and James later studied architecture.

John Prinsep was Mabel's maternal great-grandfather. Seven of his eight sons worked in India, Charles as Advocate-General in Calcutta, Toby, who spoke several Indian languages, and was described by the Governor-General Lord Auckland as knowing 'more about India than all the rest of the service put together', and became Chief Secretary to the Government of India, and Thomas as a Bengal Engineer. He surveyed and mapped the swampy Sunderbans, notorious for killing off Europeans, and survived long enough to supervise the digging of a canal joining the area to the Hooghli river, and to paint some good watercolours of his surroundings as well.

Mabel's grandfather, William, who was an independent merchant in Calcutta, was a gifted painter, and a tender-hearted, humorous man, who has left his descendants a memoir of his life as well as many charming pictures; but he was less successful in business than his father, and indeed went bankrupt once.

At the age of eleven he had been put into the Royal Navy as a Midshipman. He was rather small for his age, a sensitive and perhaps a timid boy in an era when boys were even rougher and more inclined to torment each other than they are today, so it is not surprising that he was teased, pushed around and made generally miserable by his fellow Midshipmen. He was rescued by the Captain who had noticed that the child could draw well, and who used his talent to draw maps. While sitting drawing maps in the Captain's Cabin William felt safe and happy, until, with a certain amount of string-pulling by his father he was extracted from the Navy. This happened after the battle of Trafalgar and the death of Nelson, when William's ship was sent to take part in the procession of vessels accompanying the *Victory* as it carried the body of the nation's hero back to Portsmouth for a state funeral.

William was in his early twenties when the family lived in Bristol at 7 The Mall, Clifton. He didn't have much idea what to do with his life at that age. Among the jobs he tried his hand at was that of salesman to a Bristol wine merchant. He had to travel all over the West Country on horseback with sample bottles in his saddlebags. What the wine tasted like after all the shaking they must have endured on the rough rural roads can only be guessed at.

His father was acquainted with a gentleman who owned a large estate near Bristol, and whose son, a lad not yet twenty, one day shot and killed a poacher on his land. The young man was terribly distressed and frightened when he realised what he'd done; and his parents were distraught. They could try to compensate the unfortunate wife of the dead man, but they couldn't save from the gallows their son who had committed murder. What could they do? He must be smuggled out of the country somehow; and William offered to smuggle him.

The two of them boarded the next coach to London, where without delay they caught the coach to Dover, and the packet-boat to Le Havre, where they put up at a small inn. William, whose French was good, told the innkeeper that his friend was

11

ill, and would need complete rest and quiet in a private room. There the young man hid himself and waited, while every day William walked to the port and around the harbour enquiring if any ships from New York had come in. After five days a boat arrived whose captain was willing, for a fee of £5, to carry a passenger to New York, no questions asked. And so the young man sailed off to the land of the free, whose arms were willing to embrace the hunted, all those running from poverty, tyranny, unwanted wives, creditors and the hangman's noose. 'Freedom,' says an old Chinese proverb, 'is the distance between the hunter and the hunted.' None wider than the Atlantic Ocean.

William's brother-in-law, Mr Haldimand, a wealthy Swiss business man who had married William's eldest sister Sophia, was impressed by this exploit. He thought it showed that William was of the stuff needed to make an independent East India merchant. So Haldimand offered him a place in the Silk Trade for which he would have to travel to India to buy raw silk. He was, however, sworn to secrecy as to his mission, because the East India Company, which held a monopoly on silk, would refuse him permission to travel in their territories if they knew his purpose.

William was first sent to Carr and Dodson's Winding and Throwing Mill near Waltham Cross to learn about the work. It was all done by 200 little girls who sang hymns as they worked under the eye of their Methodist employer, 'sometimes very prettily in parts', in which William joined. On finishing his apprenticeship he gave the girls 'a holiday feast for my fellow labourers', and received from Mr Carr a bible to read on the voyage out.

All this time his sister Sophia was secretly cutting and stitching an outfit suitable for him to wear in a tropical climate. He seems to have acclimatised fairly easily. No doubt his days in Calcutta were made pleasant by the painter Chinnery, from whom he took lessons. He was soon sketching the strange and colourful scenes around him. He was also enjoying musical evenings, learning to play an old harp given him by a lady who was returning to England, and playing the flute to the piano accompaniment provided by a Scottish girl, Mary Campbell, whom in 1822 he married. She stands examining a drawing by William in Chinnery's charming painting of them, now in a museum in Hong Kong.

As to business he didn't stick to Silk, but in time diversified into various trades with various partners. One of the mistakes his company made was to insure the lives of young Englishmen in India without properly assessing the risks. Such was the loss of life in those days that there was a disastrous outflow of capital to young widows who made claims on the firm. This probably added to the speed with which he fell into bankruptcy, when a partner in William Palmer's and the bank collapsed along with six other Calcutta 'Agencies'. He had to sell his house and all he possessed, including his wife's jewellery. (His brothers bought back Mary's 'trinkets' for her.) Eventually he recovered with the help of friends and brothers.

Was his conscience too tender for the times? He has recorded how he once spent the greater part of one night arguing the pros and cons of the opium trade with a friend from Penang. Was it morally wrong though so profitable? Well, it had to be lucrative to justify the dangers traders faced, what with that poor sailor being crucified when caught selling it on Chinese soil... . And of course the Chinese must have the stuff, whatever laws their emperor decreed against it. And if we didn't sell it, the French and Dutch would. There were those who said that encouraging the Indian peasant to grow poppies, and even indigo, prevented his growing enough rice to feed himself; there were others who said the juice of the poppy seed made more money for the peasant than rice did, so he was eager to grow poppies. Someone referred to De Quincey's *Confessions of an Opium Eater.* William remembered reading it when it first came out in serial form. It made quite a furore and everybody was talking about it. Well, no doubt the drug expanded the imagination of that young writer, and helped him to make a bit of money out of his dreams, but nobody ever thought the habit of taking opium for pleasure was anything but reprehensible. So was it any better for the Chinese? He'd never liked the trade himself, but Dwarkanath Tagore, his friend as well as his partner, actually relished the danger of it. He kept within the law by anchoring his ship outside Chinese waters, and selling to Chinamen whose junks approached him by night. It was they, poor devils, who took the greater risk. And Dwarkanath was certainly making money. He was also giving away large sums to be distributed among the poor of Calcutta. Queen Victoria awarded him a medal in recognition of his philanthropy.

One day his wealth (though William could not have foreseen such a future for it) would enable his grandson Rabindranath Tagore to be educated in England, to study at Oxford, and to write the poetry that later brought him and his nation the Nobel prize for literature in 1929.[3]

William came home for good during the First Opium War.

Fanny Louise was his second daughter. She was a gentle, pious, sentimental girl. An early photograph from the 1850s shows her leaning soulfully against her elder sister, Amelia, who married Rev Arthur Wilkins. Fanny Louise hoped that she too would find a good kind clergyman for a husband. Meanwhile she helped in charitable works among the parish poor, always plentifully with us, went sketching with her father, and sang with her mother at the piano. It has come down on the family grapevine that she had a wonderful soprano voice and could not only reach top C but could produce it clearly and sweetly. And William no doubt added to the music-making with his flute.

In 1854 when Fanny Louise was eighteen they were living in London at 8 Hyde Park Place West, near enough for her to visit Little Holland House, Holland Park, where her distinguished uncle

Toby Prinsep lived with his wife Sarah. There Fanny could meet her cousins Henry, Val, Arthur and Alice on Sunday afternoons, when Sarah held open house. Sarah was one of the Pattle sisters famous for their beauty and their artistic temperament; and to her parties came artists, poets, writers and even the occasional politician, Disraeli among them. The chief attraction, apart from the easy-going atmosphere of the house, was Watts, the great Victorian painter-sage, whom Sarah housed and cosseted for thirty years. He was using her son Arthur as his model for a painting of Galahad in search of the Holy Grail, while Tennyson was preparing to publish his *Idylls of the King*.

Virginia Woolf, who was Sarah's great-niece, has described those garden parties of her mother's girlhood, the image gleaned, as she herself was not yet born, from conversations with many relatives who had been there:

'I think of it as a summer afternoon world... . Long windows open onto the lawn. Through them comes a stream of ladies in crinolines and little straw hats; they are attended by gentlemen in peg-top trousers and whiskers... . Tea tables with great bowls of strawberries and cream are scattered about the lawn. They are "presided over" by some of the six lovely sisters, who do not wear crinolines but are robed in splendid Venetian draperies; they sit enthroned and talk with foreign emphatic gestures...to the eminent men, rulers of India, statesmen, poets, painters. My mother comes out of the window wearing that striped silk dress buttoned at the throat...that appears in the photograph[4]...and there she stands silent with her plate of strawberries and cream... . The sound of music also comes from those long low rooms where the great Watts pictures hang; Joachim playing the violin; also the sound

15

of a voice reading poetry – Uncle Thoby would read his translations from the Persian poets.'[5]

Toby Prinsep, William's elder brother, had returned from an eventful life in India with a fortune of £50,000. He was now a Director of the East India Co, and attended meetings of the directors at East India House in Leadenhall Street in the City, and gave advice on Indian affairs, for which he was paid a salary of £1,500 a year, so he could well afford to indulge Sarah's passion for entertaining the famous.

Not all her visitors saw her parties through a golden Tennysonian glow. Elizabeth Barrett Browning reacted sharply against 'the new fashionable London entertainment' because it was impossible to be quiet there: 'People tear us in pieces, Robert and me.'[6] In other words they were lionised. This didn't stop others. Trollope came, and used Toby, who had been trying unsuccessfully to enter parliament, as his model for the MP Phineas Finn in the novel of that name, and Sarah as Madame Max Goesler, whose Sunday entertaining he describes: 'There is a Bohemian flavour of picnic about it which, if it does not come up to the rich gusto of real wickedness, makes one fancy that one is on the border of that delightful region in which there is none of the constraint of custom...where men and women say what they like and do what they like.'[7]

Virginia Pattle, the most beautiful of the sisters, was often to be seen, followed always by a flock of adoring men, not all young, among them Thackeray. Watts had painted her while Fanny Louise was still in the schoolroom; and when the portrait was hung in the Royal Academy it caused such excitement that a barrier had to be built around it to keep the crowds at a safe distance. The painting made her so famous that, like film stars of a later era, she was sometimes mobbed in the streets; and when it was known she was at Little Holland House a crowd collected at the gate to see her leave, though on these occasions she usually escaped by the back door. All this didn't deter Viscount Eastnor, who'd fallen in love with her portrait, from pursuing her till he met and married her. A few years later he succeeded to his earldom, and Virginia became Countess Somers. This indeed was a step up the social ladder for a daughter of James Pattle, whom the Prinseps had known in India as Jim Blazes, 'The Biggest Liar in India'.

It must have been exciting for Fanny to meet such celebrities, especially the artists. Watts, nicknamed 'Signor', was regarded with awe. It was an honour to be permitted entry to his studio and hear him speak so modestly about his work, so nobly about his ideals. He seldom ventured into the outside world; he was a recluse who let the world come to him. He usually had one or two society ladies in tow, from whom, protesting that he laboured for the love of Art and not for Money, he extracted substantial sums for painting their portraits. He sought always to depict the beautiful, and believed his symbolist paintings might exalt the soul of the viewer, and even perhaps purify the depraved. He even went so far as to marry his very young and very pretty model, Ellen Terry, who came from a family of actors and actresses, in order to remove her 'from the temptations and abominations of the Stage'.[8] He was forty-six and she sixteen when they married, but it took no more than a year for her to size him up, and leave him and Little Holland House behind her, before returning to her sisters and the more robust atmosphere of the theatre she'd been brought up in.

It would have been a thrill too to see Ruskin, the famous art critic and champion of the Pre-Raphaelite brotherhood, and later Val's friend Edward Burne-Jones, whom in her motherly way Aunt Sarah took into her house and nursed through an illness. Fanny Louise had always admired the Pre-Raphaelites, especially for their more religious paintings. She did too love tea and croquet on the lawn. And her cousins were so handsome! All this romantic heart-palpitating stuff must have agitated a girl like her. But where in this social whirl could she find the good kind husband of her dreams? Clergymen did not, it seems, frequent Aunt Sarah's salons.

She confided her doubts to her father, pouring out her scruples about the worldly atmosphere of social life. And did not balls and parties stimulate frivolous, even wicked thoughts? And should she not renounce these pleasures? William replied with a charming letter written from Esher, Surrey, where he was busy painting his hostess's house:

'I would not for the world dear girl seek to lead you into anything which your conscience tells you is wrong, but...even in...a quiet tea party there may be more of wrong than in the exhilaration of the dance...[If] all were to act upon your principle...social life would become as sombre and pharisaical as in the days of Cromwell when to wear a pleated ruff was looked upon as an abomination... . Your plan if carried out fully would lead you to found a convent of sisters of Demurity and perhaps self sufficiency... . Now my idea is that a Marchioness of Malmsey or a Countess of Confectionery may be just as good in all relations of life, although in the midst of court-balls, operas, déjeuners etc. etc., as any quiet country girl in a Welsh glen who does all the good she can around her... . Before making up your mind, therefore, to this kind of separation, reflect seriously upon it. ...'

Between the lines we can read his anxiety: How on earth could he get this girl married and off his hands if she didn't meet suitors, and where on earth could she meet suitable suitors except at social gatherings, especially balls?

In time the term bohemian attached to the Holland Park circle did begin to assume a rather darker meaning than the one attached to the loose flowing dresses worn there, the informality and easy mixing of the sexes that went on during tea and croquet on the lawn, and the unstilted conversation and free and frequent laughter in the drawing room. Rumours began to circulate about Millais, that he was having an adulterous affaire with Effie, wife of the great and good Ruskin; and it wasn't long before the couple eloped together. Then there were hints circulated that to Holman Hunt his model meant rather more to him than an image on his canvas; and as to Rosetti–! Voices dropped at the mention of him. And to crown the misdeeds of the whole sorry decade was that dreadful business, so publicly flaunted by Dickens, of his repudiation of the wife of twenty-two years who had borne him eleven children. Val was a visitor at Dickens' new home, where his daughter Kate kept house for him after the separation, and was to be seen too much and far too openly in her company after her own marriage went awry. But Fanny Louise escaped untainted by all this scandal; she was safe in India by then. She had fallen in love and married in 1860, not a clergyman, but a dashing young man in the Indian Civil Service.

Clarmont Daniell was born in Macau in 1835, his father being then in the East India Co's China trade. After school at Rugby, and the East India College, Haileybury, Clarmont Daniell joined the Bengal Civil Service in 1855, but during the Mutiny two years later was suddenly turned into a soldier when he had to defend Agra against rebellious *sepoys* (the Freedom Fighters of our era), and received a bullet wound in his jaw. He returned home a hero, accepting as his due the adulation of Fanny Louise, and married her. He became a member of the reformed Indian Civil Service after the Mutiny, when the Crown took control of affairs in India.

The first Daniell to set foot in England was a de Anyers from Normandy, who crossed the Channel with William the Conqueror. Having survived to answer the roll call after the Battle of Hastings he was rewarded with land in Cheshire. A further gift of land was awarded to his descendants by another Prince for courage on another battlefield.

'The Manor (of Lyme) was given by King Richard II to Margaret...daughter and heiress of Sir Thomas Daniers of Bradley, Knight. This brave knight had taken the Chamberlain Tankerville prisoner at the Battle of Cressy, and relieved the banner of the Black Prince, for which service the Prince granted him an annuity of 40 marks out of the Manor of Frodsham to him and his heirs with lands of £20 per annum...of Hanley in Macclesfield Forest.'[9]

Later generations added to the family possessions by judicious marriages with land-endowed maidens. But all the acres they acquired were not enough to support them, for the Daniells were a fertile lot. So by the eighteenth century they had to go into trade to forage further. Clarmont's grandfather had been a director of the East India Company, a *nabob* who had made a large fortune for his large family of fifteen children. James Daniell had married Jane Anna Le Geyt, a highborn lady claiming descent from Scottish nobility. Whether this made it necessary to move in the highest society, or whether the young couple just had expensive tastes, much of the family fortune was spent during the Regency. It was said later that money had been lent to the Prince Regent, or perhaps given in the expectation of favours. The main favour received was not of great value to the next generation of seventeen children. It was the honour bestowed on James Frederick Nugent of being a Page in Waiting, and on his sister Aurora May of being permitted to strew herbs before the new King George IV at his coronation. That was before the invention of photography; but a marble bust of Aurora shows a beautiful girl.

Fanny Louise brought to her marriage with 'her own dear Clare' a loving heart, a high soprano voice, and an excessively pious disposition, but very little money. She had a few shocks waiting for her in India. She had been brought up to believe that a true Christian gentleman was always courteous to all, regardless of class or caste, so she was horrified by Clare's rudeness to the servants, and worst of all by his swearing! When she gently tried to remonstrate she learned that she herself was in many ways a disappointment to him. And then she discovered that dear Clare had learned the spending habits of his forbears, and had debts of £900 (over £30,000 today). She couldn't imagine how such a large sum could ever be paid off; but she trusted in God, and said her prayers.[10] Unfortunately Clare probably never did clear himself of debt. At any rate by the time their youngest girl Alice Mabel left St Michael's Hall School in Brighton the cash needed to launch her on a London season in a manner fitting a Daniell daughter was simply not available.

This didn't worry Mabel in the least. She wasn't interested in marrying well, nor in marrying at all. She cared nothing for fashion, balls, flirtations, and all the girlish hopes and disappointments, little secrets, coded messages in *billets doux*, the thrills and blushes, the little joys and sudden tears of adolescent love that her friends seemed to enjoy or suffer from in the 1890s; she read very few of the romances they eagerly devoured to fill the idle hours between 'coming-out' and wedding day. The only thing she cared about was music.

She had been fortunate in her piano teacher at school, Fraulein Ida Stothman, who had once been court pianist to his Royal Highness the Duke of Mecklenberg-Schwerin, and in M Rene Ortmans, who gave her violin lessons. They were both professional musicians of sufficient standing to appear in public concerts given in the Royal Pavilion Brighton and in the Clarence Room of the Hotel Metropole. They were also good teachers. Fraulein Stothman could be a severe critic, but she praised Mabel's work enough to encourage her to further willing effort; and, when she sat at the piano and played her pupil's pieces to show how they should be played, Mabel was transported to another more wonderful world. M Ortmans, too, was kind, even gallant to his young ladies; he liked showing them, with his own arm round their arms, how to hold the bow. For Mabel, there were never enough hours in the day for practising both instruments. Music was to her 'the life of the soul'. What she most eagerly desired was to study at the Royal Academy of Music in London.

Her father disapproved of the idea. He didn't care for serious music himself. A few hymns in church one had to put up with, and a bit of ta-ra-ra-boom-de-ay was all very well in its proper place, but all this practising on the piano, and the violin too–dammit! all that interminable Bach!–hours and hours of it, got on his nerves. And the girl had no conversation. What man in his senses would want to marry a girl who could only talk about *sforzando* (whatever that was) and Paderewski's *cantabile*?

'She did get a distinction in her French exam last term, Clare,' his wife reminded him.

'That might be of use,' he conceded, 'if she were to marry a Frenchman.'

The fact was Clare was desperate for money. He had retired from the ICS on a pension that he considered inadequate for his needs, and although all his older children were by this time off his hands he still had fees to pay for Mabel's boarding school in Brighton. He was no doubt looking forward to the day when she would leave school and find some other younger man to support her in matrimony. A penniless musical spinster was the last thing he wanted hanging round his neck. This music-mania of Mabel's was, he believed, due to that Fraulein Stothman, whom she had a schoolgirl crush on. It was all her fault. What if she had once been Court Pianist in the Duchy of Mecklenberg-

Schwerin? No doubt the townsfolk there were in the habit of genuflecting in the street to the escutcheon on the door of the Duke's carriage whenever he was driven out for an airing, but was that any reason why he, Clarmont Daniell, should bow the knee to this old Fraulein who had once tickled the ivories to amuse a German princeling? Certainly not!

Fanny Louise suggested they might live abroad, in Belgium, which would be cheaper than England, and Mabel could then attend the Conservatoire of Music in Brussels; but nothing came of it. In the winter of 1890-91 Clarmont applied for the post of secretary to some bigwig in London, which necessitated a move into lodgings while he waited to be interviewed. Mabel joined them for the Christmas holidays at 15 Cambridge Street, Hyde Park, where there was no piano for her to practise on. And she had to learn her part in Schubert's *Grande Marche*, which she was going to play as a piano duet with Fraulein Stothman at the school concert next term. She managed to find the Ladies' Industrial Club, where she could hire a piano for sixpence an hour, and thither she 'tramped' for two hours of practising every morning. Dads was kept waiting anxiously after his interview, 'as the men who arrange it will not decide'. He took Mabel out to the National Gallery, and also to a Variety Concert, hoping perhaps to help her enjoy more average pleasures, or even to share some pleasure with her. She laughed at the comic songs, but confessed to her diary: 'The music was wretchedly low, how people can compose such things I do not know… . Why is good music so little understood, so little appreciated by the English? Truly it is an unmusical country.' Elgar, the genius of her more mature appraisal, was yet to arrive upon the scene.

The next two years saw no improvement in Clare's affairs. He had not managed to find paid employment. 'All is uncertainty,' Mabel wrote. She went back to school, where she was happy; but she began to dread the holidays. Dads was not well, and often morose; she feared his anger when she had to ask him for money for a new bow for her violin, as M Ortmans said she must; she waited apprehensively for Dads to leave the house, because it was only when he was out that she dared to play her instruments; and that difficult passage in the Bach toccata needed a lot of polishing. She was afraid that from want of practising, the pieces set for holiday study were not up to the standard expected by the exacting Stothman, nor by kind M René Ortmans.

Then came the day, on January 11th 1892, when she asked her father's permission to make music her profession. She had been screwing up her courage for a long time to face him with this, her heart's desire. His answer was a simple 'no'. She pleaded with him eloquently enough to make him yield in so far as to say, 'We will see how things stand when you are twenty-five. Till then you must do as other girls do.' But how, Mabel asks her diary, when they were so poor could this be done? There could be no London season, no 'coming-out' for her such as her school friends were expecting.

The next entry in her diary is to record the Duke of Clarence's death on 14th Jan. 'National mourning. Poor Princess May! Her sweet token for the funeral: a Welsh harp in silver with 3 gilded strings – 2 broken.'[11]

By the time Mabel left school at eighteen they were living in lodgings in Westbury-on-Trym, Bristol. It was then that an aunt suggested to her the idea of trying to win a scholarship to the Royal Academy of Music.

Whatever the obstacles to her ambition she always worked at her music, and wherever she was she always managed to attend concerts. She heard several in Bristol, at the Victoria Rooms, and at the Colston Hall, where Paderewski gave a recital on 1st December 1893.

On 31st January 1894 she entered for the preliminary qualifying exam for entry to the Royal College of Music Scholarships, and passed; but in February of the same year she was eliminated at the second hurdle.

There are very few entries in her diary after this. It must have been a time of terrible disappointment, almost despair for her. She had to accept the hard fact that being a star performer at school concerts was a different thing entirely from being a professional musician in the big world. She must have remembered bitterly her evangelical headmistress, Miss Purton, criticising her for 'pride', though it was this self-confidence in her ability that had fuelled her dreams, had uplifted and carried her through an adolescence happier than it is for many girls. She had never lost sight of her goal, nor swerved from her dedication to the programme of work she set herself. Now she had to face a bleak future at home, weeks of feeling guilty dislike for her father, and worse still impatience with her mother, who had revealed to her that Clare had published at great expense to himself some book in two volumes that nobody could understand.

'What's this book about?' asked Mabel.

'Something called economics, he says.'

As Fanny Louise understood, or perhaps misunderstood it, Clare believed that in spite of the poverty seen everywhere in India it was a potentially rich country. There were, he said, vast reserves of gold being carried about idle and unused on the persons of Indian women. Why, even a poor village wife carried her gold, sometimes in substantial amounts, in the form of bangles, earrings or necklaces. If this gold could be gathered and stored in some strong-room in some Bank of India it could be loaned out for profit; it could float Indian ingenuity, enterprise and effort; it could subsidise Indian trade and make India rich; it was a way out of the poverty. That was his notion, Mother said. But how could this be done? And did he need to write a whole book about it, Mabel wondered.

'He says it's important. And so he's got himself into more debt.'

25

And that of course meant there was less likelihood than ever of Mabel's entering the Royal College of Music as a student. He couldn't afford the fees. But to publish his book... . 'He could afford to do that!' Mabel thought bitterly.[12] She had to endure too, advice from friends, Job's comforters with their proverbs and their clichés: 'It's no use crying for the moon,' and 'You must cut your coat according to your cloth.' Well, that was true in more ways than one!

Her mother must have understood something of what Mabel was going through, the painful process of adaptation to adult life, of her changed expectations, and her changing image of herself; she tried to help her daughter by visits to friends and relatives in Dorchester. Here the house Hardy had designed and built for himself, Max Gate, was of course pointed out to her. The recent publication of *Tess of the D'Urbervilles* in book form had made Hardy world-famous; he was, in modern terminology, a bestseller, in America as well as at home, and his novel had become an exciting subject of conversation at every middle-class social gathering. Could Tess really be 'pure' although she'd borne a bastard child? And was her beloved Angel Clare, idealist and moral philosopher, who spurned her when she confessed her past sin, a prig and a hypocrite? Mabel often peeped at Max Gate as she passed by, and wondered about Hardy, and laughed too, thinking of a certain ignoramus she knew, who on being shown the outside walls of Hardy's house by a proud local yokel had asked: 'Who is this Hardy?'

'Why, he be a grovellist.'

'What's a grovellist?'

'He do grovel I suppose.'

Grovelling was not something Mabel could imagine Hardy doing. A few years later he published *Jude the Obscure.* It was reviled by most of the literary critics of the day, the *Pall Mall Gazette* going so far as to rename the book 'Jude the Obscene'. Hardy was certainly disheartened by all the hostility, but he didn't grovel. He simply stopped writing novels.[13] He took to writing poetry instead, and then produced some of the most marvellous poems in our language.

They also went to see the strange tomb William Prinsep had designed and built in Bristol: strange, that is, to be standing in the Christian cemetery of Arno's Vale, since it was reminiscent of a Hindu shrine, and with a strange story attached to it. William had been home on leave in Bristol in 1833 when the Hindu reformer and prophet Raja Ramohun Roy was sent to England as envoy from the Mughal Emperor Akbar Shah II.[14] He travelled down by coach from London to visit William, and preached once in the Unitarian Church in Lewin's Mead, but sadly was taken ill suddenly during his stay and died. 'He was the noblest man I ever knew,' William said of him. Roy had preached religious tolerance, declaring that all the great religions of the world held certain beliefs and goals in common; he had spoken out against *suttee*, the burning of widows on their husbands' funeral pyres, and was far in advance of his time in advocating women's rights. The best William could do was to design a tomb fit for him. It still stands decaying in Arno's Vale cemetery; and from time to time a delegation of devotees from London descends on it to pay respects to the great Brahmin reformer.

Mabel went by train to hear Paderewski play Chopin at a concert in London; and perhaps this strengthened her determination to pursue music still. She wrote to the head of her old school in Brighton, offering herself as a pupil-teacher. Her services were accepted, at first in return for board and lodging only, but later, when she was giving sixty piano lessons a week, she was paid a salary of £70 a year, and had to pay income tax on it. To her father's intense fury this had just been raised from sixpence to a shilling in the pound; but he showed her how to fill in her return. Her parents followed her then, renting a house in Burgess Hill not many miles from St Michael's Hall. It was a happy time for her. Fraulein Stothman had by now retired, but Mabel took violin lessons from a professional violinist, George Menges, who had provided her with a few private violin pupils. She made friends with his musical family, and was soon invited to become a member of a string quartet with whom she played often at weekends. This happy period came gradually to an end with the illness of her father, for when Dads died her mother decided to move nearer to her sister Amy, who was living in Bath. So rather sadly Mabel resigned her post as teacher in order to look after her ageing mother in Weston, a village on the outskirts of that city.

Her favourite brother, Harry, who had been travelling continually all over the Middle East in the service of the Imperial Ottoman Bank, met in Jerusalem a party of Anglo-Irish tourists who were 'doing' the Holy Places. Among them was a girl, Maud Phibbs, whom he fell in love with. They corresponded by letter after she returned to Ireland, but he followed her home to Sligo, where he married her. Harry described his bride as 'splendid'. Mabel found her a rather formidable new sister-in-law, but she did have a London house where from time to time, after the prescribed year of mourning for Dads was completed, Mabel could meet Harry and his friends and enjoy a little social life.

Maud's nose, nearly as large, and certainly as commanding as the Duke of Wellington's, was able to detect the slightest whiff of *hoi polloi*, and would lift with disdain over the smallest deviation in speech, manners or appearance from what was *comme il faut*. Unfortunately, it seemed, Mabel's appearance just simply wouldn't do. To be *à la mode* in 1899 you had to have a wasp waist with a large bust above it. Mabel's shape, Maud pointed out, did not comply with the one required either at the waist or above it.

'I won't wear tight corsets,' Mabel declared. 'They give me indigestion.'

28

Maud was shocked. One had to suffer a little for the sake of fashion, you know; but Mabel was not at all abashed. She was not alone in objecting to tight corsets. Watts, no less, was President of the Anti-Tight-Lacing League. And he was still regarded as a wise man and a great artist, though his reputation as a painter was slipping a little and would fade in the coming century.

'And who,' Maud pursued, 'who is your dressmaker?' She was horrified to learn that Mabel made use of some little dressmaker in Weston nobody had ever heard of. And how much, she enquired, did Mabel allow herself per annum for dress?

'Twenty pounds a year,' said Mabel. It was what Mother paid their cook, and a bit more than she paid the housemaid. Mabel didn't admit that she was saving some of it to buy a better piano of her own. You could buy an upright Erard in a rosewood case for £60; and Paderewski himself had praised the Erard's tone.

Maud was horrified. 'You cannot dress on twenty pounds a year, you can merely clothe yourself,' she said. She drew herself up and, looking down her formidable nose at her sister-in-law, she said, 'You're getting a reputation for being strong-minded, Mabel. And it won't do, you know. No man wants a strong-minded woman for a wife.'

# References – Chapter One

1. Sophia Auriol married John Prinsep in India in 1782. She was related to the Dashwood family who own the painting by Zoffany in which she is shown sitting near John Prinsep in a garden. She was descended from the Comte d'Auriol, a French Huguenot who left Languedoc to cross the Pyrenees into Portugal in the seventeenth century.

2 Thorne, R G, *House of Commons*, Secker and Warbourg, London, 1886: p.892.

3 Kejariwal, O P, *The Prinseps of India: A Personal Quest, National Archives of India*, Vol XLII, Nos 1-2, 1993.

4 Virginia's mother, Julia Stephens (née Jackson) was much photographed by her aunt Julia Margaret Cameron, the Victorian romantic photographer, who was one of the Pattle sisters.

5 Woolf, Virginia, *Reminiscences*. Quoted by Hermione Lee in her biography of Virginia Woolf.

6 *Letters of Elizabeth Barrett Browning to her Sister*, ed. L Huxley, 1929.

7 Dakers, Caroline, *The Holland Park Circle: Artists and Victorian Society*, Yale University Press, 1999.

8 Watts in a letter to Lady Constance Leslie, quoted by Caroline Dakers in her book *The Holland Park Circle: Artists and Victorian Society*.

9 Lyson, *Magna Britannica*, Vol 2, Part 2: p727.

10 Daniell, Fanny Louise (née Prinsep), Unpublished Diary 1856-1880.

11 Princess May of Teck married her dead fiancé's brother in 1893, became Queen Mary when he was crowned George V in 1910, and is recorded in many photographs of a later date as a straight-backed full-bosomed woman wearing a toque hat.

12 These essays followed the publication by Kegan Paul Trench Trubner and Co Ltd (London, 1890) of his *Industrial Competition in Asia. An Inquiry into the Influence of Currency on the Commerce of the Empire in the East*, in which Clarmont John Daniell argued that "a stock of gold bullion wholly useless for commercial purposes" lay like buried treasure hidden and jealously guarded by Indians both rich and poor, a stock which if utilised, or loaned out in the world's money markets, would make India a powerful nation.

13 Gittings, Robert, *The Older Hardy*, Heinemann, 1978.

14 Raja Rammohun Roy's resting place (Kejariwal, OP, *The Prinseps of India: A Personal Quest*, National Archives of India, Vol. XLII, Nos. 1-2, 1993).

## 2

Mabel at twenty-six was still unmarried, and almost certainly on the shelf that winter when the Queen lay dying at Osborne House on the Isle of Wight. When the news of her death broke at the end of January 1901 a chill wind blew through every home and into every heart as in churches great and small throughout the land funeral bells tolled. She had lived so long she had become almost a personal relation, a mother figure to many families; she had presided over such an unprecedented rise in wealth and power in England, such unimaginable innovation and headlong rush into the modern mechanical age, her influence spreading ever wider the rule of Christian virtue and civilisation under the British Empire that it was felt by all that history was passing away, that the nineteenth century itself had gone with the old queen.

She had given detailed instructions about what was to be done for her last journey. For her it was a joyous occasion because she was going to be reunited in heaven with her beloved Albert. She wished her body to be clothed in white and draped with her wedding veil; Albert's dressing-gown was to be in the coffin beside her, with a plaster cast of his hand, and a number of family photographs, among them one of John Brown, her much loved servant from Balmoral, were to be placed in her hand. The coffin was covered with a white satin pall with the Imperial crown, Orbs,

Sceptre and Collar of the Garter superimposed on it.[1] There was to be no mournful black about her, even the conventional black Belgian horses so typical of contemporary funerals were forbidden. Her gun carriage was to be pulled by the eight cream-coloured horses that had always served her in life to her last resting place beside Albert in the mausoleum she had built for him in Windsor. She could not, however, command her mourners to dress in white for the occasion. Apart from those in military or naval uniforms they all wore deepest black.

On Friday 1st Feb the coffin left Osborne House to the music of the Highland pipes. A great crowd of family mourners, of royal servants, tenants and military officers followed, moving to the music of a Beethoven *Adagio* alternating with Chopin's funeral march. At Trinity Pier the coffin was placed on a ruby velvet bier on the *Alberta*. The Grenadiers escorted her, Bluejackets carried her aboard. And so, followed by the new King and other royal mourners in the *Victoria and Albert* and the Kaiser in his Imperial Yacht, and quite deaf now to the thunder of guns booming their last salute, Victoria left her best loved home to sail across the Solent through a corridor of ships, on one side the massed vessels of her own fleet, on the other the ships of foreign navies, including the battleship *Matsuse* sent by the Mikado from Japan, all gathered to pay their respects to her who had been called Mistress of the Seas.

The following morning, Saturday, 2nd Feb, the cortège travelled by train from Gosport to London's Victoria Station. Even along the track people gathered wherever possible. Many fell on their knees as the coffin in its railway carriage passed by. At Victoria Station it was placed on a gun carriage. Military bands playing funeral marches led the great company representing Officialdom: the Army, the Indian Army, the Royal Navy and the Royal Household. Around the Queen herself there was no music; the horses and carriages of the family mourners moved in silence past Buckingham Palace, up the Mall, down Piccadilly and through Apsley Gate into Hyde Park.

It was here that Mabel stood with Maud in the middle of an immense crowd eagerly awaiting the procession. Mabel being small could see nothing over the shoulders, nor between the bodies in front of her; but she found an empty chair and managed to climb on it. A burly policeman stood stalwart and immovable just in front of her, keeping the crowd in order; but as the silent procession drew near there was a sudden push forward, and Mabel's chair all but toppled over in the surge. To steady herself, she placed a gloved hand on the bobby's shoulder, and smiled down at him as he smiled up at her from under his peaked helmet. Maud noticed this exchange, and on the way out of Hyde Park she scolded Mabel for being too familiar with a common person.

'Oh!' exclaimed Mabel. Surely Maud's respect for decorum was a little excessive? And wasn't she, with all her adherence to good form and the fashion of the day, a bit out of date herself? Mabel couldn't help thinking as she rode on top of the horse-omnibus taking her to Paddington and the train back to Bath, that Maud belonged to the century that was passing away. It had been Victoria's, great and glorious but full of pettifogging rules of behaviour that were fast becoming absurdities. 'Strong-minded' spinsters were beginning to appear on the scene in greater numbers, who were to change forever the role, and even the face of woman, in the new century that was struggling to be born. And Mabel was glad that so many restrictions that had tripped her up were now being confined to the dustbin of the past. She felt inclined to laugh, because in spite of Maud's disapproval, in spite of the sadness of that sombre day, her heart was singing. In a few weeks' time she would be skimming over the sea on her way to India. Her sister Fanny Cruikshank, who had been home on leave, and was returning to India very soon, had agreed to take her out with another young friend for a season with the 'fishing-fleet'. And her mother was delighted with the idea.

Fanny Louise could vividly recall those cool seasons of the Indian year when swarms of English girls came out to meet young bachelors on the lookout for wives. Like dragonflies they were, those girls in their bright gauzy dresses, flitting from one amusement to the next. It was the married *memsahibs* who arranged the parties and the matchmaking. And not always for the young unmarried girls either, she couldn't help reflecting bitterly. She'd tried, but could never forget certain occasions when unscrupulous female persons had worked out their designs on her own dear Clare. But Mabel would enjoy herself, and would, she knew, be safe with Fanny.

Mabel was very happy in Gorakhpur. She liked her brother-in-law Alexander Cruikshank, an able and cultured man who had served under her father Clarmont during his time in the ICS. As Commissioner of Bareilly he had been busy trying to cope with a famine in his district the year before Mabel's arrival, but was now political adviser to the Nawab of Rampur, and a member of Viceroy Curzon's Legislative Council. He had many vivid tales of Indian life to tell her.

'Was your Nawab one of the rajahs Cousin Val painted for that Durbar?' she asked.

'Probably his son or nephew. And however did Val get that picture back to England by the way? I heard it was twenty-seven feet long!'

'I believe he made sketches during his tour of India. He only painted the picture when he came home.'

'A bit of a white elephant, wasn't it?'

'Well, white elephant or not, the Queen took possession of it when she was proclaimed Empress of India. And he wrote a book about his travels. Mother had a copy. Some marvellous drawings in it too.'

It was lovely to gossip leisurely with Fanny, to sit on the verandah reading when Fanny wanted to spend a morning sketching, and a great luxury to be taken to so many picnics, to watch polo and cricket being played, and to dress up in the evenings for dinner and dancing to music supplied by the Regimental Band. On one occasion she danced three times with a naval officer who later in life rose to the rank of admiral in the Royal Navy. Fanny hoped he'd call again to pursue his advantage, but he never did. Nor was Mabel unduly disappointed when he didn't. He was not bad looking, and danced well enough and in time to the music without treading on her toes, all considerations of some importance, but he had little to say to a young woman, and she less to him. It was all very amusing to be fishing with the fleet, but with so much entertainment organised on her behalf she had little time to practise her instruments; in any case she felt she couldn't inflict hours of violin work on her kind hosts. She began to miss the long hours of quiet music-playing at home. One afternoon when it happened that she and her sister were alone over the teacups she broached the subject.

'It's lovely here, and I love India,' she said, 'but d'you know, Fanny, I'm a bit homesick.'

Fanny put her cup down on its saucer very gently.

'You're missing your music?'

'I know it's churlish of me, but I think I am.' They sipped in silence as the little silver kettle steamed on its methylated spirit stove.

'I've been thinking of old Aunt Sarah,' said Mabel. 'She gave me my first grown-up violin you know. I was ten when we visited Aunt Sarah. I was sent to the kitchen for crumpets and butter with the housekeeper while Mother took tea in the drawing room to do her begging. Aunt Sarah gave her £10, so it's her I have to thank for that violin. Perhaps she thought I'd be another Joachim. She was inclined to hope that all her geese were swans.'

'That must be all of sixteen years ago. How time does rush by!'

Sarah was widowed and living in Brighton then. The era of pampering the painter Watts and entertaining the famous in Little Holland House was far behind her; gone too were the Freshwater days when she and Toby lived at the Briary, a cottage on the Isle of Wight wedged in between her sister Julia Margaret Cameron, who was always in full pursuit of the beautiful and the famous in order to photograph them in romantic poses, and the poet Alfred Tennyson, who often tramped across the fields to engage in a battle of wits with Toby. There was nothing Toby enjoyed more than a good argument.

Fanny wondered whatever Aunt Sarah did in Brighton.

'It must have been rather boresome for her. Poor old dear!'

'I think she liked the smell of incense.'

She had grown rather religious in her old age, and looked after the vestments in the High Anglican church of St Michael and all Angels where she could gaze enraptured at the stained-glass windows. All made by her friends and protégés.[2] There was a lovely *Flight into Egypt* that Mabel remembered seeing there. She knew the church quite well, as it was so near to her old school. Aunt Sarah might have liked the smell of incense but it must have been rather dull for her. And, all in all, it must have been a bit of a come-down. Toby had been made a Director of the East India Co on his return to London, where he continued working for the Government of Bengal. And wasn't he offered a baronetcy, which he refused on the grounds that he couldn't afford to keep up the necessary appearances?

'He probably spent far too much money running Sarah's Sunday salons in the past.'

'He wasted a lot trying to get into parliament.'

Of course Sarah was bored and lonely without Toby and his argumentativeness.

It was this trait that landed him in hot water in earlier days.

He was a tall man with a high forehead, a dominating nose, and a warm and happy temperament. He arrived in Calcutta in 1809 and rose to be Chief Secretary to the Government of India. Primarily a linguist he had immersed himself in ancient Hindu texts, had come across fragments of Vedic hymns, been suddenly thrilled to discover the poetry and the wisdom in the Upanishads, and tried to translate some of it into English verse. It was inevitable then that he would quarrel with Macaulay, who arrived in Calcutta in 1833 to establish a system of education for young Indians, with English as its basis. Of course Toby wanted the Indian languages to be retained. Moreover he had the backing of a petition from thousands of Moslems and of the Hindu Sanskrit College asking for the Indian languages to be used in the new schools. Macaulay was visiting Calcutta for the first time, had no personal experience of the country, no understanding of Indian attitudes, and indeed mocked the ancient Indian cultures.[3]

Lord Auckland, the Governor-General, described the confrontation in a letter: '...he [Prinsep] and Macaulay butted at each other like bulls, blind to everything but their own joust of brains, and the contest was not advantageous to either... . He [Prinsep] knows more of India than all the rest of the service put together...and has extraordinary readiness with his tongue and pen; but he has more than common honesty, shrinks from no labour, and shines in ability and good humour withal.'[4] Perhaps it was this readiness with the tongue that had made him fall foul of a previous Governor-General, William Bentinck, who backed Macaulay.

Macaulay was eventually the winner. Although Salman Rushdie has scornfully suggested[5] that all Macaulay's Minute on Education required was enough English for 'minute men', or clerks, history has proved the economic value of establishing English as a *lingua franca* for India in today's global market, and perhaps after all we should give Macaulay a few thanks for something he did not foresee: the great cornucopia of English literature spilling out of the sub-continent today.[6]

Music had always meant so much to Mabel, Fanny knew. So perhaps, after all, music was more important to her than marriage. It seemed an unusual choice, but there was no accounting for tastes. She reminded herself that it was her own muse of painting in watercolour that had kept her going during some arid seasons in India when she'd longed for her absent children so far away in boarding schools in a cold country, and all the news she had of them always four weeks old by the time she got it. And young women seemed to be so independent nowadays. One of her own daughters had refused to promise to obey her bridegroom during their marriage service, and another was threatening to declare herself openly a suffragette.

So with many hugs and kisses on the quayside at Calcutta and with many orders to 'Write! Write!' as Mabel boarded the P&O steamship that was to carry her home, the sisters parted. She had not found a husband, and was now quite resigned to a life of spinsterhood dedicated to music and to looking after her mother in her old age.

It was probably owing to her family connections that Miss Daniell was allotted a place at the Captain's table in the dining-saloon. Opposite her sat a young man who was introduced to her as John Reid, and who, she learned, was in the ICS, just going home on long leave from some isolated jungle station up country to which such young recruits were sent. He was very handsome she thought, looking up across the table at him furtively as he helped himself to mustard. He didn't talk much, but when he did she caught the Irish brogue in his speech. And she didn't like his table manners either; she considered them rough, rough enough indeed to make her ask the steward to change her table.

'What's happened to Miss Daniell?' he asked the steward at lunch next day.

'She asked for her place at table to be changed,' was the reply.

That put him on his mettle. By the end of the voyage they were engaged to be married.

'When you came out to India with the fishing fleet did you catch Daddy in a net?' I asked my mother.

'Not at all!' he exclaimed. And I could detect the soft Irish brogue letting slip his words in such an easy-going way, though he was far from being an easy-going man himself. 'If you want to know the truth of it, 'twas I caught her!'

'It was on the boat going home,' she said. 'And without jumping into the sea I couldn't escape!' And she laughed her wonderful rich laugh that told me she was teasing him.

In old age Mabel wrote: 'We found we had many ideas in common.' Four weeks at sea provided plenty of time to exchange them.

They had fallen in love, and all the differences between them seemed insignificant beside this shibboleth-shattering event. It remained for Mabel's relations to shake their heads over the disparities in religion, race, class, in speech and social rituals.

'Of course he's quite unsuitable!'

'I suppose at her age she must catch what she can.'

'But he's Irish my dear, and a papist!'

'Certainly not one of us.'

'Her own mother finds him quite unsuitable.'

'But Mabel is one of these new strong-minded young women. There'll be no stopping her if she's made up her mind to it.'

'And I hear he's not quite a peasant. His mother farms a hundred and fifty acres in somewhere called Carlow.'

'But a scholarship boy–! Very clever of course. Mabel says he's learned Sanskrit!'

'Got into the ICS by brains and his bootstraps, don't you know.'

'And he can ride. A good hand with a horse...'

'Very handsome too, I hear. And we all know what blue eyes and a trim moustache can do to a poor girl's heart.'

'Well, we can only hope. But I fear this particular ship may be bound for the rocks.'

Mabel's godmother told her she was a traitor to her religion. 'The Jesuits will snatch away your children to Rome,' she warned. Maud's comments on the affair might have singed the hair behind her ears had she been able to hear them, but dear Harry said, 'You're old enough to know your own mind, Mabel, and if it's love–well, what else matters?'

'And all that hoity-toity Daniell breeding–!' said Mabel. 'And that Daniell crest–! What does it signify anyway?' They both thought of it: an Irish wolfhound bending his long body to catch his tail between his teeth.

'In my opinion,' said Harry, 'he's forever trying to make both ends meet!'

Mabel stood firm against all assaults; and John admired her more than ever for standing up to her family prejudices. 'You are my own independent little lady, my twentieth-century girl,' he told her. He looked forward to the new century, hoping it would wipe out a lot of hidebound old ideas, believing it was going to bring greater rights for women, and more freedom for the oppressed and poor, especially in Ireland. She glowed under his praise, she blossomed with love, and happiness brought such a vivid bloom to her cheeks that her friends remarked on it.

'Mabel has grown quite pretty since her return from India.'

'It certainly seems to suit her to be engaged.'

'Let's hope this Irish chap is not the philandering sort.'

'He seems a rather serious fellow.'

'Not one of these Radical Johnnies, is he?'

In fact his politics had been shaped since one memorable day in September 1879 when as a child he had gone with his father to a certain field in Tulloh where Charles Stewart Parnell was to address an open air meeting. He remembered an enormous sombre crowd, the intensity of attention all around him, the sudden thrill of hearing the orator's voice speaking of the wrongs of Ireland, of the Great Famine of the Forties through which John's own Dad had walked as a little hungry boy, of starvation and worse still, if that were possible, of the eviction of starving tenants by their landlords. Then the voice had lifted as it spoke of the Land League, and how every true Irishman must join it. Afterwards, there was cheering, and women weeping, and excited talk; and later still his father helped to form the Tulloh branch of the Land League to fight for tenants' rights.

Parnell had been the hero of John's boyhood, but it was Gladstone who became the political god of his maturer judgment. He was the 'People's William' who had promised to back the masses against the classes, had during the famine years written in a letter to his wife: 'Ireland! Ireland! that cloud in the west, that coming storm, that vehicle of God's retribution!' He had toiled for twenty years to alleviate the sufferings of Irish peasant farmers, tried tirelessly with the help of Parnell's parliamentary party to bring about Home Rule for Ireland, and John admired him for all this; but it was after Parnell's fall from influence following the Kitty O'Shea scandal, when neither Catholic Ireland, nor Nonconformist England would vote for an adulterer, and his death, when Gladstone had commented, 'A marvellous man, a terrible fall,' that John had loved that wily old English politician.

Those heady days of hope in Parnell had long since vanished, and the great Gladstone was dead, but John still hoped that Home

Rule would come in the new century, so that when he'd finished his service in the ICS he might go home to an independent Ireland.

Mabel's mother couldn't overrule her, since she was no longer a child, but she begged her to wait at least a year after John went back to India before getting married. She hoped that time and distance would cool her daughter's ardour, forgetting perhaps the renowned reliability of P&O boats in the matter of love letters as well as business correspondence. And Mabel, to please her mother, agreed to wait a year. Meanwhile she spent happy days with John, one of them in woods near Bath where in May the ground was ablaze with bluebells. It seemed to Mabel that the sky had drifted down to earth, just as heaven had taken possession of her heart. The glory of that day she tried to express by writing her first song: 'Bluebells'. It was a sentimental Victorian love song. If her mother heard her composing it at the piano in their sitting room, and sang it with her from the manuscript, history does not relate, but the words would undoubtedly have touched her romantic heart: *Come sweet love, and when day dies / Bluebells linger in your eyes...* . Though he had no ear for music and couldn't sing a simple phrase in tune, John took it to Novello's in London. It was later published, to Fanny Louise's great delight.

I never knew my grandmother, but my brother John remembered her as a stout old lady in black, who, when he was a small boy at a convent-school in Bath, invited him to tea at her house in Weston and gave him a magnificent feast one Sunday afternoon.

John Reid's ancestor was a Protestant Scot from Aberdeen who enlisted in Cromwell's army for the conquest of Ireland and the banishing of Popish rule, and no doubt as a means of earning his daily bread. Being on the winning side in those wars he was awarded a portion of land in Waterford, where in time through intermarriage with the local Irish the family turned its coat to a Catholic hue. John Reid's father married a girl from Carlow called Catharine Murphy, who owned 150 acres of good land which they farmed together. It was this place, Mount View in Tulloh, that he called home. His father had died while he was away in India but his mother, a strong matriarch who had somehow managed to find money to send four of her seven boys to Clongowes Wood Jesuit College, and then with the aid of scholarships and bursaries pushed them into university education, welcomed him home. He was her first-born, blue-eyed boy, a strong-willed child to whom his younger brothers had to give way; and she adored him. He was always deeply attached to her, and knowing that her life, though not poverty stricken, had never been easy, he regularly sent her part of his earnings till she died.

When his leave ended, he said goodbye to Mabel and sailed for Calcutta, there to wait for her to join him. They were married in January 1903.

'And then you were happy ever after, like in fairy stories,' I said.

'It seems a long time ago, Jack,' said Mummy.

'Nearly twenty years, Mabe,' said Daddy. They smiled at each other across the top of my head, and Mummy said something in French, which I couldn't understand. It was no good their speaking in Hindustani any more because I was beginning to speak that better than she could.

If you climbed one of the ancient banyan trees on the edge of the compound you could see the town of Patna half a mile away, and the great river rolling down to the delta and the Bay of Bengal; but we didn't often climb those trees because they were monkey territory. Instead, Selim and I used to tease the monkeys, jeering at them and throwing pebbles, and Selim, whose aim was better than mine, sometimes hit one. Then they ran shrieking and chattering up and down and along the tangled branches. One more thoughtful than the rest sat still, his unsmiling eyes flicking from side to side as he wondered what to do next, while the biggest of all, who must have been the grandfather of the tribe, swung down and tried to grab Selim by the hair. But Selim only laughed and ran away; and I ran with him. And Sukie, my little brown and white King Charles Spaniel with innocent pop-eyes, ran with us, her shrill bark adding to the excitement.

'Selim is bad boy,' said Ayah. 'He will lead you into bad ways.' Selim was the gardener's son. He was older, though not much bigger than I was. I loved playing with him because he was a daredevil and did exciting things.

'Why are you not good like your little sister Dodie, and sit here in the shade with me?' Dodie was two years younger than me; she was docile, and prettier than me, and somehow always managed to be everybody's pet. 'Why do you want to run about like a pie-dog looking for trouble?'

A man was climbing the palm tree above our heads. He wore only a loin cloth. An earthenware pot was suspended from his waist, and in his teeth he carried a knife. He tied the pot to the trunk of the palm tree, and made a cut in the bark above so that palm juice could drip into it. Then he pulled away another pot full of juice that had been fermenting in the heat, and climbed down with it. Ayesha often bought palm toddy from him. He used to pour the liquor into a little cup she kept tied to her girdle with a string. I must have mentioned this to Mummy; it came back to me a few days later.

'You tell tales of me to *Memsahib*,' she grumbled. 'Bad tell-tales. *Memsahib* is not pleased.' But that didn't stop her sitting about and waiting for the palm-toddy man. Dodie and I managed to escape from her quite often when the toddy made her fall asleep.

The compound was large, and there were many workers, all doing interesting things, from the half-naked man who banked slow-burning fires to heat the drums of water for the bungalow baths, to the Untouchable woman who lived alone in a hut full of smoke. And there was always the daily ceremony of water-drawing to watch.

The well was deep and dark and had a little palm-thatched roof over it. From a beam under this hung a pulley, and in its groove ran a rope to one end of which were attached a series of buckets, to the other a white bullock with big curved horns. The patient beast trod slowly backwards and forwards dragging up buckets full of water to be tipped into the clay basin round the well. Servants drew water from the basin for their various needs. There was always noise at the well, a lot of talk, laughter, clanking of buckets and shouts at the bullock. And often Selim used to climb on to the beam below the roof and swing there just to scare me, and I used to squeal with fear and pleasure, imagining him falling down, down into the dark water below. He would, of course, have caught the rope and let himself be pulled up with the buckets, but I imagined him drowning.

One morning when Dodie and I ran back to Ayah we found her asleep and snoring under the palms, so soundly asleep that we couldn't wake her either by pulling the sari off her face, or tugging her hair, or shouting in her ear. We ran to Mummy, who emerged from a verandah into the blazing sun. She leaned over Ayah and shook her shoulder. 'Dead drunk,' she said. 'Palm toddy I suppose.'

So Ayesha was sacked, and I wasn't sorry to see her go. Mummy was less outraged by her drunkenness and neglect of duty than by the fact that she'd failed her own religion, as being a Moslem she should have abstained from alcohol.

After Ayesha came Agatha, who was Christian, a very small widow, who although only in her thirties already had a son of seventeen working somewhere far away. She called me Nonie, never *Babamemsahib*, so she immediately made me feel older and more responsible. She was more active than Ayesha and liked taking us for walks outside the compound, although it was often very hot and we had to wear topees to keep the sun off our heads. They were heavy and made our foreheads sweat, but Agatha's walks were interesting. She took us once to see a Hindu festival on the banks of the Ganges, where many-armed and brightly painted plaster gods were carried in procession by chanting priests and devotees; and there were naked men with long hair who swam out across the strongest part of the current pushing bowls of red hot embers before them.

'They will burn their fingers!' I cried. She nodded.

'The crocodiles will eat them!' I objected.

'Sometimes,' she agreed. 'They do it for their gods.'

On the way home we saw a very ugly man. His cheeks were lumpy and he had no nose. Agatha drew us quickly to her side.

'Is he Untouchable?' I asked.

'He is a leper.' After a moment's pause she added, 'Jesus touched the lepers and healed them. To Him there were no Untouchables.' I knew then that Jesus was good and kind.

Our Untouchable woman lived apart from the other servants. Neither she nor her shadow were permitted to touch their food. The strands of her long black hair, plastered with mud, stuck out in spikes from her scalp, and Agatha said she smelt bad because she made cowpats out of bullocks' dung to fuel her cooking fire. I didn't mind her smell because I hadn't yet been trained to find that sort of smell bad. When I ran away from Agatha I sometimes went to the Untouchable's patch and sat down beside her to watch her weaving baskets. One day she gave me a miniature bamboo armchair and matching table. I was overjoyed. It was the most wonderful present.

'For your dolls,' she said, smiling a gappy smile, pleased by my joy. 'Will you come in my house?'

46

Clutching my new toys I crawled after her through the opening into her hut, and into the eye-stinging smoke over which a cauldron steamed. She scooped a handful of food from the pot into a little earthenware dish, and gave it to me. The food was *daal baat*, rice and lentils, and was delicious.

How long I was hidden in that hut I don't know, but I was eventually found by a distracted Ayah, who had been searching everywhere for her lost child. She was horrified to find me in that dirty place, and screamed a few Hindustani vilifications at the woman before dragging me away. To me she wailed: 'Ay! Ay! Ay! You will get bad tummy-aches! You will get cholera!'

I didn't get either, but perhaps I picked up threadworms from her. I didn't object to threadworms as much as Ayah and Mummy did. What I hated and dreaded was the treatment to get rid of them: the horror of it, the Enema that Mummy had to administer. It was the worst thing anyone could imagine; and I often did imagine it as a torture for my Enemies.

Agatha used to play with us, adding good ideas to our games; but I was sometimes naughty with her although I loved her. Dodie and I shared a tin tub for the evening bath, and once I persuaded her to stand up with me in it, naked, and pee on the sides. We made a shatteringly loud musical drumming, and shrieked with laughter as poor Ayah ran to fetch Mummy, who smacked us smartly on our bare bottoms.

'No bedtime songs tonight for naughty little girls,' said Mummy. Then Dodie cried. The bedtime song was something she especially looked forward to. But Mummy was adamant. She tucked us up in our mosquito-netted beds and left us.

'Let's sing her song ourselves,' I suggested. So we did our best. We couldn't remember the words of more than one verse, so we had to sing it over and over again: *O my babby, my little darkie babby, / Your Dada's in the cotton field a workin' for de coo-oo-oo-*

*oo–oon*. We must have fallen asleep at last with Ayah asleep on the floor between us, her whole body and face completely wrapped up and safe from mosquitoes inside her quilted *resai*.

On Sunday afternoons Mummy sat at her desk in the drawing room and wrote to her other children, those brothers and sisters at school so far way across the seas. I never thought of them except when I saw her writing weekly letters Home to them. I could hardly remember what they looked like; they weren't real any more, they were just a name I'd heard, Lulu-Mary-John-Daffy-Pat to whom Mummy had to write every Sunday. It made me feel uneasy to watch her pen flying across the paper. I could feel her thoughts flying away from me to some distant place that I didn't like. And then I remembered. It was a Dublin shop; I was weeping into a striped blue and white apron for my lost mother, and a kind butcher was bending down to console me before she came back to me. It was a dark room into which I'd been locked by my baby sister's Irish nurse to cool my temper tantrum, and my big sister Mary came and unlocked the door and let me out. It was a beach at Bray where my biggest sister Lulu found a heart-shaped pebble that was a mermaid's heart, and gave it to me for my fourth birthday. It was excited voices and feet running and a big sausage in the sky that had drifted from Germany across the Irish Sea and was called a Zeppelin.

And then we were in a big ship. It was very cold but we all had to stay on deck wearing lifejackets and drinking Bovril in white cups because a lurking German U-Boat might hit us suddenly. Of the long journey out to India on the big P&O steamer I could remember nothing except the children's fancy-dress party: Dodie dressed in pink silk and sitting plump and pretty on a cushion, a bowl and spoon in her baby hands, and a white frilled cap on her golden curls, beside her a spider made out of eight pipe cleaners dyed black and bent into legs and tied together with black tape. Everybody said what a perfect Little Miss Muffet she made; and of course she won a prize. Nobody noticed the skinny elf in a brown cotton shirt with a brown paper cone of an elfin hat on my straight brown hair. A feeling of disappointment, of failure, drifts down the years to me. The sting of jealousy can last a lifetime...

I wanted to be noticed, so I pushed myself against Mummy; and still her right hand flew across the page as I leaned on her, winding my right arm through her free left one.

She missed those children, and hated being separated from them, though they seemed happier now in Ireland, and perhaps because they were older, than in the dreadful early days of the War when she'd had to leave them all in a convent in Bath, when Granny was no longer alive and able to keep an eye on them, and everybody said there was very little food to go round at Home. She remembered her brother Frank's letter written after he visited little John when on leave from his regiment. He had found the child ravenously hungry for the great feast he gave him in a teashop. He also pitied the boy for being left alone among nuns, whom he regarded as austere women not knowing much about having fun. Dear kind Frank! Well, he was far away in Australia now, with a wife and children of his own.

'Agatha!' she called; 'Agatha!' exasperation entering her voice; 'Could you please take Nonie out?—Out!' she repeated. So I had to go.

After tea on Sundays Mummy showed us holy pictures and told us stories about them: The boy Jesus working in a carpenter's shop, Mary in a white nightie sitting on a hard bed to pay attention to an angel arriving with a lily, and a man in a long shirt with long hair and a beard. This picture was called The Light of the World. The man was knocking on a door. He carried a lantern, but its light wasn't bright enough to light up the path, so how could it light up the world? These prints were reproductions of paintings from an earlier generation. Mummy must have seen them herself as a child. Fanny Louise had been a worshipper at the shrine of Pre-Raphaelitism for years till her adoration was modified when a few scandals began to leak out: Rosetti in love with William Morris's wife, and Millais running off with Ruskin's; and then there was that strange business of Rosetti throwing his poems into his dead wife's bosom to be buried with her. 'A rather excessive display of uxorial devotion,' in Clare's opinion. But then, of course, Rosetti was a foreigner.... Stranger still when it was rumoured that he'd dug them up to publish them. Clare had called that 'a piece of gruesome Gothic'.

I found bible stories rather boring, except the one about Judith, who cut off the head of Holofernes, the enemy general, while he was asleep.

The next naughtiness I was guilty of happened at Betty Ezekiel's birthday party. We all wore fancy dress. I was a fairy with a gorgeous pair of silver tinsel wings tied to my back; and she was an Armenian girl in black silk trousers and black silk jacket. It was rather hot playing blind-man's-buff so Betty suggested we went outside and took off all our clothes. When we'd thrown them on the floor of the verandah we ran back to the crowd of mothers and children in the drawing room. We twirled about shrieking with laughter at our own wickedness. Betty was stark naked, but I had the sense to keep my drawers on. These did not, however, save me from sharp retribution from my mother.

'But we wanted to be cool,' I argued tearfully. 'Why was it naughty?

Next day I saw brilliant coloured lights swirling under my eyelids; and then I felt a very bad pain in my head, and vomited. 'It's like a bird clawing at my eye,' I said. When the doctor came he called it 'acidosis', but Mummy said it happened when I got too excited. She gave me sips of boiled milk diluted with soda water to drink. It was disgusting, especially the nasty skin on the surface of the milk.

'She's so wild,' I heard her telling Daddy. 'And she asks questions all the time.'

'Well, I suppose it's time to let the nuns teach her,' he agreed rather reluctantly. He liked answering my questions himself, but of course was usually far too busy to listen to me.

So Dodie and I were sent to school at St Joseph's Convent. Agatha took us and sat outside in the shade all morning till our lessons were finished. They were dull lessons. We were promised that as soon as we were good enough we could go on to the four Rs: Reading, Riting, Rithmetic and Religious Education. Meanwhile we had to draw pot-hooks repetitively between parallel lines. To make it more interesting I tried to draw them in different positions all over the page. It seemed to shock the supervising nun.

'But they are so erratic!' she complained. Soeur Monique, who was French, called my hooks 'airatique', but I guessed what she meant, because I could see they were flying about all over the place.

'You must make them all stand in line like soldiers,' she said. She peered over the double-desk I shared with Dodie. 'Look 'ow well your little sister 'as done them!' And it was true, of course, Dodie, though not yet five, could already draw remarkably neat hooks. That made me feel very cross.

Next time she peered over my work she was no happier. 'Mon Dieu!' she cried. 'What 'ave we 'ere? Is it a Worr or something?'

I explained that I was trying to get as many soldiers in line as possible.

'But what 'ave they stuck on their 'eads?' she demanded. 'Can it be Chinamen with pigtails?'

'No,' I said, thinking her very stupid. Daddy would have understood at once. 'Those are rifles on their shoulders.'

She straightened up. 'Please do not decorate the 'ooks.' Then her voice became pleading. 'I only want a few 'ooks at regular intervals all in one line. I do not ask too much.' She pointed at Dodie's exercise book again. 'Look 'ow well Dodie makes them.'

That made me so mad with rage that I threw my pencil on the floor and absolutely refused to draw any more hooks.

Soon after that I was moved up in class to learn the four Rs. I shared a desk with Helen, whose education Mummy was paying for. She was an orphan Eurasian adopted by the nuns. I liked Helen. She came to tea sometimes at the bungalow, and played with my dolls. She was quite naughty too, so we were friends. Under cover of the desk-top I pulled out of my pocket a little Japanese wooden doll and gave it to her, and she drew funny faces on a bit of paper to make me giggle. When I got too restive I was sent to practise the piano. It was not like Mummy's big piano at home; it was a little piano with a keyboard that made no sound, however hard you struck the keys. Mummy had taught me how to read music, the different values of notes and their positions on keyboard and on the printed page, and had impressed on me the importance of rhythm and time-keeping. I was able to play one or two simple tunes from my child's album of pieces, so it was humiliating and very boring to have to sit and strum this silent piano.

'It is good for five-finger exercises,' the presiding nun explained. 'It will make your fingers strong.' But it was an instrument that positively asked for a good loud bang of its lid to shut it up, and not at all like Mummy's big black grand that Daddy had given her, at which I was sometimes allowed to sit to make little bells tinkle in the treble and drums and trumpeting elephants shout out loudly in the bass.

Dodie and I were not considered old enough, nor to have the music manners necessary for Mummy's musical parties. On those afternoons ladies in flimsy frocks and big flower-laden hats arrived in cars and dog-carts at our front verandah to sit among the pink roses of our chintz-covered chairs. The carved wood camels that stood on either side of the drawing-room door raised disdainful nostrils at guests taking sweets or cigarettes from the brass trays that replaced the usual humps, and later the ladies drank tea out of pretty cups served by Bearer; but Dodie and I were sent out to tea with Charlie Whelan.

When Ayah brought us home she took us in through the side entrance, across the verandah where the *dhurzi* sat behind a sewing-machine, stretching the cloth between two toes. I often stopped to watch him. I admired him greatly, more for the skill of his toes than for his tailoring. If the music was still in full swing he would lift his head from time to time and listen. I wanted to join the concert at once. It was annoying to be excluded; but Bearer comforted us by beckoning us into the dining room.

'*Babamemsahib's* favourite,' he would whisper as he removed a net and bead anti-fly cover to reveal two small pink-iced sponge cakes he'd saved for us. Their sweetness was of a heavenly intensity surpassing even the taste of custard baked in individual moulds.

As we ate them we could peep through the open door at Mrs Ezekiel, our soprano, slow moving and pompous as an elephant, her fat white throat wobbling through the melancholy phrases of Dvorak's *Songs my Mother taught Me*, and her face getting redder as she stretched out the top note. Then everybody clapped; but we didn't because we were not supposed to be there. Then smart Miss Patel, who had been accompanying her on the piano, stood up and gave a little bow before sitting down again to play a Chopin mazurka. She played very fast, and I could see her high-heeled shoes press energetically on the pedals, her short skirt slipping up above her slim knees, her long earrings swinging as her bobbed black hair nodded and jerked above the keys.

'She is Parsee!' hissed Ayah in my ear. I wondered if that meant she was born in Paris, which would explain her fashionable clothes, so like the pictures in Mummy's catalogue from Bon Marché. 'She is a very modern Miss,' I'd heard Mummy say of her.

53

Modern Miss she may have been, she was also an excellent accompanist to Mummy's violin. When they played Dvorak's *Humoreske*, I stood entranced. The lilting rhythm soared, making me want to fly up and up, high above the highest mountains in the world, that Bearer said were far away in the north, too far for us to see, and were called the Himalayas.

On another occasion when Ayah brought us home from Charlie's house too early I caught sight of a stout baritone bellowing: 'Du meine Seele / Du mein Herz!' Blue eyes starting out of his head, words shooting out of his red face, rage bursting out above his bow-tie, he was truly alarming.

'Why was he so cross?' I asked Mummy.

She laughed. 'He wasn't cross, dear; it was a love song.' She pushed a strand of hair out of my eyes. 'We'll have to cut your fringe, Nonie. It's getting too long.' She stroked my cheek absent-mindedly. 'He's not really out of the top drawer, you know. But he can sing in tune.'

I was puzzled by the idea of such a fat man being able to squeeze into a large bottom drawer let alone a small top one; but I did understand from her tone that singing in tune was a much more important feat than squeezing in and out of chests-of-drawers.

'It is time she made her First Communion,' said the nuns. 'She is old enough now to understand.'

So I was introduced to the exciting but sad, sad story of Jesus who was so cruelly killed but gave his body to feed the hungry five thousand. It was magic how he did it. And Mummy promised me that when I knew it all by heart I would have a white dress, with a white veil like a bride, and white canvas shoes, and hold a white-leather-bound prayer book in my white-gloved hands as I stood at the communion rail with all the other little girls waiting to receive the Host.

Mummy, who ordered her clothes from Paris by post, let me have her old catalogues from Bon Marché and Galleries Lafayettes. They were full of smart ladies dressed up in the latest, just what I needed to cut out as dolls for my communion game. I was able to make them kneel without toppling over. Their backs did bend a bit, but that was only properly reverential. I was the priest, and they were my communicants. I saved some bits of bread from my teatime slices, and I pressed these into tiny discs with my thumb on the bare floorboards. By the time I'd finished my wafers weren't as white as the Host held up by the priest at Mass when the little bell rang to tell us that the miracle was happening, but I didn't think my paper dolls would mind too much.

What I did not possess was a chalice, which was annoying, till I remembered seeing among the tin soldiers in Charlie Whelan's box of toys a small Chinese metal cup. It had a dragon carved around the stem; but I didn't think that mattered, as it looked so like the devil in my catechism book. So I pinched that cup from him next time we went to his house to play. Charlie wasn't a Catholic so he didn't need it to say Mass as I did. And anyway Charlie was wet, literally. He was a pale child who drank enormous quantities of water, and often wet himself. And his chalice was just what I needed.

I began to wonder if I might convert Selim enough to play my new game.

'You can be my altar boy and ring the bell,' I said. I could see he wasn't too keen on the idea. 'It's the bell *Memsahib* uses to call Bearer to the dining-table,' I urged.

Selim's eyes brightened at the thought of being like Bearer, so dignified in his brown serge coat, his red cummerbund spread across his stomach, and his elaborately twisted turban carried proudly on his head like a crown, but even that didn't tempt him enough.

Selim wasn't going to be easy to convert; but I knew it was a good thing to be a missionary, so I decided to try it out on some of the other servants on the compound. And thus it was that Agatha found me, to her great embarrassment, sitting in the middle of a circle of men, all nodding and joking together.

'Moslems,' I told them, 'are better than Hindus, because they have only one God, but Hindus have hundreds.' I couldn't understand why they were all laughing when I was telling them such important truths.

As the day of my First Communion approached every day grew hotter, the heat stupefying at noon. Even Mummy put aside her violin in its case and sighed: 'It's too difficult, that double-stopping passage!' She went to lie down for the siesta; and Agatha took me and Dodie off to rest. As soon as she was rolled up in her *resai* and fast asleep between us I got up and crept out to the verandah, where I put on my shoes before running to the walled garden. That was where Selim worked with his father, the *Mali*. I was rather afraid of him. He had angry eyes; and sometimes he beat Selim with a stick. 'That troublemaker!' was what Ayah called him. 'He is Moslem, too, and no lover of Gandhi.' I'd heard of Gandhi. He was the *Mahatma* who had promised to give his life for India, and Ayah loved him beyond all other men. But Selim Senior would by now have been struck down by the heat and would, I guessed, be safely snoring in his hut at the bottom of the garden, and so beyond trouble-making.

Selim was asleep in the shade of the wall where the peaches grew. I could smell the scent of their ripening sweetness as it spread into the hot still air. He woke up when I shook his shoulder.

'Let's eat one,' I said.

We were forbidden to pick the peaches, but because any that fell bruised so easily and rotted so quickly in that climate we were allowed to eat fallen fruit.

'Only one,' said Selim guardedly. 'My father will count two missing gone.' But he found a stone and aiming skilfully he hit a branch exactly in the right place so that a single peach fell on the soft earth. He picked it up and cut it with his knife and gave me half. I had already learned that forbidden fruit is sweetest.

The heat must have made the monkeys more irritable than usual. At any rate the next time Selim teased them, which was the Sunday of my First Communion, when my thoughts were very far away from him and the monkeys, the grandfather of the tribe swooped down and with his sharp nails tore a piece of scalp from Selim's skull.

We were in the dining room enjoying a special First Communion breakfast of boiled eggs and bread and butter with slices of mango to follow when it was interrupted by loud voices on the verandah outside, men complaining and women wailing. Bearer hurried from the room to see what was the matter, and came back with news that Selim was badly injured and bleeding copiously. Daddy and Mummy rose from the table simultaneously, and I tried to do the same.

'No, Nonie,' Mummy said. 'You stay where you are.' So I didn't see Selim in the arms of his angry father, nor his black-veiled mother uttering ululations, nor the bevy of relatives clamouring behind them. But in my head I saw Selim's bloody face hovering over my special breakfast like Banquo's ghost at Macbeth's feast.

Daddy ordered the *syce* to harness the pony to the trap and drive Selim and his parents to the mission hospital to have his scalp stitched up; and Mummy tore open a pillowcase and wrapped poor Selim's head in it. It was like a white turban. He'd have liked that.

After I went to bed that night I lay awake watching all sorts of pictures flashing under my eyelids, white dresses and white veils, little girls kneeling with eyes closed murmuring prayers, little girls with mouths open to receive the Host, and Selim's mouth open as he yelled, blood streaming down his nose.

I could hear Daddy and Mummy talking on the verandah. I pulled up my mosquito net, and stepping over sleeping Agatha I ran to join them. Daddy put aside his cigarette and his *chota-peg*, and though it was against the rules to get out of bed like that, he let me climb up on his knee.

'It's a big problem,' he said, 'all this monkey business.' Selim's father had come to the office that evening with a crowd of his relatives and friends, to lodge a complaint. 'He wants us to exterminate the monkeys. There are so many of them now they really are a pest.'

'Worse than that, a danger,' said Mummy. 'And Selim's father will certainly stir up trouble among the Moslems if nothing's done.'

'But shooting the monkeys would cause a Hindu riot, since they're sacred, and probably former souls reincarnated.'

'Possibly ancestors,' Mummy interjected.

There was a pause while Daddy sipped his whisky.

'Chaudhury has come up with a possible solution.' He puffed at his cigarette. 'He suggests we catch them all in nets and convey them by boat to the island in the middle of the river.'

'But it's a desert island!' Mummy protested. 'There's nothing whatever there for them to eat!'

'Water, water everywhere and plenty of drops to drink,' said Daddy, 'so they won't be thirsty. But yes, they'll certainly starve to death.'

' "Thou shalt not kill, but needst not strive / Officiously to keep alive," ' Mummy said. And Daddy laughed.

There was a long pause. Then Daddy said: 'I'm afraid it's what we'll have to do.' And Mummy said to me, 'I think you'd better go back to bed, darling. I'll come with you. We won't wake Ayah.'

She kissed me before tucking me up. 'It was a lovely First Communion, wasn't it?' she whispered through the net.

'Yes,' I said. It made you feel good to have God inside you, especially after you'd got rid of all your sins by telling them to a dimly seen someone inside the dark Confessional cupboard, smelling of unwashed hair, and had been told by a kind voice to say the blessed names of Jesus, Mary and Joseph three times, and to go in peace, my child.

'Perhaps you'd better say a prayer for poor Selim,' Mummy said.

But there were other things on my mind now. If God could feed the five thousand with five loaves and a few fishes, couldn't He make bananas grow on that island? It might be worth trying the Virgin Mary too. It would take a great many Hail Marys, a hundred perhaps, to persuade them, but it was something I knew I must do. Selim could have one, possibly two Hail Marys, but all the rest had to be spent on turning that desert island into a banana grove. It wasn't Selim I had to pray for now, it was the monkeys.

# References — Chapter Two

1 St. Aubyn, Giles, *Queen Victoria*, Sinclair-Stevenson.

2 Hill, Brian, Julia Margaret Cameron: *A Victorian Family Portrait*, Peter Owen, 1973.

3 "Medical doctrines that would disgrace an English farrier... . Astronomy [laughed at by] girls at an English boarding school... . History abounding with kings thirty foot high, and reigns thirty thousand years long...and Geography made up of seas of treacle and butter." Quoted by Christopher Hibbert in 'The Great Mutiny', from Edwardes' *Red Year*.

4 Kejariwal, O P, *The Prinseps of India, Indian Archives, Vol XLII*, 1993.

5 Rushdie, Salman, *The Moor's Last Sigh*, Jonathan Cape,1995.

6 Toby Prinsep is buried in the graveyard of All Saints church in Freshwater on the Isle of Wight. His wife Sarah Monkton Prinsep (1816-1887) lies beside him under a simple headstone. Beside them under a small tombstone lies Annie May Prinsep (1848-1932), daughter of Toby's brother Charles, a barrister who was made Attorney General in Calcutta. She was orphaned early in life and adopted by Toby and Sarah, much photographed by Margaret Cameron, and married Robert Hitchens, the author of a then popular novel The Garden of Allah. After she was widowed she married again, her second husband being Hallam, son of Alfred, and thus became Lady Tennyson. Separated from them by an old yew tree lies Emily M Tennyson under a more ornate tomb. Her famous husband has been removed from her in death and lies in Westminster Abbey among the English poets.

# 3

The plight of the monkeys, and even Selim, were soon forgotten in a much worse business when the Bubonic Plague invaded Patna. It ravaged the city, and then began to creep out into the surrounding villages. A nervous silence fell upon the servants when the subject was mentioned; their eyes slid away from your face, and their hands moved aimlessly. The big gates of the compound were closed, strangers were not allowed in, nor were we allowed out, and schooling suddenly stopped.

I managed to persuade Ayah to go down to the gates to see what was happening, which I could easily do by putting my nose through one or other of the many-shaped spaces in the ironwork. Funerals were passing. They were not solemn processions moving at a dignified pace, they were hurried affairs, the corpses rolled untidily into white cotton cloths and thrown on to stretchers which were carried on the shoulders of half-naked men, who ran chanting: 'Ram! Ram! Sita! Ram!' over and over again. The bundles bounced about a bit as the men ran, and one or two nearly fell off into the dust.

'They are taking the bodies of the dead to be burned on banks of the Ganges,' said Agatha. 'And there are so many there will not be time to burn them through and through.'

'What will happen then?' I asked.

'The pie-dogs will eat them,' she said. 'And the kites will fly down and pick their bones.' I must have shivered; I didn't like to hear the shriek of those circling birds calling each other by name: 'Cheel! Cheel!'

Mummy said, 'The rats will eat them.'

'The Public Health Department will have to deal with the rats,' said Daddy.

'Kill them?' I asked. 'But rats are dead souls too, aren't they?'

'They are indeed. And too many of them about.'

But Ayah said, 'The Ganges will wash all away.'

That evening when I sat on Daddy's knee before bedtime and we talked about the funerals going on outside the gates he said, 'Tomorrow and tomorrow and tomorrow.... We must work for the future, Nonie. It'll be better one day.'

'Better than now?'

'It's going to be.'

So I learned early in life that somehow Daddy and Mummy and I would gradually clear up the mess, the bad smells, the sickness and death. Perhaps we would plant flowers everywhere, I thought; but I knew that flowers withered quickly in India, so it must be something else, something more lasting that we had to plant.

One visitor who did manage to get through the guard on the gate was a big man with a spade-like blond beard and a deep bass gravelly voice that made jokes. He was a Dutch Jesuit missionary who had converted Mummy to Catholicism during the early years of her marriage and the births of her first two babies, so he was an old friend. There were very few Europeans at that up-country station in those days; and Mabel saw no European woman for three years. She had been an interesting curiosity to the natives when, soon after their wedding, she and John arrived in a push-push carried by four men, and the travelling party had set up camp. The first thing she asked for was a bath.

A tin tub was provided in a tent, and she undressed and gratefully slid into the cool water. While splashing herself she became aware of the tent-flaps twitching, of eyes peering in at her. The news of her coming had spread quickly, and a crowd of native women had collected to have a look at her strange white skin. They had never before seen a white woman.

As to religion John didn't care at all what she believed. He had in Mabel's opinion become lax in the practice of his own. She had no intention of becoming a Catholic, but she thought that since her children were to be brought up in their father's faith she'd better know what it was, so she set about receiving some instruction in it. There was a Jesuit Mission not too many miles away where this Dutch priest was stationed; it was he who fulfilled her godmother's prophesy. He didn't exactly snatch her and her children into the Church of Rome; he beguiled her into it with his deep honeyed voice. It wasn't difficult to persuade her; she had already begun to travel along the path taken by Newman through High-Anglicanism. 'There were only two obstacles,' she said. 'One was the Immaculate Conception, and the other was Papal Infallibility.' As to the Immaculate Conception, God being all powerful could certainly see to it that his mother-to-be would be born without stain of original sin, and of course would like her to be so before He decided to enter into her womb as a helpless babe. Mabel could accept that supposition as reasonable; but Papal Infallibility was a stumbling block. In time she stepped over it. Perhaps in wild up-country jungle, while struggling to rear and protect from dangers more sinister than teething her three infants born in three years, these matters of dogma didn't seem very important. She was never able to nurse her babies on the breast for more than three months, however hard she tried, so she had to feed them on *dudh*, or milk, carefully boiled—or dried milk in cartons, when she could get them sent up from Calcutta—and keep the bottles and teats scrupulously clean from infections rampant in that climate. She knew how easily infant lives were lost from fevers of all sorts, had heard about the British cemeteries in India full of children's graves, and remembered that her own mother had lost two babies within three weeks, and had been powerless to save them.[1] Infant welfare was a problem more pressing than Papal Infallibility then. Moreover the strong, warm-hearted Dutchman, who had indeed given up all the wealth and comforts of his homeland to follow Jesus into exile among the Indian poor, was a true friend when she contracted malaria at a time when the only drug available for its treatment was quinine. So she had trusted him.

Daddy liked talking to him. 'He is, like all Jesuits, a clever man,' he said; but Mummy said, 'He is a saint.'

Did the heavenly choirs of the Church Triumphant he promised her nourish 'the life of the soul' in those starved-of-music years she spent in the wilds with her young District Commissioner?

This Dutchman one evening brought us news from plague-ridden Patna; and we all gathered on the verandah to hear it. He was a big man, and the cane armchair creaked when he sat in it. Bearer brought him a whisky chota-peg and lingered to hear him speak. 'It is on the wane,' he said. 'Fewer people dying.' I stood beside his chair and listened to his voice and the words that he spoke in a funny way because he was Dutch, but Dodie climbed up on the black *soutane* that covered his knees and plunged her fingers into his beard and pulled it till he cried, 'Ow! Ow!' and we all laughed. Before he left he told us that one of the nuns had died of the plague.

Mummy stroked my hair. 'She'll go straight to heaven,' she said. 'She was so good.' Perhaps it was death and the funerals that gave me nightmares, or perhaps it was simply the heat.

'What are you afraid of, Nonie?' Daddy asked me.

It was not the cobra I'd seen killed by the *mali* in the garden. Daddy had read to me Kipling's story about Rikki-Tikki-Tavy, the brave little mongoose who attacked and killed snakes, and I'd watched one running about the house, swishing his bushy tail and searching for them with his quick bright eyes, so I knew we were well guarded from that danger. Nor did I fear the jackals that howled and howled at nightfall; they were all far away outside the compound. Whatever it was I began to wake up crying in the middle of the night.

'Some nasty thing is trying to catch my feet and pull me down into a hole!' I wailed.

Ayah patted my back and told me there was no tiger under the bed. 'They are all in the jungle waiting for the Sahib's bullets,' she said.

I have sometimes wondered whether the other nightmare was the result of listening to Alice in Wonderland who swallowed medicine to make her grow gigantic, and then more medicine to make her shrink smaller and smaller. It amazed me to watch grown-ups laughing and saying how clever it was; to me it was a silly story, but it did have some alarming thoughts. In my bad dream I was standing on a long road, and I was watching myself walk away from me, growing smaller and smaller till I could hardly see myself any more. Then I woke up thinking I had disappeared. That was desolation. Ayah rocked me in her arms. 'I will hold you,' she said. 'Go to sleep now.'

When the heat became unbearable, Daddy ordered the servants to put camp beds up on the flat roof, and there in the relative coolness we slept fitfully. We were woken one night by a clap of thunder. Bedding was hastily rolled up, and in a sleepy blur of excited voices we were carried downstairs as lightning flashed and thunder rumbled. And then we heard the rain.

In the morning Dodie and I were allowed to run out wearing only our drawers and stand under the flooded gutters, letting the water pour down over our heads while Ayah watched us from the verandah, clapping her hands and laughing. We shrieked with laughter, pelting each other with splashes, stamping in the puddles, delirious with joy. 'It's the monsoon!' we shouted. 'The monsoon! The monsoon!'

The longed for, sweet, impartial rain was falling.

'Sahib is not well,' said Agatha. 'Sahib is not himself. Always he shakes his head and sighs. Perhaps he will go Home.'

'Home?' I echoed. 'When?'

This time it was Agatha who sighed. 'Who knows? Ay! Ay! Ay! What will happen to me then? Such a lot of trouble everywhere!'

There was no more talk of going home as yet, but my parents decided to go on holiday, taking our little dog Sukie with them. A holiday was what the doctor advised. He lent Mummy a sphygmomanometer in order to measure Daddy's blood pressure and record it day by day. They were to travel by rail and by car to visit Benares and Shiva's gold-roofed temple.

'Who's she?'

'Shiva's not female,' Daddy said. 'He's one of the three great gods of the Hindu Trinity.'

'He's a good god,' said Mummy.

'But he's bad too,' said Daddy. 'He's lots of different things. That's why he has so many arms, so his left hand doesn't know what his right hand does.'

Mummy laughed, but she reproved him too: 'What things you tell the child, Jack!'

'He has three eyes and four arms,' he insisted. And I knew he was right because I'd seen them that time Ayah took me to see the procession by the Ganges. 'And he shows off his Lingam.'[2]

'What's that?' But that they did not explain.

I had seen Mummy's Great-uncle James's book *Benares Illustrated,* and knew about the temple he'd saved from falling into the river, but now I learned that it wasn't Shiva's golden temple, it was a lesser one among the many in Benares. 'And he built a great tunnel under the city to drain the festering swamp that lay above it,' Mummy said. 'And I do believe that drain's still working, more or less.'

Daddy was interested in Great-uncle James for other reasons. 'He was really a Renaissance man,' he said. 'After a decade in Benares he went to Calcutta. There's a statue of him still at Prinsep's Ghat.'

In Calcutta he threw himself into the study of archaeology. He became Secretary of the Asiatic Society of Bengal, and recorded the meetings at which all the enthusiastic archaeological researchers into ancient Indian history gathered. He is chiefly remembered for having deciphered an inscription on an ancient stone that led to the discovery of a whole era of unrecorded Indian history and a dynasty of Ashokan kings. He was honoured by being made a Fellow of the Royal Society in London. And all the time he was making wonderful sketches of the landscape and people around him.

'And he did something else for the India of his day. He tidied up the ancient coinage during his work as Assayer of the Benares Mint.'

But all that went above my head. What I wanted most of all to see was the Taj Mahal, one of the Wonders of the World, and Cawnpore, site of so many horrors during the Mutiny. Mummy had been born in the Collector's House next door to the notorious House of the Ladies in which the women and children who survived the siege were incarcerated and later murdered. The *sepoys* refused to murder women and children, so local butchers were employed to cut them up in pieces, which were thrown into a well. A terrible revenge was exacted by the British after the defeat of the mutineers. The murderers were hanged, but first they were pushed into the murder-room on their hands and knees, and forced to lick clean the bloodstained floor after it had been watered by natives of the lowest caste. They were punished by death, and also by being forced to pollute themselves, breaking their caste in this filthy way, and being beaten by British soldiers whenever they faltered in their task. This peculiarly nasty retribution was invented by Brigadier-General James Neill, who arrived in Cawnpore to clear up the mess after the mutineers had been defeated in battle and driven up north. 'I hope I shall not be interfered with until the room is thoroughly cleansed in this way...with the blessing and help of God,' he wrote. 'I cannot help seeing that His finger is in all this.'[3] Any uneasiness he felt about his methods of dispensing justice was quickly soothed by his trust in the approval of the Almighty.

Five butchers actually perpetrated the massacre, but hundreds of villagers as well as *sepoys* were summarily hanged, it being considered in those days of rage by the British soldiers who arrived there soon after the event that all Indians were probably guilty. The hangings continued daily for three months. Soldiers visiting the House of the Ladies snatched bits of hair and bloodstained clothing to send home as souvenirs, while swearing solemnly to revenge the innocent dead. Throughout India they wreaked revenge for the murdered *memsahibs* of Cawnpore. After the defeat of the mutineers at Lucknow and Delhi, where no prisoners were taken and *sepoys* were hunted down and slaughtered, a 'Cawnpore dinner' was six inches of bayonet steel in the stomach.

'Can't I come too? I want to see the Taj Marble fairy palace,' I begged.

'It's not a fairy palace,' said Mummy. 'It's the tomb Shahjehan built for his beloved wife Arjumand.' That the beautiful queen had died giving birth to her fourteenth child she didn't tell me; and perhaps it was a fact omitted by the guide books.

Dodie and I were too young to appreciate this Wonder of the World, so we were sent with Ayah to stay with old friends, also in the ICS, Harry and May Foster. Daddy handed over his responsibilities as Secretary of Land Reform in Bihar and Orissa to his deputy, Guy Dain, who lived in a smaller bungalow on the compound. Dodie and I were fond of Mr Dain because he was so tall and strong that he could throw us high up in the air and make us squeal with terror of falling, so we had to run off to kiss him goodbye before climbing into the waiting car. We had to hug Sukie too, who was trying to scramble into the car with us as we were being driven away.

We stayed with the Fosters for a month. I can still feel the happiness of it. Looking back now in old age I know that it was one of the happiest months of my whole life. No doubt they were missing their own children, who were all in boarding schools in Europe, and perhaps this was why they showered on Dodie and me so much affection and playfulness. Mrs Foster remarked once on the steadiness of my gaze; but the fact was I couldn't take my eyes off her. She was a small woman with big kind eyes, and a tentative smile that could quickly spread into an all-embracing welcome, a person of no great presence you might think on first meeting her, but she had a magician's tongue, and with it she wove around me a web of words that held me spellbound. Like Desdemona who, listening to Othello's yarns, loved him for the dangers he had passed, I had fallen in love with her for the tales she told. So wonderful were they that I wanted them to go on forever. She showed me Arthur Rackham's illustrations of fairy stories; she showed me where elves lived hidden away from human sight in little houses under the roots of trees, and told me how they ate their dinners on toadstool tables growing on a carpet of moss. I must have expressed a little doubt about the reality of her world, asking why it was we never saw any of these magical beings.

'Fairies live their secret life at night while you're asleep,' she said. 'They don't like humans to watch them.' But she showed me the doorstep to her verandah. It was cut out of granite, and its surface glittered with tiny silver flecks. 'That's fairy stardust,' she said. 'It shows where the fairies danced last night.' It was proof positive.

The legend of Camelot she read to me in the sonorous language of Tennyson's *Idylls of the King*, illustrated by pictures of King Arthur and his Round Table and all his knights good and true. How the boy Arthur drew the sword Excalibur out of the massive stone, thus proving he was going to be a great leader of men, how the magician Merlin guided and taught him till he was ready to be king, and the sad, sad story of his betrayal by the beautiful Guinevere and his lion-hearted friend Sir Lancelot, all took possession of my imagination; but the wickedness of Mordred, and the last battle beside the lake when Arthur was mortally wounded, were almost more than I could bear.

'So all day long the noise of battle rolled
Among the mountains by the winter sea,'

was what she read to me. The words rolled and resounded inside my head like music.

Then the dying Arthur told Sir Bedevere to take the sword Excalibur and throw it into the middle of the lake, which Sir Bedevere naturally didn't want to do at all because it was such a good sword with a precious jewelled hilt. So he hid it under bushes, and said it was done; but Arthur saw through his lies, and was angry. And in the end Bedevere obeyed the king.

'Then with both hands I flung him, wheeling him;
But when I looked again, behold an arm,
Clothed in white samite, mystic, wonderful,
That caught him by the hilt and brandished him
Three times, and drew him under in the mere.'

She paused to give me time to imagine the scene. 'And the great sword Excalibur still lies deep down at the bottom of that lake,' she said.

After that came the barge, black 'as a funeral scarf from stem to stern', and in it three black-robed queens with crowns of gold, who took the king and laid him down, his head resting in the lap of the tallest. Then Bedevere cried out in his terrible grief, asking what he would do without his lord.

> 'And Arthur answered slowly from the barge:
> "The old order changeth, yielding place to new,
> And God fulfils himself in many ways
> Lest one good custom should corrupt the world...
> But now farewell. I am going a long way...
> To the island valley of Avilion, ...
> Where I will heal me of my grievous wound." '

May Foster's maiden name was Digby. She came from an old Catholic family descended from Sir Everard Digby who was hanged, drawn and quartered for his part in the Gunpowder Plot. He was a romantic figure, a handsome man not long married, and at his execution there were many in the watching crowd who cried out and wept that such a gallant young gentleman should come to such an end.[4] Owing to his treason in England his descendants had to live for generations on the continent of Europe, often in Italy.

Harry Foster, who was a high court judge, was very much a man of his times. He owned something we'd never seen before: a gramophone with a horn. He used to place a shiny black record on the turntable, wind the handle up, lift the arm carrying the needle and delicately drop it into its groove, and hey-presto! like magic the music poured out of the horn. And then we all danced together in a ring, Dodie and I in our nightgowns barefooted, Harry in his socks.

His brother Ned had been manager of the Alhambra Theatre in 1916 in London during the War when the musical comedy *The Byng Boys* was produced, and Harry often sang snatches of the songs from it, especially the pop-song of its day, 'If You were the Only Girl in the World', in which May joined. We didn't see much of him by day, because he was working in his office; but he kept us amused in the evenings. At bedtime, just before May came to tuck us up for the night, Harry crawled under the bed, waiting for her; and when she bent over to kiss us goodnight he started barking and growling like a dog, and snapping at her ankles; and she would cry out, 'Down sir! Down! You naughty dog!' over and over again; and Dodie and I would scream with laughter, breathless and ecstatic with hilarity. Although we all knew the identity of the dog under the bed, we played the farce night after night for all it was worth. We never tired of it, and the comedy seemed as fresh at the end as at the beginning of that month's holiday.

'Did you see the murder-house?' I asked Daddy.

'Yes. And the house where your mother was born, too.'

No thinking tourist could visit Cawnpore, and Bibighar, the House of the Ladies, originally built by a British officer for his mistress, without being chilled by the knowledge of what had happened there, and perhaps reflecting on how war releases long dammed-up hatreds in a flood of cruelties, loyalty to race and religion being used to justify their infliction. My mother, in spite of having seen the sites, and knowing that her own father was wounded at Agra, looked back over the long years of peace, the Pax Britannica, since those times, and seemed bewildered that the Mutiny had happened at all. My father was surprised to learn that so few old India hands had been prepared for it, each army officer and civil administrator believing that his own men would always remain loyal to him.

'Why did they want to kill us?' I asked.

'Well, the *sepoys* were afraid of being forcibly converted to Christianity,' Daddy explained. 'And there was bad feeling in some native states that had been taken over by the British. And then there was all that trouble over the new cartridges because they were greased with animal fat. Moslems wouldn't bite off the caps in case the grease was pig-fat, Hindus in case it was beef-fat.' He sighed. 'And after all we were just *firinghis* to them, to be endured as rulers for a time, but not forever.'

'All well at Cawnpore,' wrote General Wheeler to the Governor-General in Calcutta on 20th May 1857. Ten days later refugees were streaming into the military barracks begging for asylum.

'General Wheeler was Irish,' said Daddy.

He had won his commission in the East India Company's militia at fourteen, had spent his whole life in India, married an Indian wife, and loved his men, whose language he spoke as well as they did. He was relying for help, in the event of 'trouble', on his friend Dhondu Pant, Maharajah of Bithur, known as Nana Sahib, who belonged to the same caste as Wheeler's wife. Nana Sahib was not the son, but the adopted son of the last Peshwa of Bithur, and therefore under a much hated new British law, was not regarded as the legitimate heir, a matter about which he understandably felt bitter. When the time came for decision he sided with the mutineers, and agreed to lead against his friend the 3,000 *sepoys* from various regiments who had gathered in the town.

There was no fort at Cawnpore as at Agra, and no stout stone buildings for shelter as in Lucknow. The military barracks, partially surrounded by a mud and brick wall only four foot high, had been built by the East India Company to protect an important trading post on the River Ganges and the Great Trunk Road to

Delhi. Nana Sahib thought the siege, with such pitiful defences, would be over in a few days.

Wheeler was sixty-seven when it began on 6th June. Inside the barracks and a few ramshackle outbuildings, were crowded about 800 people, 400 of them were women and children, and 100 men were civilians. There were 200 European soldiers, 100 European officers from native regiments, and a few native servants who chose to stay with their employers. Eighty of his own *sepoys* wished to remain with Wheeler, but, very sensibly and humanely, he ordered them to return to their own homes. He had four guns, plenty of muskets, and a good supply of champagne, but food stores were inadequate for a prolonged siege, and the water supply was precarious. There was a well inside the walls, but it was exposed to enemy fire, and very soon the brickwork and the machinery were smashed, and all water then had to be pulled up under fire by men hauling buckets hand over hand from a depth of sixty feet.

Temperatures reached thirty-eight by day, and terrible thirst was suffered by all, especially the children. One Ayah with great daring crawled out to the well to get water for her *babamemsahib*. Some soldiers, who were drawing water under cover of darkness when firing was desultory, sold it for eight shillings a bucket to those who had money.[5]

When the bombardment began the confusion and noise in the camp were 'terrific', a survivor recorded, the sound of explosions being echoed by the screams of terrified women and children; but after the first day the non-combatants were quiet. Families huddled together in corners, many of the women tore up their petticoats to make bandages, others carried water to the wounded. Casualties were terrible. Mrs Williams, the Colonel's wife, had half her face blown away, and died two days later. She was tended by her daughter, who herself had suffered a bullet wound in the shoulder. Women gave birth where there was space enough for them to lie; and the newborn died of dehydration, dysentery, or gunshot wounds either before or after their mothers. General Wheeler sat on a mattress in one corner of a small room, trying to direct operations, while his wife and two daughters sat in another. On a sofa sat his son, Lieut Godfrey Wheeler, 'recovering from a wound, while one of his sisters fanned his face, when a round-shot came hurtling over the mud wall and knocked his head clean off. No less than three of his fellow officers were later killed in the same way.'[6] Each day, when darkness fell, the corpses, 250 of them, were thrown into a well outside the walls.

On 25th June Nana Sahib, informed by a spy that the garrison could not hold out much longer, sent a Eurasian woman to the camp with a letter offering safe passage to all who laid down their arms. General Wheeler agreed on condition that the defenders were allowed to march out under arms, that carts were provided for the wounded, the women and the children, and that a sufficient number of boats were made ready for the journey downstream to Allahabad. This was agreed.

Crowds of townspeople gathered to watch the raggle-taggle procession of dirty, haggard, once grandee Europeans make their way down to the Ganges and wade out to the boats. As soon as these began to push off the sandy banks two hidden guns opened fire, and immediately *sepoys* began to shoot from all directions. Screaming women and children jumped into the water to escape the bullets, and also the fires that had been started by embers hidden in the thatched awnings of the boats and were quickly taking hold. Many were drowned, others hacked to pieces in the water by *sepoys* on horseback, many shot; but one boat, laden with wounded as well as able-bodied men, women and children, got away. The rudder had been blown off, and it had no oars, but planks were torn up and used as paddles, and slowly it made its way downstream while *sepoys* on the river banks shot at it. Only four souls survived to tell their story, all young men, two

British officers, and two Irish soldiers, one of whom died later in hospital.

The women and children who were still alive after the massacre were herded together on the sandy bank of the Satichaura Ghat, and taken to the house known as Bibighar for use as possible hostages.

The only women who survived the Cawnpore massacres were two Eurasian girls captured by Muslim *sepoys* who married them after converting them to Islam. One of these was General Wheeler's daughter, Ulrica. She disappeared from history till half a century later when, on meeting a Roman Catholic priest in the bazaar in Cawnpore, a very old woman revealed to him her identity.

'But the best thing was the well,' said Mummy. 'The bodies of the women and children were thrown into it, you see; but now there is a beautiful white marble angel standing guard over it.' She looked up over my head and added, 'Though how long that statue will survive remains to be seen.' She had uttered a prophecy. Today in place of the angel there is a bust of Tatia Topi, Nana Sahib's general.[7]

Mummy showed me a picture of the angel standing over the well, encircled by pillars and turrets inside the memorial gardens. My father's travel diary describes them thus: 'The gardens are large, probably fifty or sixty acres. It strikes me that part of them should be utilised as a playing ground, the memorial being railed off. About ten acres should do for this purpose. It looks like racial domination—the idea of keeping such a large space in a populous city as a permanent memorial of an atrocious massacre.'

In Allahabad they stayed at the Grand Hotel. In spite of the necessity for daily blood pressure readings John was quite well on holiday, but Mabel visited an American dentist in Allahabad and had a tooth extracted, 'without much pain'. For the remainder of their tour they travelled by car, resting overnight in Dak Bungalows. At one point near Cawnpore they passed a notice: 'Motorists forbidden to drive more than 20 miles per hour,' which made Mabel comment: 'Road so bad that driving above 10 miles an hour impossible!'

Besides sightseeing, they visited some industrial areas. My father had in mind the possibility of importing Indian goods to England after he retired. One carpet factory they visited was run by an old German, Mr Waylandt, whose many complaints about his workers (mostly young boys) they had to listen to. 'They give trouble. Always trouble. They ask more pay. They say they are men now, and so need money. It is the Mahatma who is to blame!' Mr Waylandt was seventy-four and had worked in India for fifty years, but now he'd had enough. He was going to leave it to Gandhi and the rest of them, and was going home.

At Agra Sukie got lost for nearly two days, but was found by a soldier on sentry at the Gate to the Fort, and returned very dirty and very thirsty to her owners.

'The Taj is the most beautiful thing I've ever seen,' said Mummy. 'It is a prayer in marble exquisite in its whiteness against the blue of the sky,' John wrote in his diary. And the Jasmine Tower that Shahjehan built for his beloved wife in the *zenana* overlooking the River Jumna was full of airy spaces with marble floors and a rosewater fountain to cool and scent the rooms. 'It is a glimpse of paradise,' said Mummy. She looked over my head far away, and I knew she was remembering her vision.

In Benares they stayed at Clark's Hotel, which they found in a rather dilapidated state, its owner, Miss Clark, also rather dilapidated, declaring it was impossible to run at a profit.

'Did you see the golden temple?' I asked.

'Yes,' Mummy said. 'And thousands of pilgrims waist deep in water, chanting prayers, washing their sins away in the river. And

I've brought you both presents from Benares.' It was a box full of painted animals, a tiger, an elephant, two camels and two monkeys for Dodie and me to share. We quarrelled over the painted animals, but we were glad to see our pop-eyed Sukie again.

Trouble had not ceased while they were away. Daddy frowned often, and sighed because of more Sissy Fuss, and Ayah sighed too. Bearer said Gandhi was at the bottom of it.

It had been suggested that India might be given Home Rule, or Dominion Status within the British Commonwealth, but the Congress Party, led by Gandhi, wanted *swaraj*, or complete independence from Britain. He wanted to obtain the separation by *satyagraha*, or non-violence, but unfortunately his followers were not all as patient, nor as far-seeing as he was himself. There were riots, people got killed, there were arson and assassinations, and the police did not react with non-violence. Political prisoners, thrown into gaol for sedition without trial under the hastily passed new Emergency Laws, had to be visited to make sure they were being treated fairly.

I was allowed to go with Daddy in his big Overlander motor car to the prison where carpet-weaving was being done by prisoners for occupation and remuneration, the so-called penitentiary carpets. One of these men, whom Daddy had known in more peaceful times, had his family with him when we dropped in. Above an enormous loom his small son sat twisting and rolling a handful of scarlet wool. He must have been about the same age as myself. He grinned down at me from his perch; and we made faces at each other as our fathers talked.

Daddy looked worried as we left the place. 'He is an able man,' he muttered. 'He should be out and about, helping to maintain order—not in gaol!'

'Was the boy helping to weave the carpet?' I asked.

'Probably, probably,' he said. 'I shall certainly buy that carpet and take it Home.'

'Are we going Home? —Home to England?' It was a country far away that I had never seen, difficult to imagine, resonant with voices of longing, of exile, a place full of new motor cars, and in the very cold winter smothered with something white called snow.

'Maybe, maybe, who knows when? Impossible to tell these days.' He sighed. 'There's such a lot to do before—before I—'

After the rains that year came the plague of frogs. I squawked when I put my foot on one hiding in my shoe. Frogs swarmed in every corner of the compound; they invaded the house; they hid under the sofa in the drawing room, behind curtains, they got into cupboards, under beds and even under rugs; there were so many of them everywhere that you tripped over them and squashed them underfoot.

'Something must be done,' said Daddy.

Bearer did it. He led two men, each armed with a pair of tongs to catch the frogs and pop them into empty oil drums too high for them to leap out of. At first the men were not quick enough and the frogs escaped, only to be caught later in other hiding places. There was a certain amount of jesting, the hunters became competitive, and Dodie and I, who were following their every move, laughed when they laughed. The froghunt had become a game. When the oil-drums were half filled with the leaping, panting creatures they were taken away to the edge of the compound and left there.

'It's not nice for the frogs,' I said.

'No,' Mummy agreed. 'But perhaps they'll come back in another life one day.'

It was amusing to speculate on what forms they would take. Perhaps a nice fat frog would be the next Babu Chaudhury, leaping out of his seat from time to time to croak at the drowsy *punkah-*

*wallah*; another might turn out to be a Bearer, turbaned above his rolling eyes, padding on splay feet across a dining-room floor to serve plates with his neat damp hands. Mummy and I laughed together at the thought.

The rains stopped at last, followed by cooler weather, and then the best season of the Indian year, winter, began. Daddy was more cheerful. In Ireland the Troubles, though not exactly finished, had decreased with the declaration of a Truce. But in India things were not so good. Gandhi had just been released from prison and was spreading the gospel of non-violent resistance, but somehow inciting folk to violence. And there were some words, I learned, like 'Amritsar', which were bad words. People stopped talking when they heard it, and looked down at their hands. It was like that time of the plague when all the servants in the compound were afraid. When I asked what was this Amritsar I was told it was a place where Indian men, women and children were massacred, by order of a British General.

'It was nearly two years ago, in April,' Mummy said.

Several Europeans had been murdered, there had been rioting and looting of banks, and buildings set on fire, and an English lady missionary had been pulled off her bicycle and beaten so badly she would have died if Indian friends hadn't picked her up and taken care of her. So General Dyer decided: 'This must stop.' He marched his soldiers through the city, standing now and again to read the Riot Act forbidding Assembly. It was market day, and thousands of people had come into Amritsar not only for the market but also to hear some Congress leaders address the crowds in Jallianwala Bagh. General Dyer had two armoured cars with machine guns, but couldn't get them through the narrow entrance into the place. Instead his fifty riflemen took up their positions, and when he gave the signal they opened rapid fire, and continued shooting for ten minutes. There was nowhere for people to hide, and the narrow entrance to the square blocked their getaway. When the soldiers marched away they left four hundred dead and over fifteen hundred wounded.

'An atrocious massacre,' said Daddy. 'Unforgivable. And foolish too.'

In government circles it was generally recognised that India must fairly soon be governed by herself. But how? The discussion went on, and arguments went round and round. The Indian National Congress, formed in 1884, had at first been only a voice for India, but as the process of Indianisation, or the taking of posts by Indians in Civil Administration, the Police, in Public Health and Education, in the Public Works Department and the Railway increased, that voice began to assume power. Then arrived the Mahatma to lead the Congress Party with his totally new ideas of how to persuade the British to give way and go home: *satyagraha*, or non-cooperation, by days of strikes, or *hartal*, holy days of prayer and idleness, refusal to obey British rule through non-violent passive resistance. This strange new idea in the brain of an eccentric holy man was spreading through India like a forest fire in the dry season. Everybody listened to Gandhi, everybody respected him, even the hotheads in his own party who wanted immediate action, even the diehard element of British military opinion, though many regarded him as a fanatical fakir performing absurd antics in a loin cloth. Not so John Reid, who remembered the boycotting of oppressive landlords by Parnell's Land League in Ireland. He also understood why Gandhi had discarded his shirt and cap in favour of a loin cloth, or *khadi*, of home-spun cotton. It was to advertise an Indian cottage industry, and to show his identification with the poor. In another year he was to organise the burning of foreign textiles in a great bonfire in Bombay; but that was yet to come.

Gandhi will have to take on my problem here, John told himself, and that was the whole vexed question of land tenure and bonded labour. The land reforms department had been able to do so little to change that ancient system under which a landowner, or *zemindar*, could sell a plot of land to a penniless peasant in return for his labour. In practice the debt was seldom paid off in the peasant's lifetime, and his son took on the debt, and often his son's son, who were all forced to toil thus endlessly on the *zemindar's* land while eking out a poor existence from their own small portion. It was nothing but a form of slavery.

He would have to talk to Gandhi. Gandhi would have to do something about it. He had already spoken out on behalf of Untouchables, or *Harijan*, who were importuning the Viceroy with petitions and the like, begging him not to allow the British to quit India. Gandhi was trying to modify caste prejudices, especially the worse than snobbery, the contempt in which Untouchables were held by higher castes. He was clever enough to understand that being so numerous, 60,000,000 of them, they would be a voting power to be reckoned with in any new democracy. At the other end of the social scale were the princely states, many of which strongly objected to the idea of being taken over by an Indian parliament. Gandhi, poor man, was going to be left with a basket of troubles in his hands!

Whatever happened the handover of the reins of government must be peaceful. Nobody wanted another Easter Rising in Calcutta followed by an even bloodier war than had been going on in Ireland, with its nasty ambushes and assassinations, or what they called reprisals, as Ulster looked on, fully armed, her many volunteers in training, and, after Carson's slogan: ULSTER IS RIGHT AND ULSTER WILL FIGHT, ready to invade the South if any treaty with the British put their province under Irish rule. John feared that in India too, as soon as the British Army went Home, Moslems and Hindus would set about cutting each other's throats.

The year ended in a flurry of excitement because of the Prince of Wales's tour of India. Prince Edward (later Edward VIII) had been very unwilling to embark on this tour. He had only a few months before returned from a long tour of Australia and New Zealand, which he had found intensely boring, apart from the few occasions when he was able to dance with pretty girls (described as 'bits' in the letters he wrote daily to Freda Dudley Ward); and many advisers spoke out against it, fearing for the Prince's safety in the present unstable state of law and order on the sub-continent, but others thought his royal presence might stimulate a surge of loyalty to the Crown, and so calm the seething resentments threatening India. Moreover his father, King George V, was anxious to get him out of England and away from Freda Dudley Ward, as rumours about their long-term love affair were spreading, and he believed were damaging the monarchy.

Prince Edward was expected to arrive in Patna soon; and Daddy had to arrange for his reception. Gandhi had called upon the people to show their hostility to the tour by boycotting the Prince's appearances with holy days of prayer, and strikes of public services.

Prince Edward landed in Bombay with his friend and cousin Lord Louis Mountbatten, and in spite of Gandhi he received a tumultuous welcome. Thousands thronged the streets to see him and cheer him on his way. He boarded a special train with spacious accommodation to carry him and his entourage round the country to meet the upholders of empire, to smile and shake hands and exchange the small talk that he always found so boring. The driver of his train was proud of his responsibility, and of his engine, and so eager to show off what speed he could attain, that as soon as the royal party was aboard he started frantically to pile on coal and force up steam pressure. The train gathered speed quickly, but soon began to rock, and the Prince became alarmed by its motion and the noise it made. He looked quite ill with fright, till finally orders were sent forward to the engine to slow it down. The order was obeyed no doubt reluctantly by the driver, who then proceeded at a more dignified pace of thirty-five m.p.h.[8]

Meanwhile at the Rice Collector's bungalow in Patna parcels were arriving from Paris. There was a lovely midnight blue voile dress spattered with white flowers for my mother, and a dark blue straw hat under whose wide brim a big pink rose bloomed. For me and Dodie, who were always dressed alike, there were new dresses too, of a lighter blue than Mummy's, with several pairs of white socks, and new shoes for each of us of black leather, but not the new shiny patent leather, which Mummy considered rather vulgar. We had a dress parade in Mummy's bedroom while Ayah sat on the floor and watched it all with smiles and exclamations of pleasure. Mummy would wear her new outfit at the garden party to be held on the *maidan*, to welcome the Prince; Dodie and I were not invited to this party, but would go with Ayah to an Indian lady's house near the river. Here we could stand on the flat roof to see the Prince in his open landau, attended, it was hoped, by enthusiastic crowds, as the procession passed from Commissioner's Ghat to Government House.

Invitations to the great garden party had been issued; but Daddy's spies had informed him that all the important people, including the local *zemindars*, intended boycotting the whole thing. So a few days before the event Daddy decided to drive out to the surrounding villages in his Overlander.

'Can I come too?' I begged.

'No, no,' said Mummy and Ayah both together. There might be some violent demonstrations. There might be some *badmash* men in the villages determined to use fists and sticks and even knives.

Daddy sat in the open car with two muscular servants behind him. As soon as the Overlander approached a village the inhabitants lay down in the road. Daddy had to stop. Then standing on the driver's seat, while his two stalwart servants stood up on the backseat, he made his speech: 'The heir to the throne of England has come to visit India and its people. He will arrive in

Patna in a few days' time.' He was heard in sullen silence. After pausing for a moment to allow his news to be understood he continued: 'Who among you would like to see the future King of England?' He waited again for a second before shouting suddenly, 'You may come to the garden party on the *maidan*. No tickets needed. Entry absolutely free.'

This was followed by a moment of silent disbelief. Then an excited babble of voices broke loose as people began to stand up and form argumentative groups; but they moved to the side of the road as he tried to turn the car; and there were a few friendly shouts as his party moved away.

While these arrangements were being made in Patna the Prince and Lord Mountbatten, mounted on elephant howdahs, were shooting game in Nepal; and with the help of the Maharajah and a large number of elephants, beaters, and hunt followers, each noble guest got his tiger. Mountbatten records in his diary of the tour: 'It is reputed that this shoot has cost Nepal 46 *lakhs* or about £300,000...about 30 head of big game have been obtained all told, and so each animal may be considered worth £10,000.' Moral hindsighters of our own times can be reassured that British India can be exonerated from this extravagant expenditure of cash and wildlife; it was undertaken by the ruler of Nepal, an independent state not under British rule.

On the day of the Prince's visit to Patna, Thursday, 22nd December 1921, Daddy felt ill. It was his duty as Deputy Commissioner of Patna as well as Secretary of Land Reforms to meet the Prince at Commissioner's Ghat when he arrived by boat. Although Daddy felt ill he was able to note with some amusement how the Prince escaped from his military escort on landing, and in spite of their fears for his safety dashed forward to shake hands with Indians closely pressed against barriers, but eager to see him. They were cheering wildly. Some fell at his feet and tried to kiss his boots, till pushed back by police with *lathis*. 'These are the people I have come to India to see!' he announced; and his message was immediately passed over the bush-telegraph to the swelling crowds as he took his place in the carriage for the long drive to Government House.

On the flat roof among Indian ladies in their gorgeous red, blue, and yellow saris edged with gold, Dodie and I stood to watch the Prince pass. We got a good view of him, a dapper little man, smiling and waving cheerfully at the crowds lining the street. As he drew near someone threw him a bunch of flowers, and immediately the aide who was sitting beside him leaped up and caught the bouquet in mid-air; and all the ladies round us uttered a hissing gasp.

'That was a brave man! There might have been a bomb among the flowers!'

'But all's well, there was not!' And everybody laughed with relief.

Daddy was able to get away and retire to bed in our own bungalow, and remained there, cosseted by Bearer with soups and *chota-pegs*, while the Prince was given lunch in Government House. Daddy was still unwell next day; but Mummy took her place with the reception committee to receive the Prince for the garden party at the *maidan*. She couldn't help noticing from afar a number of furtive figures creeping through the cordons around the guests. Mountbatten's diary describes the event thus: 'The landed "magnates" gave a garden party in Hardinge Park, which we all attended...[which] started with the super pomp of native India and finished with a truly democratic crowd of every conceivable caste, creed and odour. In fact it resolved itself into a football scrum, like it used to be in Australia and New Zealand.' [on the previous royal tours.] [9] Little did he know that the 'magnates' were missing, nor guess that some of that odour came from Bengali peasants, and even perhaps from Untouchables.

The royal party left that evening for Calcutta and for some rather more elaborate celebrations.

The next few weeks were filled with preparations for travel. This time we really were going Home. It was January, and quite cool. There was even a fire in the drawing room sometimes; and Dodie and I wore thick serge skirts and long socks; but it was not too cold to sit out on the verandah to watch a group of traders and buskers from the north display their wares and perform with their monkey-theatre. The drama was of the simplest kind, a sort of Punch and Judy Show, in which the female monkey, wearing a short red skirt and uttering many chattering squeaks pinched and pulled the hair of the bigger male monkey till he lost patience and chased her round and round inside a rope circle screaming with rage and showing all his teeth. He was caught by the ringmaster before he actually thumped his wife, which Dodie and I were hoping he would do. Daddy sat with Dodie and me and Ayah to watch this performance, while Mummy was examining the turquoise necklaces and silver bracelets she eventually bought as presents for those other sisters I would soon meet; but she joined us to see the snake-charmer draw a sleeping cobra out of a basket. It rose up, swaying its hooded head as he played high-pitched notes on a kind of flute. I was fascinated too, but I was afraid as well, so I hid behind Mummy, peeping over her shoulder. I'd been told this cobra would obey his charmer; but even when hypnotised he was still the king of snakes and possessed the deadliest of strikes. So although it was a weird and wonderful thing to witness I was glad when it was over.

'There are no cobras in England,' I informed Ayah.

# References – Chapter Three

1 Fanny Louise Daniell's (née Prinsep's) unpublished diary 1850-1880 describes the illness of her three little girls in 1869 in India. The eldest, Fanny aged eight, survived, but the younger two, Aurora aged five and Maude aged three, died within three weeks. She gives a very good clinical description of the disease: sore throat, fever, a whitish exudate on the tonsils growing and spreading, hoarseness and finally obstructive breathing (due to smothering of the airway by the thick exudate), which leads me to diagnose diphtheria. There was no specific treatment for this at that time. In her diary she blames Clare (who was away and had the only available transport, a horse-drawn trap) for the delay in getting a doctor; but it is unlikely that the doctors (two eventually, one English, one Indian) could have done much to help.

What was needed was tracheotomy, or cutting open from outside of the breathing tube to allow air entry. It seems from her diary that the doctors didn't realise what was going on. The children died of suffocation. She had also lost, in India in 1865, another girl aged five from an unknown disease.

2 Lingam: the phallus of the god.

3 Hibbert, Christopher, *The Great Mutiny*, Allen Lane, 1978.

4 Fraser, Antonia, *The Gunpowder Plot*.

5 Hibbert, Christopher, op. cit.

6 ibid.

7 A bust of Nana Sahib's general, Tantia Topi, now covers the well (Wild, Anthony, *The East India Company. Trade and Conquest from 1600*).

8 Mountbatten, Lord Louis, *Diaries: Tours with the Prince of Wales, 1920-1922*, ed Philip Ziegler.

9 ibid.

## 4

By the end of January everything was packed up, Mummy's black grand piano and Daddy's Overlander were sold, as was the pony and trap, Sukie had been entrusted to the care of a kind family, and we were ready to go. A great many farewells had to be said, and a great deal of *baksheesh* handed out before we finally climbed after our luggage into the train at Patna. Bearer and Ayah accompanied us to Calcutta, and then across the city to the quayside, a complicated manoeuvre requiring a whole fleet of carts, taxis and rickshaws, and a lot of shouting and pushing people out of the way. Bearer and Daddy had to see to the stowing away in the hold of the ship of the zinc-lined trunk, the crates and heavy baggage, while Ayah helped Mummy carry the suitcases we'd need on the voyage, and find the cabin reserved for us. It was all very exciting.

'We're going Home!' I said to Ayah as we climbed the gangway.

We were going Home to that magical place spoken of with such reverence and hope. And we were going to live for a whole month on this huge ship with its warren of corridors and cabins and decks, one above the other, and deck-rails through which you could peer down and see water moving away from under your feet. 'And we're going to travel at knots!' But Ayah didn't know what knots were (it was something I'd learned from Mr

Dain when he bid us goodbye at Patna), and she didn't seem as happy about our departure as I was.

'Ayah's crying!' I said.

Mummy embraced her, comforting her. 'Don't cry, Agatha,' she said. 'You will be able to visit your son in Madras now. And you'll find another nice family to look after.' She took out of her handbag an envelope and gave it to her. 'I've written a good reference for you. First class. Tip-top. And you'll find some extra rupees there as well.'

Ayah gave Dodie and me a branch of green bananas. She knew how fond we were of small sweet bananas, and knew that as they ripened gradually with the passing days our pleasure in them would be prolonged.

There was plenty of time on the long voyage home for John to reflect on what he was doing. He was resigning from the Indian Civil Service for reasons of ill health. He had been told by doctors that he had hypertension due to overwork and dealing with too many crises, that if he didn't live a healthier life his high blood pressure would kill him. No drug was available in the 1920s to reduce it; the only treatment was to change the way he lived: he must have fewer worries, more exercise and more sleep. What he suffered from was a tendency to sudden attacks of giddiness with a fear of falling in public places, and an unpleasantly rapid beating of the heart at inconvenient times. Today, after Freud, two Great Wars, and a lot of speculation and studies of what we now call stress, he would be labelled as suffering from anxiety neurosis, or even panic attacks. Was he sick because his was a mind in conflict, his resolve divided between loyalty to the British Crown that paid for his services and his instinctive sympathy with Indian desires for independence, no doubt echoing in his personal uneasiness the feelings of his race towards England? He believed that he helped to provide justice, efficient administration and moderate prosperity for a nation for whom *swaraj* would let loose the dogs of anarchy. Was he afraid to face the inevitable ordeal looming, with all the likely horrors of a religious war and intertribal killings? Whatever his illness was it was painful enough to force him to give up a successful and still promising career culminating in the usual honours awarded by grateful rulers for long service in a pitiless climate.

He had worked in India for twenty-five years; he was recognised as a man of unusual ability, dedication and integrity even among the incorruptible, the 'heaven born', as Indians called the new Indian Civil Service formed after the Mutiny, when the Crown took over government of those parts of India formerly administered by the East India Company and its civil servants were forbidden to take bribes, or to accept any gifts apart from the customary garlands of marigolds hung round the necks of guests. After he retired, John was made a Companion of the Indian Empire: CIE. Had he remained in office longer he would have been given more glittering prizes; these he decided to relinquish in favour of peace and quiet and a more normal family life.

Sitting up on deck as our vessel of the *Messageries Maritimes* line sailed across the Bay of Bengal he must have felt a lightening of the heart at leaving all those insoluble problems behind him. He was certainly relaxed and carefree enough to play with Dodie and me, though he must have known there were other very great difficulties ahead.

He was only forty-eight years old and was therefore retiring early on a reduced pension, which in any case he feared might be confiscated by a new independent Indian Government if and when that took over the civil service. He had a family of seven children to feed and educate; he had no house in England to go to. He'd always intended retiring to Ireland, buying a small farm, and perhaps rearing a racehorse, but the Troubles there had shaken his resolve.

In the summer of 1921, De Valera and Arthur Griffiths had

travelled to London to meet Lloyd George and discuss possible cessation of hostilities, and a Truce was agreed, but not signed. Six months later Griffiths travelled again to London, this time with Michael Collins, to negotiate the terms of the Treaty. De Valera, President of the Dail Eireann formed during the rebellion, did not attend; he did not sign any document, and so in later years was able to evade responsibility for what happened. Michael Collins, a hurley player known at home as the Big Fella, complaining that he was a soldier, not a diplomat, took his place at the negotiating table. On 6th December, after exhausting sessions of argument and diplomatic dealing, the Treaty was signed. Michael Collins and Arthur Griffiths put their names to it (in Gaelic script) opposite those of Lloyd George, Winston Churchill, Austen Chamberlain, and Lord Birkenhead. It was the birth certificate of modern Ireland, the southern counties renouncing control of the six northern counties of Ulster. Ireland now had Dominion Status as the Irish Free State within the Commonwealth.

As soon as Eamonn de Valera read the terms he rejected them, saying that the Irish delegates had 'sold out to London'. But in reality, as opposed to de Valera's misty Celtic romanticism, what else could they do? Michael Collins' ragged guerrilla army, though remarkably successful against the British Army and the rag-tag-and-bobtail collection of Black and Tans it had been forced from lack of manpower to enlist, was exhausted, the people sick of killing and longing for peace. England too was tired after her long war with Germany and the loss of half a million young men in Flanders, and ardently desired peace with Ireland; but Ulster had bought arms and prepared an army of fresh volunteers eager and ready to invade Ireland rather than be ruled by Dublin. And it was quite probable in the prevailing circumstances that had they declared war they would have been victorious. O what a tangled web lay there on the negotiating table! On the night of the signing of the Treaty, Michael Collins wrote to his lover Kitty

Kiernan: 'I don't know how things will go now, but with God's help we have brought peace to this land of ours, a peace that will end this old strife of ours forever.' But after the signing of the document Birkenhead said to Collins, 'I believe I have signed my political death warrant.' And Collins replied, 'I may have signed my actual death warrant.'

De Valera and the anti-treaty pro-Republicans were not satisfied by Dominion Status; they wanted complete separation as well as the six northern counties in an Irish Free State.

John could not then know through the testimony of witnesses to these events what we can now read as history, but because he knew Ireland well and was not lacking in imagination he must have guessed what mental and emotional conflicts Collins went through during the two months of the negotiations.

De Valera had been elected President of the underground Dail Eireann during the Anglo-Irish war. He was a much respected figure, known as the Long Fella because he was so tall and thin, a patriot with a vision of an ideal Ireland that was rooted in a romantic past. Throughout the four years of bitter, nasty fighting that Collins spent moving from cover to cover in the Irish countryside, from one safe house to another in Dublin, in constant danger of assassination by British Intelligence or in army ambushes, de Valera was safe in the USA, using his high-flown rhetoric to collect money for the Cause; now that fighting, it seemed, was over, he had returned to the political arena. Unfortunately for Ireland, de Valera's politics were not, as they were for Disraeli, the art of the possible, but were to prove a struggle to the death of others for his ideal. No sooner had he informed the press that he rejected the treaty than the Dail began to split into pro-Treaty and anti-Treaty factions. Sessions of debate in public and in private, often acrimonious, continued till 22nd January, when a vote was taken, which was won by the pro-Treaty party by a narrow margin of seven votes. Cheering crowds greeted the news as it filtered out of the House, but de Valera immediately threatened to resign, which he soon did, following vindictive abuse and angry accusations of betrayal from both sides, taking with him into enmity many who been comrades in the Anglo-Irish war. Collins pleaded with them to remain united in order to see Ireland through the difficult changeover from a war footing to peace; but they left, and the men who had fought together against a common enemy began to separate into the Irish Free State Army and the Irregulars, later to be known as the IRA. Thus the Irish Republican Brotherhood formed generations before to fight for Ireland's freedom was split in two.

It was not an encouraging environment for an exile to return to. Whatever the outcome in a country now suffering the aftermath of five years of bitter warfare against an oppressor, Mabel, good and kind as she was, would always be English, and therefore would not be welcome in his homeland. John knew very well it wouldn't do to bring his English wife home just yet. And from what he'd gleaned in letters from the boys and from his brother Dr Pat, who took care of them during school holidays, such was the climate of opinion over there that he himself might be under suspicion of treason to the Cause for having worked so long in India for British Colonialism, though in his own mind no truer Irishman ever lived. Better to wait and see how things turned out. If peace prevailed, and random murders and the firing of English houses stopped, it might still be possible for them to live in Ireland. Meanwhile he needed to consult some doctors about his health; and the combined attractions of French Medicine and a continental tour decided him.

'We're not going to England yet,' he said. 'We're going to France. That's why we're on a French boat.'

'My brothers and sisters aren't in France,' I said.

'No. But Lulu and Daphne are in Belgium; and you'll meet them there.'

'Where's Belgium?'

'Near Paris. We're going to Paris first.'

I was disappointed that I couldn't see England yet, but hopeful that I might be given one of the new dolls made in Paris. I had seen pictures of them in Mummy's French catalogues. They had lots of real hair, it was claimed they could actually walk and say, 'Ma-ma!' and I longed to possess one.

In the meantime Daddy amused himself by giving me reading and writing tests, and I gave him singing lessons. I tried to teach him to sing 'Three Blind Mice'. I made him do it over and over again, but found him impossible to teach. He simply could not sing this simple melody in tune.

'You're not paying attention, Daddy. You must try harder,' I said. But he only laughed.

'Well it's not much of a come-all-yous, is it?'

'What's a come-all-yous?'

'It's a song they sing in Ireland to get a party going.' 'Three Blind Mice' didn't have enough of what in recent years has come to be spoken of as 'the Craic'.

'Now if you'd sing me 'The Minstrel Boy' that 'ud be worth hearing. 'Tis my favourite song.' And he began to sing in a dreary monotone:

'The Minstrel Boy to the war is gone
In the ranks of de-e-ath you'll find him.
His father's sword he hath girded on,
And his wild harp slu-u-ung behind him.

'Did he die?' I asked.

'He died for Ireland. Yes.'

'Why do people die for Ireland?'

He made no reply to this but instead took me down into the bowels of the ship to watch the engines working. It was for me

95

a frightening experience: the intense heat, the palpable tremor in the chamber, the hiss of steam, the noise of wheels turning and powerful pistons plunging up and down, up and down, the sudden sharp gleam of brass, all made me tug his hand and beg him to come away, come away from this mechanical ogre grinding bones to make his bread.

John was well enough for the first few days to sit up on deck, but as soon as the sea became at all ruffled he took refuge on his bunk.

'He suffers terribly from sea-sickness,' Mummy explained. And indeed for much of the voyage he never appeared on deck or in the dining saloon at all, and his steward had to bring invalid meals to his cabin.

We landed at last in Marseilles, where Dodie and I were promptly deposited in a French convent. Mabel records that when we were left there 'Nora cried'. I don't remember crying; I can recall very little about these few weeks spent in that French convent apart from the pleasure of eating during the mid-morning break a hot *croissant* with a piece of dark chocolate melting inside it. It was my introduction to French *cuisine*. You didn't need to understand French for that, nor to appreciate the bullying that I saw for the first time in the playground. There was in my class a little lame girl, partially paralysed, probably by poliomyelitis. She was able to run about quite happily, but she was a magnet for the cruel instincts of others, who ran after her, trying to trip her up. I saw her tripped, saw her fall, and saw her tormentors run off laughing, which made me suddenly so angry that I ran screaming after them till the nun on surveillance duty intervened to console the victim and to calm me down. The bullies, as is often the case, got away in the general fuss.

It was while we were in the convent in Marseilles that the parents must have read in the French newspapers the news that anti-Treaty Irregulars had seized control of the Four Courts in

Dublin, as well as other municipal buildings. Collins did not immediately attack, but bided his time, trying to negotiate peace, and waited for a general election to show what was wanted by the majority in the country.

By early May we had joined our parents in Paris. The city, with its *boulevards*, the Bois de Boulogne, where Daddy walked with us under chestnut trees in flower, the Jardin du Luxembourg where Dodie and I rode wooden horses on a merry-go-round, the Eiffel Tower, the pavement cafés and all the tempting shops (though I didn't get the walkie-talkie doll I so desired because it was too expensive), remains in memory a happy place. It couldn't have been very happy for my parents, worried as they must have been about what was going to happen next in Ireland. John was undergoing medical examinations and therapy, including 'cupping', which left peculiar marks on his back like the bite marks of some sharp-toothed little mammal; and Mabel was hovering anxiously over the proceedings. It was here that one of the doctors remarked, 'Monsieur knows a lot of French, but we can understand Madame better.' Monsieur had in fact an accent that was unlike anything the French had ever heard.

In spite of some communication difficulties he received much good advice: smoking was not prohibited, and a little wine allowed, but he must have only one full meal a day, must rest more, keep his weight down, and walk daily. His blood pressure, however, remained too high; and perhaps living in Paris was proving expensive, so it was decided to visit Germany, where post-World-War-I runaway inflation made it cheap for those who could pay in sterling. They would visit the spa at Aachen with its hot healing springs.

We travelled first to Belgium, to the small town of Eekloo, where Lulu and Daphne were boarders at Notre Dame aux Epines, a very large convent. 'So you won't mind being there,' Mummy said. 'Lulu and Daphne will look after you; and besides, there are a hundred other English girls you can talk to.'

We stayed at Le Verger Vert, a pension near the market square. Lulu and Daphne were granted permission from the Reverend Mother Superior to spend Sunday with us there. They arrived in time for lunch, Daphne, who was nearly twelve, dressed in her Sunday uniform of white drill sailor-suit, Lulu a tiny person carrying a big cello. She was not in uniform, as she was eighteen, and about to leave school, but wore a close-fitting buttoned-up navy dress that accentuated her thinness. She had lovely hair, fair and curly and not yet put up into a bun; she had delicate features and a sweet smile, and would have been a beauty if her looks hadn't been spoiled by the weakness of one eye. When she looked straight at you, sometimes her left eye wandered away upwards, which was disconcerting.

I was shy with them at first, but Lulu was kind, and after a leisurely Sunday lunch she took Dodie and me into the garden of the guesthouse and began to tell us the story of Snow White and the Seven Dwarfs. I listened eagerly, till Mummy called us into the salon, as she wanted to hear Lulu play her cello.

She sat down, spreading her legs wide to position the unwieldy instrument between her thin limbs, so that she looked like a brown beetle, while the rest of us sat down to listen to her performance. At the end of it, Mummy, with the best intentions, moved forward to tell her that she was not holding the bow correctly, and tried to show her how it should be done; but Lulu suddenly stood up, threw the cello against the chair and said, 'Well, if that's all you think of me I shall never play the beastly thing again!' And with that she scuttled out of the room.

Dodie and I ran after her. She took our hands and led us across the market square to a sweetshop where we stopped to gaze awestruck into the window at a display of sweets such as we'd never before seen: bars of *nougat*, chocolates, little baskets of sugared almonds, and toys moulded in chocolate and coloured sugar. In the midst of all these delights was a white sugar chamber pot containing a chocolate turd. Dodie spotted it first.

'O look! Look!' she cried, and burst out laughing. I was soon laughing too, but Lulu pulled us away angrily, muttering: 'Disgusting! Typical *sales Belges!*'

Daphne went back to school that evening, but Lulu remained at Le Verger Vert to help Mummy look after us. Already, without much thought as to her own wishes, she was falling into the role assigned to the eldest daughter who was expected to stay at home to help her mother till she married, when of course she became her husband's helpmate.

It had not been a joyous family reunion. Lulu had rebelled against the tyranny of her hated cello, had angrily rejected her mother's advice, perhaps tactlessly proffered, about the playing of it; Daphne had hardly said a word all day. No doubt the expectations, nourished only by letters and imagination over the time-space of a four-year absence, were suddenly found, by parents as well as daughters, to be false. There was not much love and happy laughter about that Sunday.

Next morning we were woken by the hideous noise of market day. The square was crammed with pens full of fat pink squealing pigs tended by fat women in black with pink arms, all shrieking at once, or so it seemed, as I wended my way through the crowds towards the sweetshop clutching the centimes Daddy had given me to spend. I didn't buy the chamber pot; I bought some *nougat* which I was chewing as I tried to find my way back through the bewildering turmoil. I soon lost my way to the side street on which our pension stood. I began to cry, and immediately was surrounded by black-robed women, one of them with a squealing piglet under her arm. They were bending their fat pig-faces close to mine and uttering what must have been kindness, but in voices raised to screaming pitch in order to be heard, and in incomprehensible Flemish. Panic seized me, and I bawled louder still, till miraculously

Lulu suddenly appeared, and, taking me by the hand, led me quietly away. She may have felt disappointed in strange parents who neither praised nor appreciated her, but to me she was an angel of deliverance.

A week later she introduced Dodie and me to our new school at Notre Dame aux Epines. After the heat and dirt of that June day in the narrow streets of Eekloo, the convent parlour was cool and clean, its walls whitewashed, its high window casting a beam of light so bright it assaulted the eyes as it struck across the red-tiled floor to illumine, none too kindly, a plaster statue of the Virgin robed in blue and wearing a crown of thorns. On one wall hung a crucifix, on another a picture of the Pope. We all sat on high-backed chairs whose shiny brown seats were stuffed with horsehair. I swung my legs and stared at the crucifix opposite as we waited for Reverend Mother; Mummy commented on how cool the room was; Lulu said nothing. Daphne then arrived, bringing Reverend Mother with her; and the grown-ups began to talk in French.

Reverend Mother was tall and impressive in her black habit, the wooden rosary beads attached to her belt clicking when she moved, and her big headdress of starched white linen framing her rosy cheeks. Smiling, she bent over us and called us *mes enfants*, which I understood, as a large white hand emerged from her wide black sleeve to grasp my shoulder while her other arm enfolded Dodie. Mummy recorded: 'This time Nora didn't cry.' And so we were led away into a strange new world where everybody was talking French.

Dodie and I sat side by side at a long trestle table and drank bowls of hot chocolate with *tartines*, or slices of bread and butter that could be spread with jam, we learned, if we supplied our own *confiture*. Lulu told Mummy to buy it for us, and saw that we had plenty of it. Daphne, who was a big girl housed in another part of the school, we hardly ever saw.

100

At night we slept in a big dormitory. We each had a separate little wooden cubicle, and Dodie's was next to mine, so we could talk through the partition before 'lights out'. It was not long before we were lying there during the daytime too, because we were both shivering and feeling miserable, our faces and chests covered with spots. Dodie kept up an infuriating wail: 'Mummy! Mummy!' Short pause. 'Mummy! Mummy!'

'She can't hear you!' I cried. 'She's in England!'

But this information didn't stop her, wrong as it was, for our parents were by this time in Germany. Her cries continued till at last a nun arrived bringing with her a doctor, who pronounced: *'C'est la Rougeole!'* We had succumbed to measles. He then looked inside my throat and told Sister that my tonsils were very large. Turning to me, he suddenly barked, 'Cut out!' in his limited English and still more limited understanding of a little girl's fears. It was in an era when tonsillectomy was believed to be a cure for a good many ills. Luckily nobody else noticed my tonsils for many years to come.

After that we were wrapped in blankets and carried to the Infirmary, a small house in its own grounds, where Sister Philomène looked after us. She was a plump, smiling person who fed us well and exerted very little discipline. There were several other children there to play with as we got better. We played *cache-cache*, or hide-and-seek, in the garden where redcurrants were ripening, and she never noticed how the bushes were being stripped of their delicious fruit. Perhaps she blamed the birds. We were certainly happy there; and we were learning to speak French. I was enjoying a special pleasure daily when the postman brought me a postcard from Germany. Lulu was sending me a series of cards telling the story of Snow White, and each day another exciting episode unfolded for me.

It was during that June that the General Election in Ireland was held. Collins' Provisional Government won ninety-two seats as against de Valera's anti-Treaty Party which won thirty-two, but de Valera, petulant egotist that he was, refused to accept the majority verdict, declaring that the majority had no right to do wrong. He was never much of a democrat, and once wrote: 'I only had to examine my own heart and it told me straight off what the Irish people wanted.' Collins now knew he had the people behind him, and pushed by Churchill who wanted him to take action, he ordered the Provisional Government forces to bombard the Four Courts and eject the Irregulars. It was done with the aid of British field guns from the other side of the River Liffey; and the Irregulars inside soon came out holding a white flag. This did not however signal surrender in the country at large. All over Ireland former companions in arms joined either the Free State Army or the Irregulars and began to fight each other.

When we were at last out of quarantine and free to leave the Infirmary the school term was ending. We were to spend the long summer holidays in Germany. The parents returned from Aachen— the home town of Charlemagne, who probably liked the hot springs to wash in—to Eekloo to fetch us, and also to pick up my sister, Mary, who was travelling from Ireland.

My three elder sisters had all been at the Dominican convent in Cabra, Dublin, after World War I. Lulu and Daphne moved to Belgium in 1921, but Mary had stayed behind to study for her matriculation. The exam was held at the end of June 1922.

She was sitting bent double with concentration over her desk in the examination hall in the middle of the city and almost adjacent to the Four Courts when the intense silence was suddenly shattered by an explosion, by shouts and a sputtering of gunfire; and smoke began to billow through the open windows. This was the day the Free State Army had decided to dislodge the Irregulars from the Four Courts. The Civil War had started.

The hall was cleared quickly, and the students all sent home. They had to sit the rest of the examination a few days later at another venue. When after a lapse of two years Mary applied for admittance to London University, her matriculation certificate was not accepted, as it had been obtained in two parts; and she had to sit the whole exam again in London, to her advantage as it proved, for she won a distinction.

As soon as she'd taken the Irish exam she had to travel across Dublin through sporadic fighting. Two nuns accompanied her in a cab down the old Cabra Road into the city. There was not much traffic, but as the cab made its way towards Kingstown (now renamed Dun Laoghaire), armed men of various sorts ran through the streets from time to time, buildings burst into flames and gunfire and sudden explosions could be heard. The nuns were so frightened that they insisted on pulling down the blinds, but they were also eager to see what was going on, so they kept pulling them up.

'Jesus, Mary, Joseph! Will you lift the blind a little, Sister Theresa? What was it that just went up?' cried one. And the other, peeping gingerly out replied, 'Holy Mother of God! There's a whole row of houses blazing!'

And so they trotted through the streets, the anxious cabby urging on his terrified horse till they reached the ferry terminal.

'Thanks be to God, you're safe, my child,' said Sister Theresa. 'Now don't talk to anyone on the boat. We'll be praying for you all the way!'

Mary was seventeen, a very pretty, lively girl not marked up for demure obedience, even a bit wild, for hadn't she organised a sweepstake among the girls of the upper school, and very nearly been expelled for it? She had to cross the Irish Sea to Holyhead, then travel on by train across godless England to make her way to Belgium.

The Irish ferry was delayed, not surprisingly at the commencement of a Civil War, the boat-train had left by the time she reached Holyhead, and she had to wait a long stretch of hours before the next train. She had her travel tickets in her pocket, but very little money to spend on tea and buns, and there was very little to see in Holyhead. It was dark by the time she boarded the train for London. She slept fitfully on the journey, and arrived at Euston in the early hours of the morning tired and hungry, but no tearooms, nor even stalls were yet open for customers. She was, however, able to buy herself a cup of tea and a bun at Victoria Station before taking the train to the coast, the cross-channel ferry to Ostend, the Belgian train to Ghent, and then a smaller puffer to Eekloo, where she at last arrived in low spirits but looking forward to being greeted by loving parents eager to give her a good meal.

The reunion was not at all what she'd hoped for. Her father asked her angrily why she was more than twenty-four hours late. He had been counting the hours. He had read newspaper reports of renewed fighting in Ireland, and was undoubtedly extremely anxious about his daughter's safety; and his own feelings, perhaps inevitably, were much more violent than he could imagine hers might be.

'We have been very worried about you—ill with worry—not knowing what was happening.' His voice was alarmingly loud. 'Why did you not send a telegram to let us know you'd been delayed?'

She hadn't thought of it; she hadn't imagined his feelings any more than he'd imagined hers. She had never in her life sent a telegram. It would have cost a penny per word to anywhere in England, but probably more to Belgium; she had not been provided with enough money for a meal, let alone a telegram, so sending one was impossible. She was still too young and inexperienced to summon up appropriate words in explanation, too stunned by exhaustion to summon up any words at all. Mummy, who was standing beside him rather helplessly, interrupted him.

'I think she's very tired, Jack. And hungry too, no doubt.' She put her arm round Mary for the first time since her arrival at Le Verger Vert, and led her into the *salle à manger*, where she ordered a splendid English *fif-o'clock-tea*, a plate of bread and butter, and a slice of the local *pain d'épices*. At the *pension* they had no idea how to make English tea, let alone the strong Irish brew Mary was accustomed to, but she drank it gratefully, and was full of praise for the delicious cake.

From such events and out of such small dramas lifelong attitudes and affections are formed.

Dodie and I were still in the Infirmary, so we didn't meet Mary then. It was only years later that Mary, with her inimitable gift for mimicry, told us the story of her journey and its end.

Mary had a good soprano voice, not as high as her grandmother's had been, but good enough in Mummy's opinion to be properly trained. So arrangements were made for her to spend the summer living in the higher-school house at Notre Dame aux Epines, perfecting her French, and taking singing lessons from a good music master, while the rest of us travelled to Germany. She came to the station to see us off.

The train to the frontier was very crowded. Daddy managed to find a porter to help carry some of the luggage; Lulu held Dodie and me by the hand; Mary and Mummy, both carrying suitcases, were running up and down the platform trying to find seats for us all; and Daphne ('Daffy'), heavily loaded with baggage, brought up the rear. Daddy, who had at last found space in a third-class carriage, was shepherding us into it when he caught sight of Daffy, and, irritated by her slowness, suddenly shouted, 'Stop dawdling! And hurry up, will you!' But Daffy either didn't hear him, or was lost in her own thoughts, and simply plodded on. The train was about to leave, the guard waving a flag to signal to the driver, when Daddy rushed towards Daffy, and lifting his stick thwacked her across the back. Then Mary, who had witnessed this, ran back towards them, shouting furiously, 'No! No!' And seizing one of Daffy's bags she pushed her forward. Just in time. Daffy fell into the carriage as the guard blew his whistle. Mary, standing on the platform outside, waved us goodbye.

We were all crammed onto wooden seats, luggage pushed into whatever corners could be found in among women and their baskets, some containing live poultry, others vegetables, loaves, and parcels of butter, all being taken to the German frontier to barter, not for cash–since the mark, owing to hyper-inflation, was worth nothing–but for goods. There was a lot of talk, all in Flemish that we couldn't understand, and a lot of laughter too. Friendly gestures were made, chiefly towards Dodie, who was sitting literally pretty on Mummy's lap, and we all exchanged smiles.

And so we travelled across another frontier to Aachen, and another strange new world.

## 5

A silence fell when I entered the crowded shop. Our *Gasthaus* was only a few doors away from it so I was allowed to run into the shop by myself. Daddy had given me a fat packet of bank notes to pay for an ice cream. To my parents it seemed rather amusing that you had to pay thousands of marks for an ice cream, but as soon as I was inside the shop I knew it wasn't a joke for all the people who were staring at me and my handful of paper money. All my young life had been spent in foreign countries, but never before had I felt alien. That was something else I learned in those few minutes: that I was an enemy.

When I got back to the guesthouse Daddy was sitting in the lounge with an elderly bearded German, whom he'd invited to share a flask of coffee with him. The man smiled at me sourly as he asked me if my ice cream was *'gut'*. I sat on the floor between them and soon learned some more surprising facts. The old man was a retired professor living on a pension, which was now worth so little that he had to sell old family possessions in order to survive. I had just spent, he informed me, more than his pension for a whole week; it was just enough, he said, vigorously nodding his head to drive his message home, to buy one sausage! And this sorry state of things was brought about by that greedy Welshman Lloyd George, and even more so by that French tiger Clemenceau, who were demanding such impossible-to-pay reparations for the War that the whole German nation was being starved.

His message was brought home even more strongly later that day when Daddy took us out to lunch in a nearby restaurant. We ate well, but as we were leaving a woman with two children begged Mummy to give her the bread left over at our table. Mummy, though quite accustomed to continual demands for baksheesh in India, seemed confused and agitated by the German beggar. She sent Lulu back into the restaurant to collect the broken rolls of bread, and, opening her purse, pulled out handfuls of notes which the children as well as their mother very quickly grabbed.

My parents were taken aback by what they saw; and Mummy, certainly, felt some guilt at being able to profit from the misery of others. They had spent the years of the Great War, apart from some months' leave in Ireland during 1917-18, in India, far away from the European slaughter. The conflict, though they had read about it in the newspapers, and in letters from friends and relatives at home, had not been as real to them as to those who felt more immediately its impact. They had not known the slow, accumulating loss to a community whose young men, one by one, household by household, family by family, simply disappeared. They had not felt the intense need to seize the pleasure of the day experienced by young men released on short leave from trenches of death, and the girls who were to lose them; the importance of hedonism in these brief lives was something they couldn't imagine. Nor had they imagined what defeat and inflation of their currency would mean in terms of poverty and hunger to ordinary Germans.

In such a state of affairs we were of course rich. Sterling could buy anything. We were kitted out with new winter coats and velour hats, with new skirts and smart shoes; and Lulu was allowed to buy her first evening gown. When the professor saw all this booty he told us that tourists had to declare new purchases, for which they had to pay duty at the frontier. Only the week before customs officials at the Belgian border had caught four nuns, each wearing three evening gowns under their habits. They were trying to smuggle them out in order to sell them in Belgium at an enormous profit. It was a shocking business, a disgrace, publicised and gloated over in the newspapers.

Mummy talked about an expedition to Bonn where Beethoven was born. I knew who Beethoven was. Mummy esteemed him as the greatest of all composers. I'd heard her say so one evening to the professor when she'd just played part of the *Appassionata* on the piano in the *Gesellschaftsraum*.

'Do you know what Beethoven did on his deathbed?' He raised a clenched fist. 'So,' said the Herr Professor. I watched him push his fist into the air above his head.

'He was interested in French Revolutionary ideas,' said my father.

'So sad, *nichtwar*? So sad that so becoming deaf he was.'

There was a short silence while we all felt the sadness of it.

'Like you, Herr Reid, he took the water cure. And always he was pouring cold water on his head to clear the thinking, while he was—how you say?—composing his wonderful music.'

What would it feel like, I wondered, if I poured cold water on my head? It would be like monsoon rain falling on me. But would it help me to make up tunes?

'But there was no cure. And when he knew it he wrote to a friend like so: "As the autumn leaves fall and wither, so my hopes fade for me." '

This time there was a longer silence. It was a terrible disappointment for Beethoven. And I could see from Mummy's face that she felt it as if it had been her own.

It was the professor who suggested the expedition to Bonn. He knew a man with a car who could take us there and back in a day. I was excited by the idea. I wanted to see Beethoven's house. But there wasn't room in the car for all of us. Lulu said only one of us could go. In order to settle which one it would be she set a competition for Dodie and me. We would each have to paint a leaf of the Virginia Creeper growing on the back of the house, and whoever painted the better picture would win a place in the car. I painted my red and purple leaf with great care; it was in my opinion perfect, but for some reason that I couldn't understand Lulu decided that Dodie's was better. I had to remain in Aachen with Daffy under the eye of the hotelier while the rest of the family, accompanied by the professor and his car-owning friend, drove off to enjoy themselves in Bonn. It was a terrible disappointment; I can still feel the injustice of it. The irony of this small drama was that my sister Dodie in old age couldn't remember a thing about it. She had had no interest in seeing Beethoven's house, and was astonished by my feelings on the subject.

Nor did Daffy feel unduly sore at being left out. We were left together to amuse ourselves for the day. We sat at a table in the guesthouse lounge, and with the aid of her paint-box we painted whatever images came into our heads. It was when I saw the Virginia Creeper leaves that Daffy painted that I understood how far from perfect mine had been. And when she drew a picture of a chair at the window with a beam of light striking across it, all shown with pencil shading, it was so like the real thing that I thought it was magic.

'How do you do it?' I asked in wonder.

'Like this,' she said. But no matter how hard I tried, using all the HB, B and BB pencils that she generously allowed me to use, my scribbles and shadings never turned out to be anything like as good as hers.

Daffy was very shy and modest and never swanked about anything, but when the rest of the family came back that evening, and Mummy saw the drawing of the chair at the window, she seemed surprised. 'Well, she can certainly draw,' she said. And to Daffy: 'It's awfully good, my dear. You have a real talent.'

We were taken to Cologne to see the great Gothic cathedral, whose grey stone pinnacles summoned up in memory seem ghostly and mysterious. We took a trip on a river steamer down the Rhine to view the rock where Lorelei sat singing the song that tempted foolish sailors to their ruin. That expedition was a great thrill, slightly spoiled by Daffy's mishap. We were all sitting up on deck in our new coats and our new velour hats, no doubt partly to shade our complexions from the summer sun, when a gust of wind seized Daffy's and blew it away very quickly beyond rescue. This time it was not I but Daddy who was enraged. And poor Daffy got the blame for her loss.

One evening Mummy went to the opera. *Tannhauser* was the name of it. She went alone because Daddy couldn't stand or understand opera. So he remained at the pension after supper, and sat smoking and talking with the professor, mostly in English. They were talking about a man named Bismarck. Lulu, Daffy, Dodie and I sat at a circular table by the window and played cards till bedtime. Lulu was teaching us Whist. It was a lovely game, especially when you had a few secret trumps in your hand and could throw one suddenly and unexpectedly on the table and win a trick. That table had a red plush cover that fell down all round it nearly to the floor, so that its fringes tickled your feet when you pushed them underneath.

Mummy came home late, after we'd gone to bed, but she told us next morning that in the middle of the opera when the audience was most solemn, she'd had a fit of giggles because the Evening Star couldn't make up its mind where to appear and kept popping up first in one place, then in another. After that she had a fit of coughing and couldn't stop, and the people near her began to hiss. So she had to leave the theatre before the end of the story.

111

Daddy laughed, but she said she was ashamed at behaving so badly.

The highlight of our German holiday was a visit to the cinema. Dodie and I had never seen a film before. I have no recollection of the title of that film, but I can vividly recall a very fast moving black and white sequence of Fatty Arbuckle being chased by a little dog. Being so fat he was unable to run very fast, and the dog was immediately behind him, snapping and jumping up to tear bits of cloth out of the tail of his jacket. Somehow Fatty climbed on to a shed and lay on the roof with his head peering over the edge. The dog stood below, barking madly. Unluckily for Fatty his tie came loose and hung down, just within reach of the angry dog, who was able to keep jumping up and grabbing the end of it. At each tug the noose of the tie grew tighter and tighter round Fatty's neck, and he was in imminent danger of being strangled. Dodie and I found this so exquisitely funny that we were helpless with laughter. No sooner was the film ended than we wanted to see it again.

'There'll be plenty of other flicks to see once we get to England,' Lulu said, as she took us back to the *pension* for tea.

It was a bright future to look forward to.

My father was able to get newspapers from Ireland, and was following the course of Ireland's Civil War. That was very real to him, partly because he and Mabel were anxious about their own two sons, who were still pupils at Clongowes. They were in fact quite safe in Borris, near Carlow, with Uncle Pat, enjoying a lovely summer holiday, swimming in the River Barrow, learning how to tickle trout, cycling around Mount Leinster, and playing cards in the evening with the girls from the post office. Sometimes my brother Pat, then aged eleven, inspected the rival military camps in the area. He had friends in both, and was surprised one morning to be told that one of his friends wasn't alive any more. He had been killed in a skirmish the night before.

On 22nd August, Michael Collins was murdered in a narrow lane by a posse of Irregulars who lay behind a high bank waiting for him. A week later, John was able to see a copy of the *Cork Examiner* of 24th August. It carried a full page of news on the event. 'HEROIC DEATH OF MICHAEL COLLINS. Ireland's Woe... . National hero dies... . An appalling catastrophe has befallen the Irish people... . General Collins was shot dead by ambushers at...a spot between Cork and Macroom... . The party was proceeding by by-roads accompanied by a Whippet armoured car when they were attacked by a large party of Irregulars.'[1]

The fight lasted an hour. Collins was shot through the head. A shudder of horror passed over the whole country, and shocked England as well. Churchill immediately sent a message calling the deed 'a cruel and wanton act'. The Provisional Government's message to the people was written in patriotic purple prose: 'The greatest and bravest of our countrymen has been snatched from us at the moment when victory smiled through clouds upon the uprising of the Nation to which he had dedicated all the powers of his magnificent manhood.' And to the Free State Army the Chief of General Staff wrote with soldierly reserve and elegance: 'Stand calmly by your posts... . Let no cruel act of reprisal blemish your bright honour.'[2]

'What a hope!' was John's thought as he read this. 'There'll be bloody murder everywhere.' And that was what decided him to give up any idea of going home to Ireland. They would settle in England instead. They would leave Daphne and me at the convent in Eekloo, Mary would continue for the present in the higher school, studying French and singing, and Lulu and Dodie would travel with them to London, where they would set about finding a house near enough to suitable day schools for both their boys and their girls.

Notre Dame aux Epines was no longer strange to me, and I fell into line there as children do, accepting their environment. On Sundays, dressed up in our white drill sailor-suits and straw hats, we had to attend High Mass, which was rather long and boring, though I liked the singing, especially the mysterious words, *Kyrie Eleison*, that were the magic key that unlocked gates into a hidden garden full of tangled trees where old magicians in golden coats moved about, waving their arms and chanting their spells. After it was over I could buy from the tuck-shop a bar of chocolate-coated *nougat* and eat it while roller-skating across the asphalt playground. On feast days for dinner we had little brown pears cooked in syrup and served with almond biscuits that were nicer than anything I'd ever tasted before. Such treats almost made up for the absence of my mother.

There was one other English girl I knew. My friend was called Joan, and she was the daughter of May and Harry Foster, who had been so good to me in India. She was a little older than I was and had been at the school already a year, so she spoke French, and knew the ropes. We were two foreigners in a crowd of children all chattering French or Flemish.

As the weeks passed I began to pick out meanings in their words, and was gradually drawn into their games: skipping games, hopping games and *osselets*, which was played by bouncing a ball with one hand while scooping up little steel 'knucklebones' with the other. I loved these games, though I knew I was only allowed to play on sufferance, and was frequently teased. In India I'd been a small queen of the compound, with Ayah to look after me and many kind servants to make much of me; at Notre Dame I was an unimportant stranger, and often laughed at, which was hard to bear.

'Why are you crying?' asked Soeur Veronique. She was a tall nun with bulging blue eyes.

'They call me a baby because I believe in fairies!' I blurted out. 'They say fairies can't fly!'

*'Mais il y a des anges,'* she said. 'Angels can fly.' A large white hand appeared out of her black sleeve and rested on my shoulder. 'And you have your own special guardian angel, you know.'

My tears stopped at once. 'What's her name?' I asked.

'You'll have to ask her,' she said.

I ran off happily to wait my turn on the roller skates. When at last I took off and managed to glide the whole length of the playground without tripping I was lifted into happiness. It was magic. 'I shall call you Solange,' I told my guardian angel, who had undoubtedly just helped me to fly so fast. 'You'll be my friend.' She would be my Ayah too, and look after me, and I would boss her about. I imagined her sleeping on the floor beside me in the dormitory, wrapped in her wings, like Ayah, inside the *resai* that protected her from mosquitoes.

Joan and I had beds in adjacent cubicles. After the supervising nun had turned off the lights and shouted her last command, *'Silence maintenant! Et bonne nuit, mes enfants!'* and had padded away down the corridor, I used to rap twice on the partition. Joan replied with two soft knocks. It was our secret signal to talk.

'Did you know that nuns have red flannel petticoats underneath?'

'Nuns have no hair, you know.' Long pause. 'They have it all shaved off when they come here.'

I imagined Soeur Veronique without her headdress, looking like that old doll of mine, the one whose wig I tore off in a rage because the hair got all tangled up when I tried to brush it.

On the end wall of the dormitory there hung a picture of the Blessed Thérèse of Lisieux dressed in her nun's habit, and surrounded by roses. I used to look at her before lights-out because her smile was so comforting in the dark. I wondered if she too was bald under her veil.

It was very important to be good at Notre Dame; and it was soon obvious to me that to win attention and praise you had to be very good indeed. Every good thing you did was like popping a coin into your personal spiritual piggy-bank. Piling up treasure in heaven was what it was called. But if you did something really bad you might lose all your savings in one go, and fall into the pit of hell forever. You could win a red rosette for good behaviour, and I determined to win one. It wouldn't be easy. The Devil was about everywhere, hiding in corners, ready to jump out and tempt you to wickedness. I'd seen him one Sunday evening in chapel during Benediction. He wasn't as black as I'd imagined, but whitish from the incense escaping from the censor swung by an altar boy, and spiralling upwards, peaking into pointed ears and a sharp beard and a big ha-ha-ha of a mouth. I wasn't afraid of him; he was only smoke, and I could deal with that. It was Soeur Roget, not the Devil, who made me bad.

She was a tiny woman with bright burning eyes, and she spat speech as she scuttled about in the great hall at evening playtime. Sometimes the noise of a hundred little girls running about and shouting was more than she could bear. Then she would jump on a chair, and clanging a hand-bell would scream, '*Silence! Taisez-vous! Silence! Silence!*' With her black sleeves flapping and her eyes shooting darts of rage, she was like a crow that has blundered into a greenhouse.

Before prayers she always gave us a sermon on modesty. Modesty meant hiding your body so that no one, not even yourself, could see it. Parts of the body exempt from this rule were the head and neck, and hands and feet.

Several times during the first term we were taken to have footbaths. We sat on a row of chairs and spread out our bare feet into white porcelain slipper-shaped basins full of hot water. I daresay hot water was scarce. Perhaps that was the reason that all-over baths were so infrequently enjoyed, and always with a certain amount of ceremonial. First two young novices allowed hot water to run into the baths, each bath in its separate cubicle, then Soeur Roget put her finger in the water to test its temperature before telling us to undress. This we had to do under a cotton tent, and this we had to spread over the bath before stepping into the water, where we were supposed to wash without looking.

Joan was scornful of this custom. 'English baths aren't like that,' she said. So we simply wet the covers and threw them on the floor. Unluckily for me Soeur Roget entered the bathroom and caught me happily soaping my uncovered self. She scowled, and her lips emitted a burst of machine-gun fire, which didn't hit me as I didn't yet understand enough French words. But later I began to suspect that she didn't like me much.

'You'll have to try a lot harder if you want to win that rosette,' Solange warned me.

I even made efforts to swallow the disgusting sour milk soup served up on Mondays. It was so nasty that many girls tipped it into paper bags, which they somehow hid under their skirts and later flushed down the lavatories.

The lavatories were built round a yard, and their doors were made of wooden slats with a space below where your feet were visible from outside, and a space above where your head, if you were tall enough, could be seen.

We were shepherded to this place at regular intervals; if we needed to go at other times we had to ask permission. It was one evening at playtime that I was suddenly seized by that need. Was it something I'd eaten? Perhaps the sour milk soup? Whatever it was I had to run to Soeur Roget to ask for her permission to leave the hall.

She was seated at a high desk with her feet dangling above the floor. She glanced down at me severely before nodding. 'But keep out of temptation!' she shouted above the prevailing din. 'Be modest at all times!'

117

'Yes, Soeur Roget.'

'And when you are in bed,' she spoke agonisingly slowly, 'keep your hands above the blanket. Fold them in prayer.'

'Yes, Soeur Roget.' I was concentrating on crossing my legs.

'Pay attention, child!'

'Yes, Soeur Roget.'

'Never let your hands stray down your body to give yourself pleasure before you sleep.'

'No, Soeur Roget.' The menace in her voice made me think I must have committed, without knowing what it was, some terrible sin.

'You can go now.'

I ran.

A single electric light bulb dimly lit one corner of the yard as I stumbled towards the slatted doors. Only just in time. I sobbed with anguish and relief as I sat down on the lavatory seat. After a moment or two I examined my hands, turning them over, trying in that poor light to spot any telltale signs of wickedness on them, but could discover none. How could Soeur Roget know that I warmed my hands between my knees in bed when it was cold? She was a witch; and those eyes of hers must be magic to be able to spy like that after lights-out.

I glanced up, and there in the space above the door was the Blessed Thérèse of Lisieux, her face softly shining. She smiled at me, and offered me one of her pink roses.

'You'll never win a red rosette now,' said Solange as I stood up.

But I didn't care any more, because a moment ago I'd seen a magic holy vision and was offered a rose that was far grander and more important than a red rosette. And Soeur Roget seemed somehow shrivelled , and a lot less frightening, now that I knew Blessed Thérèse was on my side.

In London's Holland Park where the rest of the family was staying, Dodie had no need to see visions; she was getting all the attention and love a small girl could desire. Being the only child in the boarding house where my parents were living, and an unusually pretty and good-tempered child too, she was universally petted and made much of. There were staying at that time in the same boarding house a couple who worked in the newly emerging film industry. They were greatly taken by Dodie's looks and personality, and tried to persuade my parents to let her act in a film they were making; but Daddy was horrified at the suggestion. The stage, whether in the traditional theatre or in this new thing called the cinema, was to him a sink of sloth and false morality. The idea of allowing his youngest and prettiest child to get fouled up in this world was repugnant in the extreme.

'I think you're rather behind the times,' Lulu said. 'She might be a Child Star you know.'

Lulu was learning shorthand and typing at a secretarial college where she spent the mornings, but every afternoon she looked after Dodie, taking her for walks, or bus rides into town to look at the shops.

'It's not for you to criticise your father,' Mummy said. No doubt the parents had discussed the whole business when they walked together in Kensington Gardens for the daily constitutional ordered by the French doctors. No doubt she also very sensibly saw something of the traps that would inevitably be set for actors and actresses in this new profession, and agreed with his decision. In any case it was her job to look after his health, partly by keeping him calm. That meant she had to agree with what he said, as any disagreement tended to raise his blood pressure.

Daffy and I remained at the Belgian convent during the Christmas holidays in company with a few other girls whose parents lived far away in foreign countries. We placed our shoes outside our cubicles in the dormitory on the eve of the feast of Santa Claus (6th December) and found them crammed with sweets and nuts, and an orange in each heel. That was the first time I'd ever tasted an orange; and I was able to express my appreciation of it in fairly fluent French. Another term came and went with a great ringing of bells at Easter, when the bells of the convent chapel threw down little sugar Easter eggs all over the Infirmary garden, where we had to go and hunt for them.

Then the summer term began. But halfway through that term we were summoned to England with Mary, who escorted us to what was to be our first English home.

*References – Chapter Five*

---

1 Coogan, Tim Pat, *Michael Collins.*
2 ibid.

# Part Two

## HOME

## 6

No 11 Ridgway Place was a solid three-storey house built over an extensive basement on the hill leading to the Ridgway that lay on the edge of Wimbledon Common. From here a number of parallel roads, like the teeth of a comb, ran down to the lower town, the station and the theatre. The upper, older town, known as 'the village', contained small, old-fashioned shops, including Cullens the Grocer, and an ancient inn, the Fox and Grapes.

Every day Daphne, Joanie and I walked to school. We were joined by other girls: Mary Bellm, who was a neighbour from higher up the hill, and Joanie's friend Chloë Hain whose mother, a melancholy German, lived in a neighbouring street. We walked along the Ridgway until we came to a road called The Downs, where we turned left downhill towards the Ursuline Convent. John and Pat turned left down Edghill, which was one road sooner, to Wimbledon College, a Jesuit day school for boys. Immediately to the right of the Ridgway was another school, King's College for Boys. They wore red caps and blazers; but they were Protestants.

By now we had lost our baby names, Daffy had grown into Daphne, Dodie had become Joan, I was changed to Nora. We were adapting to a new school as well as to a new family. To Joanie, No 11 was a tall grey house, grim and cold; to me it was a wonderful place: This was England. This was home. The garden was nothing but a strip of scuffed lawn where the boys could kick a football about, and some dilapidated wooden sheds that John and Pat mended and made into a henhouse and chicken-run. Behind these was a shrubbery that provided the material for home-made bows and arrows and also a Sherwood Forest for my games of Robin Hood.

Inside No 11 was a hive of rooms, four to each floor, with a whole new group of interesting brothers and sisters living in them. Our favourite room was the 'Barracks'. It was where we ate, did our homework, played cards or *mah-jong*, read aloud to each other, and talked. It was a warm room with a coal fire adjacent to the basement kitchen with its great black, iron coal-burning range. The Barracks was 'our' room, into which the parents came only for weekday meals. The dining room, where we ate Sunday midday dinner, was on the first floor, as was Mummy's drawing room containing a new upright piano, her pair of side-tables shaped like camels, and the big red carpet with green and cream medallions all over it that they'd brought back from India. Daddy had a smaller room, sometimes called the study, sometimes the office, where he kept his books and laid his favourite rug, his 'blue Baluchi'. This had a geometrical pattern of red, brown and deep blue, and a thick pile. The carpet that I'd seen being made in the Patna Prison lay on the dining-room floor.

Lulu, who had attended classes in cooking at Notre Dame, was expected to be housekeeper and cook-general all in one, while my mother, who had never done any cooking in her life, devoted herself to the care of my father. She took and recorded his blood pressure twice daily. She intervened in conversations whenever she thought he might be angered by a thoughtless word from one of us. He never went out into the street except in his car, and this was only to drive to the common every afternoon with Mabel to get his two-mile walk; he never went to a public place for fear of getting giddy and falling, nor to any friend's house.

He was becoming a recluse. He never went to church. Mummy accepted this neglect of his religion on the grounds of ill health; but she redoubled her own piety, perhaps in the hope of saving his soul for him. The result of this 'health' routine was that they had no social life. They never visited other houses, and very few guests came to visit them apart from relations, the occasional old friend on leave from India, or business clients, such as the Rajah who brought his teenage son to England to buy a Rolls Royce. My father got a commission from introducing them to a car dealer; but for the Rajah and his son there was only tragedy, for the young man, as soon as he'd got the driving-wheel into his hands would suffer neither instruction nor advice. He was so excited by the power and speed of his beautiful new machine that it was not long before he drove it into a tree and killed himself.

Mummy ordered the groceries from Cullen's on the Ridgway, managed the accounts, and planned all the economies considered necessary. It had not dawned on the parents that running a big house with the few household gadgets available in 1923 required a strong labourer. Lulu was a rather frail girl; and since she was a daughter did not require the wages being demanded by English servants, that were, compared with what was paid to Indian servants, outrageously high. Lulu started work at six a.m., when she lit the coal range in the kitchen and began to cook breakfast for us all, before running up three flights of stairs to see that Joanie and I were getting ourselves dressed and washed ready for school.

We were supposed to leave the house and walk to school together, but Daphne was often late, and lagged behind. She seemed unwilling to get out of the bed she shared with Mary. Mummy, who slept next door to them, used to run in and out of their room, knocking on the door and calling out, 'You'll be late, Daphne! You'll be late if you don't get up at once!' One morning, Daddy, irritated beyond endurance, perhaps partly by Mummy's agitated attempts to get Daphne moving, advanced into the girls' room. He was in his pyjamas, and in his hand he held a stick. He always slept with a stick beside him, perhaps to ward off burglars, perhaps simply as a habit that remained with him from a day when, many years before, when they were living in a *daak* bungalow in jungle country in India, he saw a cobra fall from the lintel of their bedroom door just a few minutes after Mabel had passed under it.

He stood over the girls' bed and raised the stick. He threatened to strike Daphne unless she got out of bed at once, perhaps he actually did hit the blankets over her. Whatever really happened, Mary, who was fully dressed and combing her hair, witnessed, but the exact truth of it I shall now never know. At any rate from that day Daphne was never late for breakfast; but punctuality and obedience trailed a load of resentment and rebellion behind them.

Breakfast consisted of porridge, tea and toast and marmalade, every morning except Thursday, when we had coffee and rolls instead. On Sunday mornings after early Mass we enjoyed boiled eggs fresh from John's chicken farm. A charwoman came in on Monday mornings to do the 'rough' work, the scrubbing of the kitchen floor and the weekly washing. This entailed boiling all white clothes, sheets and towels with soap suds in a 'copper' over a coal fire before rinsing, mangling, and hanging everything out to dry on a washing-line in the back garden. Apart from the Monday work, Lulu had to do all the cleaning and cooking, and was supposed to nanny Joanie and me as well, which included 'cutting down' and very cleverly remaking clothes to fit us.

Lulu also typed out a Bath Rota and hung it on the bathroom door. As there was only enough hot water for one bath per day, and there were two parents and seven children to use it, Lulu allotted one bath to be shared by the two boys, and one for Joanie and me on Saturdays. What infuriated me was that we were described on her rota as 'The Babies'. I struck this out with an indignant pencil and wrote instead 'The Ladies'; but unfortunately, my spelling not being of the best, I wrote: 'Not Babbies but Laddies', which caused laughter in the Barracks; and I was humiliated. Perhaps that made me pay more attention to my spelling; but probably it was reading rather than humiliation that taught me to spell.

Mary became increasingly rebellious, voicing her protests in the Barracks that Lulu was being turned into a drudge, a little slavey exploited by the parents. It was a wicked shame she declared. Lulu began to lose weight. More than once when Joanie and I went upstairs to bed in the room we shared with her at the top of the house we found her in bed already, silently weeping. She vented some of her misery and rage on us by being very strict about such things as tidiness, which I considered silly. I preferred kicking off my shoes across the floor to placing them in a parallel pair under the bed; I didn't want to remove my warm woollen combinations before putting on a nightie and creeping into a cold bed on cold nights, colder on the top floor than anywhere else in the house. I used to lose my temper with her sometimes. Then she got hold of both my wrists and held me firmly while I stamped and screamed in impotent fury. She let me go when I stopped screaming. So there were times when I hated her. But I loved her when she told us stories.

She was writing a novel in a lined exercise book, and was reading it aloud to us as at bedtime. I always longed to know what was going to happen next before she'd had time to write it down. It was set in the time of the Terror during the French Revolution, and was about the last Dauphin of France, who, when still a child, was imprisoned with his elder sister and his parents, Louis XVI and Marie Antoinette, awaiting execution. He was not guillotined when his father was, nor with the Queen in October 1793. Nobody knows what happened to him. He simply disappeared from history, though it was rumoured that a prison guard had taken the boy into his own family. Lulu was inventing a thrilling life for him that never came to an end because she never finished her novel.[1] Was the poor girl writing for therapy? And was her Unconscious killing off her parents by guillotine so allowing her fantasy self to escape from the prison of her life into another existence as a boy? Her only open rebellion at this time, apart from her repudiation of the cello, was a refusal to eat what was on the table, declaring that the food, particularly margarine, made her feel sick.

When her weight fell to six stone Daddy was alarmed. He began to fear Lulu might be suffering from tuberculosis. So Mummy called in Dr Clarke whom she'd met at the Sacred Heart Church on Edghill one Sunday morning after Mass. He examined Lulu, and talked to her. No, she was not suffering from TB, he said, but from overwork and lack of nourishment. In those days Anorexia Nervosa was not a popular disease, although it had been recognised by the medical profession since the 1870s; but with hindsight I guess that's what her illness was. The cure proposed by Dr Clarke was fairly successful: She was to be given butter to eat; she was not to be worked so hard at uncongenial tasks. She was to be allowed more leisure.

Mummy found and employed an Irish cook-general called Margaret, whose face was like cracked leather, yellow and lined. Her hair, a tangle of grey wire, was kept in place by a white cap while she was cooking. She was strong and able to do the work, but she didn't waste time on pleasantries, nor bother to smile at any of us. She simply got through the day's toil, and then retired to her bedroom to smoke. No one dared to open her door for fear of releasing a blast of burnt tobacco fog on a stream of Irish invective, but Joanie and I, when we were going to bed, could hear her tramping about her room and talking to herself, often angrily, sometimes laughing. We knew she must find her bedroom cold in winter after sitting by her oven in the basement.

'I bet she doesn't take her combies off at night.'

'There's nobody to make her take them off, is there?' It was unfair.

'I expect she goes to bed with all her clothes on.'

We used to wonder what she talked about to herself. On Thursdays she took the afternoon and herself off into town; on Sunday afternoons she went to bed with a copy of an Irish newspaper that had arrived for her by post the day before. She got on well with the char, with whom she shared many a Monday joke. In the Barracks we called her Mad Margaret, but in truth No 11 couldn't have done without her.

Lulu was promoted to the post of private secretary to my father, and was paid a small salary for her work. Every morning after he'd finished the breakfast that Mummy brought to his bedside on a tray, Lulu sat down near his bed and put into shorthand what he dictated. She then typed it on the new typewriter he'd bought for her. He was writing and having printed a pamphlet about the independent insurance agency he planned to create and advertise among expatriates in India. When this business accumulated clients, Lulu was busy typing letters to them and to the insurance companies chosen.

As soon as Mary, with the help of some coaching in maths from Mother Veronica at the Ursuline Convent, had passed her London matriculation, she began to study for a degree in French and German at University College, London. Every morning after breakfast she caught the train from Wimbledon Station, and disappeared from our lives till the evening. She was given a packet of sandwiches for her lunch. She was ashamed to bring them out in the college refectory, because all the other students were ordering and eating food from the kitchen there, so she used to lock herself into the women's lavatory to eat them. After a time she persuaded Mummy to allow her ten shillings a week for bus fares and lunches, and forgot the sandwich packs.

Her first battle with her father began on the day she cut her long hair into a short bob with a fringe. There was an outcry of horror from the parents, although I thought she looked lovely. She had already shortened her skirts in spite of Mummy's opposition on the grounds that showing so much leg was immodest, and rather common too. However since short-skirted girls were everywhere, thronging the streets, the shops, the buses, and even the church, and hearing no preaching from the pulpit against the fashion, Mummy had given way on this point. I believe Mary's wickedness over the 'bob' was her failure to seek permission first. The outcry soon had to stop; after all, no amount of scolding could restore her cutaway tresses.

I loved school. I loved the lessons, and I loved all the new friends I made. I soon had a gang of them organised into the Round Table. Of course I was King Arthur; Marjorie Cole, a pale girl with magnificent long plaits of red hair was Queen Guinevere. Joanie was Sir Lancelot, and there were other girls who acted other knights for me at times, but chiefly we three played the game on our way home from school. Camelot was in hedges, in their broken spaces, a hollow tree, and sometimes a shrubbery inside the open gate of a suburban house along the Ridgway.

There was at school a girl with Down's Syndrome. She was five years older than me, and of course much bigger, but couldn't read. She took a fancy to me, and asked to sit beside me in class, so I suppose I must have been kind to her; but I certainly possessed a cruel streak. In the junior school there were a few boys. When our class was divided into two teams that had to compete for marks in lessons, and I was made head of one team, I decided that one small boy who consistently let the side down by getting low marks needed punishment. So I told him I'd have to squeeze his thumb in a pair of pincers which I drew out of the pocket of my blazer. I can see his face now; his expression of fear haunts me still with a small tweak of shame. Luckily for him he soon left the convent to go to a proper boys' school. To me boys were very dull. They didn't want to play acting games; all they wanted to do was to throw a ball about, kicking it or hitting it with a bat, an activity that to me was intensely boring. But I loved 'gym', taught by stocky Miss Hassall in a black gym-slip and black wool stockings. In the junior school it was Swedish Drill; the older girls learned to climb ropes, to balance on bars, and to vault a wooden horse. All this was more fun than marching with straight backs round the hall at Eekloo to improve our deportment.

Piety was not as all-pervading at the Ursuline Convent as in Eekloo. There were prayers in the Assembly Hall in the morning before we all trooped off to our classes, marching to the tune of Percy Grainger's 'Country Gardens' played briskly on a piano, there were short prayers at the commencement of every lesson, the Angelus rang out its bells at noon to remind us of the birth of Jesus, and there was Religious Education. That meant learning the catechism by heart, listening to gospel stories, and in the higher classes reading and learning by heart passages from the gospels. But it was a day school, which meant that we all rejoined our families in the rough, down-to-earth outside world at the end of the school day. I think at that age we treated religion as a game, full of ritual to act and colourful magic to believe in. It was not until adolescence that it began to assume a larger place in our rational consciousness.

History was interesting. It was shown as great sweeps of time: the Roman invasion of Britain, and Caesar who said, *'Veni, Vidi, Vici,'* the Anglo-Saxons and the visit of Pope Gregory, who said, 'Not Angles but Angels,' the Vikings in their long ships with shields and spears, who were very fierce, and of whom a Celtic scholar wrote that they were 'strong and angry men', and the Normans who conquered King Harold by shooting an arrow into his eye. All these periods of history were shown us in outline prints that we had to paint in with watercolours. It was a pleasant exercise.

I learned a different form of history from my brothers in the Barracks. They had been living in Ireland during the Troubles; and Michael Collins was John's hero. They had spent the summer holidays of 1922 with Uncle Pat in Borris. There were two camps in the area, one inhabited by soldiers of the Irish Free State Army, the other by Irregulars. My brother Pat, who was eleven at the time, had made friends in both camps. He used to cycle off to call on them, to inspect all the horses, motorcycles and rifles, and listen to the men's talk.

Dr Pat always refused to take sides during the Civil War, declaring that he was a doctor, and to him wounded men had to be cared for, no matter what their politics. And because he was a doctor both sides valued him and protected his life. On one occasion he was ordered by masked men to go to the nearest railway station and prepare for the casualties from a battle that was to take place nearby. He put all the surgical instruments he possessed in his Gladstone bag, and all the dressings and splints he could muster, and, having told the boys to remain indoors all day with Bridgie, his housekeeper, he went off to deal with death and the wounds resulting from one of the many bloody skirmishes in the Ireland of those days.

One evening they were all playing cards in the parlour when there came a sharp double knock on the door. Cards fell from their hands. They stood up. A minute later Bridgie came in, white-faced, to announce:

'They've come!' John, who was nearly sixteen and considerably taller than his uncle, grabbed a cricket bat and waited behind the door. Two men in long mackintoshes, their faces half hidden by trilby hats pulled well down on their foreheads, entered and stood with legs apart. There was a moment of complete silence before one of them spoke. It was to warn Dr Pat that he must not be seen about with two named friends of his. That was all. They then immediately left the house. John put aside his cricket bat while Bridgie made them all cups of tea.

Dr Pat was able to send messages to warn his two friends. One of them, a solicitor, without more ado caught the train to Dublin, and the boat to Holyhead and safety in England, where his wife and children joined him at a later date. The other, a publican, remained behind his bar. Not long afterwards he was taken at gunpoint from his pub and shot against the high stone wall of the McMurrough-Kavanagh demesne.

'What's that?' I asked.

'I'll tell you about the McMurrough-Kavanaghs another time,' said John. 'Just now I want you to help me kill a hen.'

Without a word of protest I followed him into the garden, where he had prepared the stump of a tree as a beheading-block, and laid an axe beside it. He caught hold of an old bird in the run, and tied its legs together before placing its head on the block. 'Now hold its legs there firmly,' he commanded me. I did exactly as he told me; but when he lifted the axe and struck the deadly blow I squawked louder than the hen, and let it go, when the poor thing, released from my hands but headless, fluttered off the block and began to stumble about the grass. It was horrible to watch, till it fell at last and lay motionless.

John picked up the corpse, and throwing the head into the shrubbery walked towards the backdoor. 'It didn't feel much, you know,' he said. 'That running about without its head is entirely automatic.'

I followed him into the kitchen, where Margaret took the bird from him. She patted my shoulder briefly when she saw my tears. 'Sure 'tis only an ould hen,' she reassured me. 'It wouldn't be alive at all if it wasn't for eating.' It was a harsh truth but irrefutable.

John gave me a short History of Ireland to read, and I was soon an ardent Irish Nationalist. Mary saw me reading the book and said, 'You don't want to believe all that Cathleen na Houlihan stuff!'

'It's true, isn't it? John believes it's true,' I defended him.

She went to the half-window high up on the wall of the Barracks, and stared up at the bit of grass that was visible. 'I hate Ireland! I hate the Irish!' The words burst from her. 'What sort of a nation is it whose fathers beat their daughters?'

John looked up from the table where he was struggling with a piece of maths homework. He was having to work hard, as his matriculation was looming. 'He never beat you,' he said.

'He wouldn't dare!' she cried.

They had both spent impressionable adolescent years in Ireland during the Troubles, but they didn't feel the same about it. Sometimes John sang in a good fresh baritone to Mummy's piano accompaniment a nationalist song that thrilled me: 'The West's awake! The West's awake!' To John, Ireland was his beloved country, held in bondage for centuries by a brutal oppressor; she was the glorious lost civilisation of Yeats's Celtic Twilight, the beautiful suffering woman of the poet's dreams. Mary saw Ireland with Joyce's eyes as the old sow that eats her farrow.[2]

It was our first family summer holiday. The older children travelled by train, but Daddy and Mummy drove down to the coast in his new Singer car. The cumbersome hood had been folded back, as the weather was fine and warm, and Joanie and I sat in the back with Lulu and the luggage. It was a long drive out of London to Dymchurch on the Kent coast.

The old farmhouse appeared to be sinking into the flat landscape, submerged almost by a field of uncut wheat surrounding it, its ground floor windows all but choked by nettles. We could see, as the car bumped over the potholed drive, scarlet poppies growing among the corn. I'd never seen poppies before. They were like drops of blood.

After we'd clambered out of the car we stood for a moment staring. It was so quiet on that hot August afternoon that you could hear the ripe wheat rustling, and not far off the heave of the sea. No grunting of pigs nor clucking of hens broke the silence. The outhouses were empty, wooden doors hung motionless on rusty hinges ready to creak and bang as soon as a wind blew up, and on the earth floors straw lay unswept but odourless from having been so long without the tread and dirt of animals.

'Perhaps the farmer died,' said Daddy. 'There's been no one here for a long time.' He had rented the place from an agent, and knew nothing of the former owners.

'We'll have to open all the windows and get rid of the stale smell,' said Mummy. 'I can see we'll have to clean up a bit before the others arrive.' Joanie screeched when she saw a dead mouse under the kitchen sink, but Mummy picked it up by the tail and threw it out through the window into the orchard. She put a duster into my hands before we went upstairs.

Cobwebs hung in corners everywhere, and, on the ceiling of the bedroom I was to share with Joanie, hordes of mosquitoes clung, ready and waiting to descend on uncovered arms and faces as soon as we were asleep.

It was my job to collect the fallen apples from the knee-high orchard grass that John had been ordered to cut. But first he had to slash down, with a sickle he'd found in a shed, all the nettles growing round the house, and Pat had to rake them up into a shaky old wheelbarrow they'd found in the backyard, and cart them off to a bonfire, getting stung in the process. I stood by watching and feeling sorry for the red blotches on their arms; but they didn't grumble. My father never did any menial tasks himself; he organised us into doing them. After all, that was something he'd done most of his life: organising people into working for him. Lulu was released from work; this was to be her annual holiday. As Margaret had gone back to Ireland for her annual four weeks' leave, Mary was to be cook for the month. She proved to be a mixed blessing in the kitchen. Her cooking, since she'd never done any before, was of the simplest. She provided an unvarying menu of sausages and mash followed by stewed apples (the fallers from the orchard collected by me) and junket, every day for dinner for the whole month.

It wasn't long before we were all running down to the beach and plunging into the cold sea with squeals of shock and pleasure. Oh, the joy of those seaside days! We played rounders till we were so hot with exertion we had to rush into the waves to cool ourselves. Mummy joined in all our games, but Daddy remained remote, walking alone, or sitting in some wind-screened cranny between dunes with his head in a book. Once or twice he presented me with a shell he'd found. Daphne and I were collecting shells of different shapes and colours. Fans were the prettiest, but rare. Best of all was to stand at the edge of the sea letting the advancing tide creep over our toes with a soft crepitation as it curled, broke and bubbled on the sand, and then retreated with a scratching sound.

We bathed twice, sometimes three times a day, staying in the water till we were blue with cold, and Mummy, wearing a straw hat and black sandshoes under skirts that flapped in the wind, stood on the shore and waved her arms, shouting, 'Come back! Come back! Come in at once and get dry!' Then Joanie and I crawled out shivering, and she rubbed our skins with towels, and made us drink sweet cocoa kept hot in a Thermos flask.

And oh, the terror and triumph of that time I suddenly found myself out of my depth, floundering helpless and expecting to drown, till to my immense surprise I was swimming. I could swim! I could swim!

It was when I blurted out my terror and my triumph as I sat on the sand shivering and drinking cocoa that Pat told me how he'd once nearly drowned in his school swimming pool. He had not drowned, he said, because, when he was born in India in 1910, Halley's Comet was blazing in the night sky. An Indian seer had foretold that he would escape many dangers, and live to see the next blazing of the comet seventy-five years after his birth. He kept glancing at me sideways to see if I believed him. He had some good ideas for games and adventures, and I could join in if I liked. Very soon I was his willing slave.

The boys had brought their cycles with them on the train. By lowering the saddle of the smaller one Pat was able to make it a suitable size for me to ride. I began by wobbling down the farm drive while he encouraged me, at first holding the saddle to steady me, and at last pushing me off on my own. And when we found, a couple of miles inland, a low hill with a long gradual slope, what heaven it was to freewheel down, gathering speed!

One afternoon a change in the weather with a cold wind drove us away from the beach, and we decided to play 'sardines'. With so many hiding places to choose from it was an ideal game. Pat and I waded into the wheat-field and lay down on a prickly bed of flattened stalks and thistles.

'They'll never find us here!' he said.

'It's the best hiding place in the world!' I agreed. I turned over on my back and gazed up at an army of menacing clouds marching slowly across the sky. 'It's nice having a brother,' I said.

We talked idly and amicably. And then he told me the story about the McMurrough-Kavanaghs of Borris House. They owned thousands of acres of fertile land in Ireland, he said. They were a very old family descended from the Earl of Leinster who ruled before the Normans came. Although in later centuries they converted to the new religion in order to keep their lands out of the hands of English conquerors, some of them were closet Catholics. There was in the grounds of Borris House a private chapel containing some Popish idols that worried the conscience of Lady Harriet Le Poer Trench, a staunch Scottish Presbyterian who became the second wife of Thomas Macmurragh Kavanagh in 1825.[3] She decided to remove the idols, among which was a nearly life-sized crucifix, but had to employ local men who were Catholics to do the job. It was in the year 1831. She was expecting her third child.

In taking down the crucifix from above the altar one of the workers must have slipped and lost his balance. The great crucifix fell, and, in falling, all the limbs, both arms and legs of the Christ, were smashed. It was a dreadful omen. The men shuddered and crossed themselves.

In March of 1831 Lady Harriet gave birth to a boy, Arthur, who was born without arms or legs. The child was not discarded nor neglected; Lady Harriet saw that he was loved and cared for, and he grew up to be, although so terribly disabled physically, an intelligent and strong-willed boy, who wanted to do everything that other normal children did.[4] He was put on a saddle at a very early age, and with the aid of hooks fixed to his stumps he learned to manage reins, and so he learned to ride, and from that day he went everywhere on horseback. He married and fathered several children. And when he died his spirit was unable to leave the saddle and the horse that had carried him, so that he came back to haunt the countryside. On clear, quiet moonlit nights the sound of his horse's hooves was sometimes heard; and once or twice he had been seen, a lone misshapen rider vanishing into the mists over the slopes of Mount Leinster.

'Ooh! How creepy!' I shivered.

'Our grandfather sometimes heard his ghostly galloping at night,' Pat said, 'but I don't think he ever actually saw the rider.'

We were so enthralled by the story that we lost all count of time. The happiness of that afternoon I can remember still. Pat was chewing a blade of grass, and I was tearing at the black heart of a poppy by pulling off its petals one by one, when we became

*1 John Prinsep smoking a hookah. Detail of a painting by Zoffany of Dashwoods and Auriols in India, 1780s.*

*2 William and Mary Prinsep painted by Chinnery after their wedding in Calcutta in 1822.*

*3 Mary Prinsep (née Campbell) painted by her sister-in-law Emily, 1835.*

4 The tomb of Ramohun Roy designed and built in Arno's Vale Cemetery, Bristol, by William Prinsep for his friend who died on a visit to Bristol in 1833.   Photo courtesy of H Bhattachariya.

*5 Alice Mabel Reid (née Daniell) aged eighty-five. Painting by A Mason exhibited in the Royal Academy in 1960.*

aware of a shadow moving along the edge of the field. It was a long shadow; it was Daddy watching us.

'What are you two doing there?' he called out.

Pat sat up. 'Playing sardines,' he said.

'And it's such a good place the others can't find us,' I added.

'They've all gone in to tea long ago,' Daddy said. He frowned, and I recognised his dark face, the one he put on when he lectured us about what we'd done wrong.

We scrambled to our feet and ran into the kitchen where the others sat at table spreading jam on slices of bread, and Mummy was pouring tea from a big brown teapot.

'Sorry we're late,' said Pat. 'We'd no idea it was so late.'

'Well, you've only just escaped the rain,' said John. There was a flash of lightning, making me jump, and a few seconds later thunder rolled, and the long-expected rain came down.

I thought no more about it till that night. Daddy was sitting downstairs with Joanie on his knee, reading to her some fairy tale, and I had put myself to bed early to read Kingsley's *The Water Babies*, skipping the boring bits to get on with the lovely story, when Mummy came up to kiss me goodnight.

'Have you said your prayers?' she asked. I had, though briefly.

'Have you washed your teeth?' I had, even more hastily. She sat down on the edge of the bed.

'What were you doing with Pat in the field this afternoon?'

'Playing sardines. It was a good place, so nobody found us.'

She seemed to want to talk, but unable to say more. 'Were you two canoodling?' she managed to bring out at last.

'What's canoodling?'

'I thought perhaps…sex might have…' she said.

'What's sex?'

My direct question seemed to fluster, if not alarm her. She blushed, she looked away, she picked at the edge of my blanket. 'Were you unchaste?' she asked.

139

'What's unchaste?' My zest for knowing must have seemed relentless to her.

'Well, you know dear, it's—it's being immodest.'

She had been sent by Daddy to interrogate me, but not being as accustomed as he was to dealing with defendants in a magistrate's court, she didn't know how to do it.

Modesty I had heard about. It meant women had to pull down their skirts to cover their knees. With a leap of imagination I guessed immodesty might mean pulling down my knickers to pee when somebody was looking.

'You mean, did I do wee-wee in front of Pat? Of course not! I'm not a baby!'

She couldn't help smiling then, but my innocence made her feel uneasy. She sighed. 'Well, you must remember to cover your body in front of boys,' she said. She kissed me before she left the room.

It was still light enough to read, so I opened my book and followed Tom, the little chimney sweep, into the world of water babies where mermaids were washing off his soot. He didn't have to be modest because, as was obvious from the coloured illustration, he was standing on the seabed absolutely naked, and the mermaids wore no clothes at all above their tails. I could only suppose that morals were different under the sea.

In the morning we woke to a leaden sky and the threat of more rain. When I looked in the mirror as I brushed my hair I saw with horror a face all swollen and blotched by mosquito bites.

'Gosh!' said John, as I sat down to breakfast, 'They really did have a go at you last night!'

Daddy remarked that for mosquitoes to breed there must be an undrained marsh nearby. Everybody nodded in agreement except Pat. I caught his glance at his father across the table. It was not a loving look. But he refused to meet my eye that morning.

At first I thought he didn't like the sight of my blotched face. Later when I reminded him of a promised bike ride along the coast he shook his head. 'Before it rains…' I pleaded; but he blushed and turned away. For some reason I embarrassed him. 'I've got to clean the car,' he said. I guessed he was trying to avoid me.

Next day he wasn't available for any fun either, because he had to help John dig a new pit for the latrine. There was no water-closet in the farmhouse; we had to use an earth lavatory beside the vegetable patch. Instead of flushing you had to throw a spadeful of earth over what you'd done. When the pan was full it had to be emptied into a big pit, and the contents covered with soil.

'Ugh!' I giggled. 'How smelly. 'I'm glad it's not my job!' I tried to laugh as I ran off, but I was crying really. Something had happened. It was something to do with hiding in the wheat field. Had Mummy talked to him about canoodling too? Or perhaps Daddy had. It was some grown-up thing, something suspected and sinister, like sex, something important enough to make Pat turn away from me. Whatever it was it had spoiled our lovely friendship, and things would never be the same again. All the sunshine seemed to have gone suddenly from our holiday.

Lulu was told to set me some long-division sums to occupy me. Last term I'd had trouble with long division. However much I tried, the end result of all my calculations never seemed to come twice to the same conclusion. It was something I had to practise every day till they did; and sure enough by the end of that holiday I could do those sums.

I played draughts with Joanie, but she kept letting me take her pawns, so I got bored, and began to scratch my face more than ever.

'Let's *do* something,' I said. 'Let's go and *murder* the mosquitoes.'

Daphne joined the murder squad. Armed with the old tennis racket we used for playing rounders we went up to the bedroom.

Standing on the bed I was just tall enough to ram the handle against the ceiling. We took turns in hitting it wherever the sleeping insects hung. We must have slaughtered hundreds, and we did it with satisfaction, leaving the corpses stuck up there, each in its own blot of blood. I thought they looked like poppies in a field.

During the next term, we were allowed to go every Monday afternoon after school to the local swimming baths. It cost us sixpence each. There was a chute over the deep end. What a glorious feeling it was to slide down at high speed and hit the water with a great splash! Joanie learned to dive; but I'm afraid I never did. I was too cowardly to throw myself in headfirst. What I did throw myself into headfirst was the Public Lending Library, and very soon I was book-mad. First of all I devoured the fairy-story books on the shelves, and of the fairy stories of all nations my favourites were Russian. By reading a new book each week I soon romped through a lot of children's books and began trying out novels. Daddy encouraged my reading; he never checked nor censored it. Sometimes he, too, read my book. We both enjoyed Angela Brazil's stories about hockey-playing schoolgirls in gymslips and black stockings; but after that craze was over I moved on to Dickens, and Daddy returned to Martin's *Histoire de France* in French in the ten volumes that he was steadily working his way through, while *The Tale of Two Cities* had me in thrall.

*'It was the best of times, it was the worst of times, it was the age of wisdom, it was the age of foolishness,'* Dickens begins. That good and bad can and do co-exist is a very big idea for a little girl to ponder on. And into these times Dickens threw me, flooding me with the pity and terror of catharsis, so that I was almost unconscious of the ordinary world as I saw the French Revolution through the eyes of our national storyteller. Much of the novel is melodrama awash with sentimentality. The heroine keeps fainting off and falling into a stupor at the most inconvenient times; there

are horrors unlimited, and sarcasm is of the lampooning sort, with nothing understated, except, of course, sex. But the reader reads it, reads on, and on. The attraction is intense. I think I all but drowned in its excitement and its terror. I certainly could think of nothing else while I was reading it. How does the great magician spin his webs around his readers? He did once reveal some secrets of his trade when he wrote: 'Make them laugh, make them cry, make them wait...' Nor do they have to wait too long for great memorable scenes.

After that I read in quick succession *Barnaby Rudge*, (more street rioting and persecution), *Oliver Twist, Little Dorrit, Nicholas Nickleby*, which was Daphne's favourite, and *David Copperfield*. I can still see as clearly now as eighty years ago, plump Peggotty lifting the corner of her apron as she leans down to whisper words of encouragement through the keyhole of the room where little David has been locked up by his cruel stepfather as a punishment for some peccadillo. My empathy was all the stronger for recollections of being locked in a dark room by an Irish nurse until my sister Mary rescued me. Perhaps it was the experience of many naughty children in the past.

We were all reading. There was as yet no Television nor Wireless to amuse us, though John was trying to make a crystal set in a matchbox, and kept telling us he was receiving wireless waves, though there were many more crackles to be heard than '2LO Calling'. Often we played cards, not for money but for matches, sometimes we played *mah-jong*, and occasionally roulette, in which even my father joined, acting the parts of banker and croupier, and intoning in his appalling French accent: *'Faites vos jeux, Messieurs!'* But mostly we read. On winter evenings we drew close to the fire in the Barracks, and four of us read aloud in turn, Daphne, Pat, Joanie and I. We read all sorts of novels that no self-respecting modern child would look at. It's hard to believe today that Walter Scott was one of our favourite authors. Pat liked the Crusaders in *The Talisman* and *Ivanhoe*. King Richard the Lionheart was his hero, the epitome of manly heterosexual chivalry, so that when in middle age he saw the film of *The Lion in Winter*, which suggested that Richard I was homosexual, he was outraged. He believed the film-makers were perverting history to make their film more sensational and therefore more profitable; and for quite a long time he was extremely angry with film critics, the film industry, and the world in general. Daphne loved the romantic highlands in *Rob Roy*. Believe it or not, we read that old-fashioned novel twice! Of course we skipped many a long-winded paragraph to get on with the story. I refused to read Edgar Wallace, the bestselling thriller writer of the day, because his stories, full of corpses falling out of cupboards in dark rooms, scared me so much I was afraid to go upstairs to bed, though my courage was often bolstered by the laughter we enjoyed in the basement of the house. Shared laughter is a palisade against all demons in the dark.

There were other popular novels we all devoured eagerly: Rider Haggard's *King Solomon's Mines*, and P C Wren's *The Four Feathers*, and *The Scarlet Pimpernel* by Baroness Orczy. We were learning about romance and chivalry, ancient and modern, and a bit of history too, but as to sex education there was none.

Mary told me that babies grew inside their mothers, but how they got in or out I had no idea. Mummy let it be understood that such things were simply not talked about. I speculated on a few theories of my own, thinking it possible that the baby came out through the navel, and wondering if the mother sucked the seed from the father's nipples. Otherwise what were a man's nipples for? I had seen babies suckled by women in India, and plenty of naked male children too; but it never occurred to me that the little tail that boys grew at the front instead of behind was anything more than a pipe for pissing. Girls didn't pee in that way, but I didn't ask about the cause or the purpose of the difference, so I was completely at a loss to understand what had happened in the summer of 1924, and in time those events began to fade in memory. The fears and suspicions entertained by my parents were quite beyond imagining, and certainly beyond enquiring. Even Mary couldn't bring herself to tell me much. Sex was locked up in an iron-bound box and labelled DANGER. DO NOT TOUCH.

It wasn't till 1927, when Katharine Mayo's book *Mother India* was published, that enlightenment really dawned. The book sold wildly owing to the scandal and shock it caused by its revelations of the horrors of childbirth among India's child brides, the high maternal death rate, the number of suicides among young married women, and the much higher death rate of females than of males. All this was much talked about at home, so that was how I heard that very heated debates were being held in the legislative assembly of the Indian Congress over the matter of raising a girl's age of consent to sex, within or without the marriage bond, to fourteen. Orthodox Hindus held so strongly the entrenched traditional view that early marriage was acceptable, and female lives expendable, that the more enlightened began to think any change would be impossible to enforce. A Sikh member from the Punjab was reported as declaring angrily: 'Early to marry and early to die is the motto of Indians'; and Gandhi published an article on 'The Curse of Child Marriage' quoting the case of a perfectly respectable sixty-one year old educationalist, who had just married a girl of nine.[5] It was all discussed so much, and with such shrill indignation by Lulu, that in spite of Mummy's vigilance even 'the children' learned quite a lot.

At about this time I noticed blood on my knickers. When I asked Mummy what it could be she replied that I'd know when I was old enough. It was Lulu who gave me practical help. But the talk in the Barracks about Mayo's book did open my eyes to how babies came into the world. Blood and babies and quite a lot of death got connected.

# References – Chapter Six

1 Fraser, Antonia, *Marie Antoinette*, Weidenfeld and Nicholson, 2002. Many "false Dauphins" claimed to have survived incarceration, but recent DNA testing has proved that the true dauphin died in prison. One of the doctors who did the autopsy on the boy's corpse secretly took his heart, which finally rested in a crystal urn in Saint-Denis. DNA from this heart has proved him to be related to Marie Antoinette and two of her sisters. So the little boy did die two years after his mother. His elder sister, Mme Royale, survived till the 1840s.

2 Joyce, James, *A Portrait of the Artist as a Young Man.*

3 O'Toole, James, *The Carlow Gentry.*

4 ibid.

5 Mayo, Katharine, *Mother India*, Jonathan Cape, 1927.

*7*

---

In 1925, while I was feverishly reading historical romances, conversation in the Barracks swirled around me about current events. Everybody had to see Noel Coward's *Hay Fever* being played to crowded houses in London, everybody must go to the pictures to see Charlie Chaplin in *The Gold Rush*; a literary trio, the Sitwells, whom Lulu called *'poseurs'*, were amusing the public with their antics and Edith's outrageous clothes; and there was a new poet who didn't look like a poet at all but resembled a bank clerk. He wasn't like Browning crying out with a full heart: 'O to be in England / Now that April's there!' Quite the contrary. April was to him 'the cruellest month, breeding / Lilacs out of the dead land.'

'What a dreary man!' my mother said.

'It's the waste and weariness of the War,' was John's opinion.

'We want to throw out all the old rubbish,' Mary said.

'Well I like Browning,' Daphne said. She loved his strong rhythms, his courage and high hopes, and most of all his romantic elopement with Elizabeth Barrett from the clutches of her preposterous father.

'That man T S Eliot writes about cabbage smells in alleyways,' said Lulu scornfully. 'That's not poetry! Not English poetry. The man's a Yankee anyway.'

A more lively message, dangerously bright, was drifting across the Atlantic on Scott Fitzgerald's prose with his own ambiguous feelings about the wealth, glamour and self-deception of *The Great Gatsby*, and with it the drums and trumpets of the Jazz Age sounded, a little later in London than in New York. The Charleston was all the rage. Everybody was doing it at tea-dances, which were allowed even in our house. Joanie and I soon mastered it and jazzed about when walking to school. All the girls did it when we lined up in the Assembly Hall. It was a great annoyance to the nuns, who were unable to stop this epidemic of jitters.

More serious matters were discussed at tea over which the parents presided. Ramsay MacDonald's first brief Labour Government had fallen. Lulu turned her battery of small hatreds against him over the teacups. Churchill, the new Chancellor of the Exchequer, had brought back the Gold Standard, described by Maynard Keynes as 'merely heraldic', but strongly approved of by my father. Mummy, whose brother Alfred had died of diabetes, said that some cure called Insulin had been found by two scientists in Canada. Hitler had published *Mein Kampf*, the manifesto he'd dictated to Rudolf Hess while in prison for attempting to overthrow the Bavarian Government. Unemployment was rising. It was nearly a million, Daddy said.

He had reached the Napoleonic era in his reading of French history, and often expressed his thoughts about it over the tea-table: Napoleon was a genius, not only in war but in the way he reorganised France after the Revolution, in education, local government, and his Code Napoleon still held as the law of France of that time. It was due to him that France had been a long way ahead of us in most things throughout the nineteenth century.

'He was an adulterer,' said Lulu suddenly.

Interrupted in mid-flow my father was taken aback. 'Josephine was unable to produce an heir, you see,' he explained. 'He needed an heir. That's why he married Marie-Louise of Austria.'

'He had to get divorced. Divorce is a sin.' Lulu persisted.

The rest of us were listening with amusement because Lulu had caught Daddy out. To him Napoleon was next to God, and she had discovered the Emperor's feet of clay. 'He did re-establish the Church in France after the Revolution,' he pleaded in defence of his hero. 'And anyway you can't judge Napoleon by the morals of ordinary mortals,' he added.

'All souls are equal in the sight of God.' Lulu was implacable.

Poor Mummy was in a quandary. The boys were openly grinning. She didn't want to contradict her husband in front of the children; she couldn't back him up in what was morally wrong. She was afraid of his anger and the danger to his health. Looking tired and worried she began to fiddle with the teapot lid, then lifted the teapot in an agitated rush of activity to offer everybody more tea, trying at the same time to deflect the conversation into less dangerous channels.

Mary did not usually get home in time for tea in the Barracks, so it must have been at Sunday dinner that Daddy noticed she was wearing make-up.

'Have you been painting your face?' he suddenly demanded. Conversation ceased; everybody stopped eating to look at her; and Mary flushed.

'Not exactly!' she laughed awkwardly. 'I'm wearing a normal amount of make-up, if that's what you mean.'

'Is this the result of your taking part in some amateur theatrical performance in London?'

'Well, I've been lucky,' she admitted. 'I've got a part in *The Admirable Crichton*. The university has its own Dramatic Society, you know.'

'There's only a thin line between an actress and a life of degradation,' he said. 'And painting your face is the first step down that path.'

'I think you'd better talk about it after dinner,' said Mummy, who was afraid unseemly things might be mentioned in front of Joanie and me.

When dinner was over Mary was summoned to his study, where she had to stand in front of his desk while he harangued her about the evils of the Stage, about actresses and the temptations they were heir to, and how she was playing the role of Jezebel, not in the Bible, but at No 11 Ridgway Place. Mary made matters worse by telling him he was hopelessly out of date, that all the girls in London wore make-up now, and they certainly weren't all Jezebels, nor actresses either; and anyway she wanted to go on the stage herself as soon as she'd got her degree. The fat was in the fire.

The quarrel lasted for over an hour, each shouting at the other, till Mummy intervened so that Mary could find time for an essay she had to write, and Daddy could retire to bed to have his blood pressure taken. All was then quiet upstairs. In the Barracks rebellion seethed.

Battle was resumed on Monday evening when Mary returned home from London. This time Daddy sat up in bed to lecture her, and she stood at the end of the bed to listen to him. He threatened to stop paying for her education unless she stopped using make-up; she threatened that she would then leave home and get a job, any job, in the theatre, which was of course the last thing he wanted.

'You're making your father ill, Mary,' Mummy said. 'Why can't you do what he wishes? Why must you be so stubborn?'

'He's talking nonsense, absolute nonsense,' she said. 'And he's a tyrant too. Women are not slaves any more. We do have the vote now, you know.'

The parents must have been bewildered at the way history seemed to have twisted upon them. They both in their youth had desired greater freedom for women, especially in education and in the professions; but that those young women who had now

150

acquired some degree of liberation should waste their newfound freedom on frivolities and the pursuit of pleasures instead of concentrating on improving their knowledge and their economic lot was a disappointment, to say the least. In a paradoxical way their attitude was forerunner to the 'liberation' movement of a later date. The liberation that most young women seemed to want, then as now, was a relaxation of the rules as regards codes of behaviour in manners, in respect given to elders who were no longer considered betters, in a discarding of many beliefs long held to be sacred, in dress, and a feverish desire to have fun. This bundle of attitudes is perhaps what we inherit after a national cataclysm such as war. Were the Twenties a foretaste of the hedonism of the Sixties when the Cold War spread vague but widely felt apprehensions of the possibility of nuclear wipe-out?

Certainly my parents didn't understand what was going on. My father felt himself a stranger in a foreign land. His childhood had been spent in rural Ireland, twenty-five years of his adult life in India, in England he was an alien; he did not belong. My parents were Edwardians who arrived late in an England coming to terms with post-war disillusion. They were absent from Europe through the greater part of World War I, had not watched while more and more young men disappeared into the killing machine of the trenches, had not felt, since their own sons were too young to fight, the agonising loss felt by so many families, nor the urgent need of fighting men and their girls to eat, drink and be merry today, for tomorrow was too terrible to contemplate. My parents who had seen themselves in youth as liberal and advanced in thinking were suddenly old-fashioned. To them it seemed that the 1920s' Flapper was not seizing the opportunities offered by her new status as a voter. She didn't seem interested in freedom, equality and fraternity with all men; what she was grasping in her greedy little hands was ephemeral pleasure: smoking, drinking and flirting, flashing her silk-shod legs, filling the house with the

151

sounds of drums being thumped and the double bass being plucked, and the howl of saxophones reminiscent of Patna hyenas, rushing out of town and into the byways of the countryside in fast cars, spilling out their youth in meaningless hilarity. What in the end had those serious nineteenth-century suffragettes brought about? They had opened floodgates to release folly. Thus was my father disillusioned.

When he remembered how his mother, an intelligent woman of strong organisational abilities who had been denied the opportunities of education, and been forced to put all her own yearnings into ambition for her sons, would so earnestly have desired what he was giving to Mary, it was incomprehensible that his daughter should treat her studies so flippantly.

Hidden underneath all these more or less rational views, perhaps at the deepest unconscious level, the primitive urges of a strong Alpha male ape drove him to try to keep all his females away from other males, and under his control. No doubt he was driven, too, by his own fear of sex, of its terrible anarchic power. Deep in his memory, no doubt there crouched a terror of eternal damnation that had been planted there into the turbulence, the awakening sexuality of his adolescent soul, during those days of silent religious retreat experienced in his Irish school, when the rhetoric of an Irish preacher-priest fired his already racing imagination with images of hell. Bonfires of pain and horror burning for all eternity glowed in the dimly lit chapel at evening Benediction, and later crackled in his head in the dark corridors and even darker dormitory at night.

To Mabel, who had so ardently desired but never got a serious musical training, that Mary, with all her brains and talents, and a university education served up to her as on a plate, should turn out such a flibberty-gibbet was really quite a shock. What neither of them understood was that Mary intended having fun as well as working hard to acquire an honours degree; and in the meantime she toyed with fantasies of becoming a famous actress, or perhaps a singer, or even a musical comedy Star like Evelyn Laye.

The battle raged for three weeks. Every evening when Mary got home she was hauled into the study there to be harangued, and every evening she stood her ground and answered back.

One evening when she was very late home, Daddy, not wishing to waste the lecture he had been preparing all day, summoned the rest of us, this time to his bedroom, where we all stood around the end of his bed to listen to him, and Mummy sat on a chair beside him, her sphygmomanometer at the ready, while he told us in many different ways how badly Mary was behaving, how ungrateful she was, how ingratitude was like a serpent's tooth. She was selfish too, and disobedient to her parents; she was spendthrift, wasting the money he'd earned through years of toiling and making himself ill in a tropical climate for the sake of his children; and now her stubborn hardness of heart would send him to an early grave.

'You're making a fuss over very little, you know,' said Lulu suddenly.

'Very little? Very little?' he shouted. And when John replied smartly, 'A little lipstick, that's all,' his anger knew no bounds.

Then Mummy was alarmed. 'That's enough, Jack,' she said. 'I think they've heard enough.' My mother's abnormal, you might say almost pathological patience, was at an end. She rose and pushed us all out of the room.

Next evening the quarrel began again. I was in bed. I could hear the voices through my bedroom floor, on and on, ding-dong, ding-dong, argument for argument, angry invective for more of the same. I was suddenly overcome with misery. I got out of bed, and kneeling beside it I prayed: 'Oh God, please stop them! Please stop them!' I was trembling.

My prayer was not answered at once, but after three weeks

Mummy, whose endurance must have been tattered to shreds, went to the parish priest for help.

The Sacred Heart church attached to Wimbledon College was run by Jesuits, and it was a Jesuit who came to her aid. Jesuits, through rigorous selection, are intelligent men; through years of study and long training in self-discipline they are learned, courteous and civilised, though not necessarily compassionate. Whatever else this priest was he was a diplomat; and at the request of a woman distressed and at her wits' end he came to make peace.

First of all, he interviewed my father alone in the study. For quite a long time they sat together in armchairs, their feet resting on the blue Baluchi rug, and talked. What was said we never knew, but afterwards Daddy stopped lecturing us, and his face was calm and satisfied. The anger he had been firing at us he now directed at the Inland Revenue; and Lulu typed the angry letters. This battle he continued for years.

The priest saw Mary also alone, sitting in the dining room separated by the big family dining table. Afterwards she too seemed quietly pleased. We were all waiting for her report when she came down the stairs into the Barracks.

'What did he say? What did he say?'

'He said it was all a storm in a teacup,' Mary reported. 'He said that there was no more intrinsic evil in lipstick and mascara than in a smart hat. And that these things were important to young ladies. And no harm either if the young ladies were pure in heart and observed their religious duties.' Mary was smiling. 'But he also said,' she added, 'that he is my father, that the fourth commandment tells me to honour my father, and that as long as I'm dependent and living in his house I must obey him.'

We were all relieved, believing that there would be no more rows, and we could all return to normal life.

'As soon as I've got my degree,' Mary said, 'I shall leave home. And that's that.'

Meanwhile she kept her make-up in her handbag. Every morning when she arrived at Waterloo station she went to the Ladies' Room, where she put on her lipstick and mascara before sallying forth to face her London world, and in the evening she removed all traces of make-up before she came home.

We were none of us permitted to go to see Mary act in her play, but afterwards she brought us a black and white photo of the performance. She was sitting on the corner of a table boldly swinging her legs; her silk stockings shone, and the cloche hat, low on her forehead, was black. When it was all over, and she had no more evening rehearsals to attend, she began to spend more time at home. She took to practising her singing, and Mummy accompanied her on the piano. Mummy was happy then. I believe she forgave Mary all the pain that three weeks of fighting had caused her when she played the accompaniment for one of the love songs Schumann wrote to Clara for their wedding day. They also worked together on some lovely French songs. Joanie and I used to sit on the stairs outside the drawing room to hear Mary singing: *J'ai vu passer l'hirondelle, le soleil et le jasmin…* ' Each note was clear and true, without tremolo and with no swooping up and down the melody, singer's tricks abhorred by my mother. The smooth sound was a sort of magic that made me feel I was flying.

'It's like ice-cream going down,' Joanie said.

Joanie and I were allowed into the drawing room to do our daily piano-practice, and sometimes on Sunday evenings we all gathered in the drawing room round the piano to sing part-songs, among them Stephen Foster's 'Way Down Upon the Swanee River'. Mummy seldom played the violin these days, but she played the piano often: Beethoven sonatas, some delicious morsels of Schumann, many of Chopin's works. I used to lie back in a corner of the sofa letting the sound flow over me, and gaze up at the shadows cast on the ceiling by the little chains from which the chandelier hung, and think of how my mother was chained to my father, with so much art and all those longings locked up inside her; and I felt sad, with a quiet sort of sadness.

Our musical world was not limited to our own home recitals. By this time it was possible to obtain good recordings of classical music for the gramophone. Mummy bought a number of records, including one played repeatedly by Pat of the great soprano Amelita Galli-Curci singing Rimsky Korsakov's 'Indian Love Song'. We also had several of Alfred Cortot playing Chopin, and of course many of the Irish tenor John McCormack. Once I caught my mother standing listening spellbound to the great pianist Cortot. When the music ended she gave a long sigh. 'That's just as it should be,' she said. Did she mean he played exactly as Chopin intended, or that Cortot was expressing his 'life of the soul' as it should be? And did her sigh express regret that hers was not? I shall never know.

Mummy was our first music teacher, but in Wimbledon she entrusted our musical education to Mother Imelda. I always enjoyed her lessons. She was enormously fat, and found it difficult to move about, so she walked only once daily from her cell in the main building to her music room in the junior school. It was on the first floor and overlooked the garden. She was an enthusiastic and encouraging teacher, and often said amusing things:

'Play each note, whether he be black or white, carefully and with love, and you will make sweet harmony; but careless thumping only makes a row.' She was rumoured to be related to an aristocratic French family; certainly her manners were queenly, and she was a law unto herself.

Every summer term when the visiting examiner from London came to listen to our set pieces, and hear us through our scales, exercises and arpeggios, he was met by Mother Imelda with a tray of good French coffee and some little almond biscuits; and afterwards with great courtesy and many soothing gestures she took him on a very slow walk round the garden to pick a large bunch of sweet peas for his wife. Perhaps she had been brought up in a diplomatic family before taking the veil. At any rate her diplomacy and her desire to work *Ad Majorem Dei Gloriam* did win honours for her pupils, including a distinction for myself in Elementary, but sadly never repeated in the higher piano-playing exams I took. (Joanie won Honours at Advanced Grade.)

Mother Imelda's devotion to duty was perhaps excessive a few years later, when I was due to take a written exam in Harmony. She offered to give me an extra lesson in her cell if I came to her after Mass on the Sunday morning before the exam. As soon as I arrived she made me sit down and set me a number of questions, whose answers I wrote and she then corrected. Then she wished me luck, and I went home to Sunday lunch. What was my surprise on Monday morning to find that the questions in my Harmony paper were exactly the ones she'd set me the day before! Needless to say I got ninety-six per cent for this exam. These successes I believe made my mother continue to hope that I might be a musician yet. She had even higher hopes for Joanie, who learned her pieces as effortlessly as she seemed to be able to paint, and get through her schoolwork, and wear her clothes, and of course look beautiful.

Lulu and Mary were only allowed to go to evening parties if they got home by ten p.m., and then only if they came home together. To come home in the dark alone with a young man was absolutely forbidden. Darkness was somehow full of sin and danger. As this made them a laughing stock, they refused a lot of invitations. We were becoming known in Wimbledon as the family with the strict father. But tea dances were allowed. It was quite the thing in the Twenties to roll up the sitting-room carpet on a Saturday afternoon, wind up the gramophone, and dance to the strains of 'Whooo…stole my heart away?' Lulu and John had joined a tennis club, where over tennis and tea, and sometimes tea-dancing as well, they had met a number of other young people. So we often had as many as six or seven couples dancing at 11 Ridgway Place. The parents usually took this time to drive off in the car to Wimbledon Common for their afternoon exercise, so there was a certain feeling of freedom in the house. Joanie and I tagged on to the tea-dances. Sometimes a grown-up, usually a girl, but occasionally a kind young man would gallantly lead us round the floor, which was a great thrill. So we quickly learned the steps of the Charleston, the Foxtrot and even the Tango, a dance that Lulu called *risqué*. It was accompanied by a record on the gramophone called 'Jealousy'. When people danced the Tango they scowled and moved like cats about to pounce, which made Joanie and me giggle behind their backs.

At the tennis club, Lulu met a red-haired player called Cyril Echlin who worked for an insurance company. This made him interesting to Daddy, so before very long Cyril was a regular weekend visitor to the house, and the next thing we heard was that he and Lulu were 'engaged'–a matter of great interest and curiosity to Joanie and me, but of disappointment too, because nothing spectacular seemed to happen after their engagement, which we learned would have to be a long one as his salary was not enough to marry on as yet. He used to sit smoking with Daddy in the study and talking about financial matters for most of Sunday evening, so the time he spent with his fiancée was necessarily limited. They were engaged for six years.

John was popular with the girls of their set not only because he was a good dancer and had neat clear-cut features and kind blue eyes, but because he made them laugh. He liked women, he liked their company, and so of course they liked him. So when Andrée arrived it was not surprising that the Barracks was suddenly filled with a sort of electricity. Andrée came to us on an exchange to perfect her English, while Mary lived with her family in Auxerre to polish her French. Andrée looked rather like a pretty boy, her figure slim and flat, as was the fashion then, her complexion guiltless of make-up, and her hair cut like the oak frame of a photograph about her face.

'O Jun! Jun! 'Ow can you say zat?' she used to cry, fixing her large innocent blue eyes on him when he teased her. Joanie and I watched the flirtation avidly, and discussed it when we went to bed.

'Are they falling in love?'

'Will they get engaged?'

'Will they be married in England or in France?'

'I'd like to be a bridesmaid.'

'Me too.'

But even we knew we were inventing an impossible romance. Andrée must return to Auxerre very soon. She would complete her education and in due course become a teacher in an *école normale*, and in time would marry a suitable Frenchman who lived, if not next door, at least within easy travelling distance. John had only recently become an employee of the Bank of England and would have to climb many rungs of the clerking ladder before he could afford to marry. In any case he might not stay in England. He was restless. He found the routine of commuting to London to work day after day in an office in the city terribly tedious, and longed for the open-air life. He had threatened more than once to run away and join the Rhodesian Police, which needed white recruits, and offered the exciting prospect of riding horses over great distances of untamed country in a climate cooler than India's and warmer than the weather Canadian Mounties had to endure.

Mary had travelled to France. Her journey by train from Paris to Auxerre was a long one with few stops. She was lucky in finding a corner seat in an empty carriage. Just as the train was about to start a Frenchman wrenched open the door and sat down, breathless, in the opposite corner. She studied her magazine, but was able to snatch a few peeps at him, and noticed that he was smartly dressed, and wore shiny patent-leather shoes. After a quarter of an hour had passed he addressed her politely in French, and she replied, also in French, whereupon he sat himself beside her and without more ado began to make what in those days we called 'advances'. She told him in no uncertain terms to go back to his corner seat, but he refused, and became bolder, pulling up her skirt and fondling her thighs, which she firmly held together at the knees.

'I'll pull the communication cord if you don't stop!' she threatened.

'Oh, that won't help you!' he laughed. 'I shall simply deny everything you say. And they'll probably believe me and fine you for needlessly stopping the train.'

So she stood up, and with her high heels she stamped suddenly on the toes of his thin patent-leather shoes. He uttered an anguished howl and immediately retreated; and she returned to reading her magazine. He left the carriage at the next stop.

No one had heard of sexual harassment in 1925; the term had not yet been invented, though the activity had always existed. It was one of the reasons why chaperones were considered necessary until Edwardian times to protect young ladies of supposedly greater sensibility than working girls, who had to look after themselves, and usually did. Minor encroachments on a woman's person, such as bottom-pinching, were accepted as an inevitable expression of maleness. For a female traveller in a warm climate it was simply a tourist hazard. In Italy, it was a humanitarian gesture, along with cries of *'Bella! Bella!'* that greeted any young girl as she walked out alone, or with a female friend. In Rome, if you didn't get your bottom pinched you began to wonder what was wrong with it. It was all part of growing-up and learning how to cope with the world.

There was another form of sexual harassment nearer to home that we took entirely for granted. In one or other of the leafy hollows where we lodged our Camelot or Sherwood Forest a dilapidated 'Priapus in the shrubbery'[1] sometimes crouched, revealing what he should have kept covered. Daphne was the one subjected to most frequent exposures. Joanie and I thought him funny, and used to laugh as we ran past him, but Daphne blushed and turned away her eyes. He never did us any harm, and in time moved off to pastures new. Perhaps it was he, or another unhappy ill-adapted man, who some years later managed to crawl through a gap in the hedge that screened the convent tennis court from the road. One day two Spanish girls were playing tennis with my friends Biddy Kelly and her sister Nancy, who noticed that the Spaniards made the sign of the cross each time before they served a ball. My friends supposed it was a Spanish custom till at the end of the set they changed positions on the court and walked towards the hedge. There sitting comfortably cross-legged to watch the game was a man with his flies undone and his great purple indecency bulging out. All four players were much too shy to breathe a word of this to the nuns, but somehow Reverend Mother got wind of it. She took to walking around the tennis court with slow and measured tread, reciting her breviary; and the intruder very soon fled, never to return

Christmas was a time when our lives were allowed to blossom with many pleasures. The day began with Midnight Mass and a sleepy return home to bed, but a very early waking next morning to seize the Christmas stockings hanging up on the ends of our beds. These were filled with small presents, sweets, oranges and apples. One year Pat left us each a second sock of his own filled with stones wrapped in many layers of paper, a piece of coal in the heel and a potato in the toe.

We did not deck a Christmas tree, but on a table in one corner of the dining room there was a brown paper cave containing straw to represent the stable at Bethlehem. It was occupied by miniature figures of the Holy Family with attendant shepherds and angels, and Three Kings approaching outside. We ate Christmas dinner in the dining room, the table laid with a white damask tablecloth, the centre decorated with holly and crinkled red paper surrounded by a ring of Christmas crackers and little silver dishes containing almonds, muscatels and pieces of Turkish Delight, crystallised fruits and my mother's favourite *marrons glacés*. After roast turkey there was Christmas pudding filled with tiny silver trinkets, a thimble for the future spinster, a ring for the bride-to-be, and horseshoes for luck. It was served with brandy butter beaten to a creamy lightness every year by Daphne, and it was set alight with a flame of burning brandy by John before being brought to the table. My father drank whisky with his dinner, but the rest of us sipped Stone's Ginger Wine.

In the afternoon we were given our big presents wrapped in brown paper, tied with string and sealed with red sealing wax. They were hidden one by one in the drawing room, and we each had to hunt for our own while Mummy played 'Mrs Gallagher's Jig' on the piano, softly when we were looking in the wrong place, loudly when we got near. When I was nine I got a very large present hidden in the folds of the curtains. It was a scooter, when scooting was the current craze at school. All through the hunt, Daddy sat in his big armchair smiling benignly, sipping his whisky and soda and smoking a special cigar. Even Lulu had called a truce in her guerrilla war of words with him. I remember the smell of that cigar as a perfume of harmony and happiness. In the evening we all sang carols round the piano. And so (like Pepys) to bed.

We were invited to Christmas parties, and we were allowed to give one ourselves. It was a fancy-dress party. Joanie and I were decked out as gipsy dancers complete with tambourines. Each of our guests, after various games and a splendid tea, was given a present wrapped in brown paper. The parcels contained painted Indian animals that Daddy had imported, hoping to sell in England, but had proved a loss commercially when no London stores showed the slightest interest in them. Joanie and I thought these animals dreadfully boring, but mercifully our guests seemed to like them.

Parties were exciting, but nothing like as wonderful as the matinée of the pantomime at Wimbledon Theatre. That was a theatrical performance we were allowed to watch. I believe it was *The Babes in the Wood*, but to me the story was irrelevant. It was the ballet danced by fairies in a woodland glade that I found magical. I wanted to see it again; I wanted to be a ballerina, to learn to dance on the tips of my toes, and wear a tutu made of layers of tulle. Lulu told me brutally that ballet dancers had to begin training before they were five years old to be any good, and that we couldn't afford dancing lessons for me anyway. In fact, I did persuade Mummy to send me to dancing lessons in a small local dancing school; but was soon bored by the dull lessons in foot positioning I had to practise before I was allowed even to put on a pair of ballet shoes. Needless to say, I was no star in the ballet class, but balletomania did possess my soul for some time to come.

We also went to the pictures, black and white and silent then. Daddy had less objection to the cinema than the theatre, provided we attended daytime performances. So the four of us, Daphne, Pat, Joanie and I, were able to enjoy thrills of fear and screams of laughter watching Harold Lloyd being chased across roofs and dangling from window ledges of New York skyscrapers, and to have our hearts wrenched by Beth's long-drawn-out dying in *Little Women*. We girls watched it dry-eyed; it was Pat who cried. I'm afraid we laughed at him.

We also laughed unrestrainedly, when we saw the first Talkie, *The Jazz Singer*, at Al Jolson when he sang 'Sonny Boy'. It was an excruciatingly sentimental performance decorated with many whines and sobs. Had my mother been there she would have walked out in protest at the singing and the poor taste of it. He did, however, say something in that film that seems to have become an aphorism, both as to the Talkies and to life in general: *'You ain't heard nothing yet, folks.'*

But the greatest joy that Christmas holiday was skating. There was an exceptionally long and hard frost; the ponds on Wimbledon Common were frozen for more than a fortnight; Mummy found hidden away in a cupboard several pairs of old skates made of wood with steel blades, and these Daphne, Joanie and I made the best of. Every day, all day till darkness fell, we skated. People brought sandwiches and hot drinks in Thermos flasks, and picnicked on the grass verges. Someone brought a gramophone, others brought records, and soon there were couples gliding smoothly to the music of a waltz. A few of the more expert skaters danced the foxtrot to the rhythm of 'I Can't Give You Anything But Love'. The glow from the exercise of our own muscles prevented our feeling the fall in temperature as the light faded. We were too happy to notice the hours passing. It was a fortnight of bliss.

*References – Chapter Seven*

1 Eliot, T S, *Mr Apollinax*.

---

## 8

I was twelve years old, growing fast and always in such a hurry that my talk became balletic: when I couldn't find the words needed to express my thoughts my arms and legs tried to dance their meaning. John, who was nervous and quick-moving, and like me sometimes suffered from attacks of migraine, used to laugh at my antics. When Dr Pat came over from Ireland to visit us for a few weeks John asked his opinion on my 'jumpiness'. Was it normal? Uncle Pat seized me by the arm and told me to stand still, which I did.

'Well, it's not Chorea[1],' he said, 'so it must be high spirits.' And turning to me he asked, 'Would you like to come to the races with me, No-ree?' That was how I was taken to Kempton Park on my first visit to a racecourse.

Uncle Pat was a very small man, not much taller than me. During his adolescence he had fallen from a tree and broken several vertebrae. Although his spinal cord was luckily not torn, so that he escaped being paralysed, he did not grow in height after the accident; but he had strong arms, could lift heavy weights, and was a powerful swimmer. He seemed to like people, chiefly I believe because he found them comical. I found him easy to talk to.

We travelled to Kempton Park on top of a bus so that he could look down on his surroundings: London suburbs, to me a boring vista, but to him who lived among green fields in Ireland it was no doubt strange and interesting.

He pressed a florin, or two-shilling piece, into my palm. 'That's for you to back the horses you fancy,' he said. 'But don't put it all on one. If he doesn't win you lose all. So spread your bets.' He looked out of the window as I thanked him. I got no regular pocket money at home, so it was a fortune to me.

'That's the secret of a good life, No-ree.'

'What is?'

'Modtheration in all things. The Golden Mean.'

With this good advice in my ears I descended the swaying staircase of the bus and joined the crowds pushing their way into Kempton Park. The day was overcast but dry, the tension in the air palpable; people moved briskly and purposefully towards the Tote, or over the field towards the stands or the bar, but we made straight for the bookies on their pedestals shouting their strange lingo in hoarse voices, some of which Uncle Pat was able to translate for me. When we had made our bets, we moved towards the white railings marking the course, and were lucky enough to be able to squeeze to the front of the crowd, and so have an excellent view of the first race. My heart began to beat very fast when it began. I strained my neck to see the approaching knot of horses, to pick out the colours of the jockey I'd chosen, and watch him gaining ground, then losing it. Oh! The excitement as they drew near! I screamed encouragement with everybody else, caught and submerged in the roar of a thousand shouting with one voice for the five seconds it took for the galloping to come and go, the sound moving like a wave following the horses, as a thousand necks craned towards the finish. The pleasure of it all was still with me long after I knew I'd lost my bet. Of such moments belonging to the human race is made.

After it was all over we moved slowly towards the exit gates. Neither of us had won anything. 'Did I ever tell you, No-ree, about my friend Patrick Maloney's dream?' he asked. He was holding my hand for fear of losing me in the dense crowd. 'Well, I'll tell you when we get on the bus.' He continued the story when we were seated, and on our way home. 'Well, Patrick Maloney was a great one for horse racing. And one night before the big one at Leopardstown in Dublin, he dreamed the wind blew off his hat, and he had to chase it as it went bowling along the road. ''Tis an omen!' he told me. 'The winning horse will have a hat in his name. Mark my words!' So as soon as he'd got his racecard he looked down the list of runners, searching for the right name. 'That's it!' he thought when he found a horse called Trilby. 'Sure Trilby's the name of a hat!' So he put all he had on Trilby.'

'Did it win?' I asked.

Uncle Pat shook his head sadly. 'No. The horse that won was *Mon Chapeau.*'

'What a shame!' I cried.

'Sure, the poor man didn't know French,' he said.

I was quietly happy when we got home, and slept well that night. A day at the races with an Irish uncle is wonderfully therapeutic for a hyperactive child.

Mary, who had spent an Easter holiday in Borris with Dr Pat, asked about her other uncle: 'And how is James?'

'He's well, and hopes you'll be back in Borris soon, so he can take you for another jaunt in his car.'

'I'd like that,' she said. She knew it wasn't a motor car. 'And is he still following the horses? And the ladies? I always thought of him as like Dr Johnson who would have liked to spend his life driving briskly in a post-chaise with a pretty woman.'

'For James 'twas a pony-trap,' he said shortly.

'It was a wealthy widow he was chasing,' said Mary laughing. 'But I don't think Samuel Johnson was a lady-killer. He was rather an ugly man, and Uncle James is a very, very handsome fellow.'

'Not all wealthy widows are taken in by good looks,' said Dr

Pat. 'Some guess that the good-looker is not always the best bet.' His voice was unexpectedly bitter for a man of 'modtheration'. Was he thinking of the family farm that James was neglecting, or did he feel a stab of jealousy for a brother who was so attractive to women?

'So he hasn't found one yet?'

'He has not.'

❦

*The Constant Nymph* by Margaret Kennedy was the best-selling novel of the season, but too shocking, so Lulu said, for me to read. I was still enthralled by historical romances. My favourites were set in the eighteenth century with its horses and highwaymen, post-chaises and pistols, its powdered wigs, top boots and long satin coats. I had just discovered a beautiful Irish actress called Peg Woffington. Garrick was her patron and her lover. Besides being beautiful, talented and successful on the London stage, she had a generous heart, and founded a hospital when at the height of her career she made money. She died in poverty, like so many actresses of that period. It was she who inspired me to write in a lined exercise book my first novel, complete with illustrations painted with the help of my Windsor and Newton paintbox. Its title was *The Gay Diana Walks the Boards*. I hid it from the others in the Barracks, especially John, who was strong on derision. He had already made fun of some flights of fancy in an essay Daphne wrote about a laburnum tree. I ought to explain that in those days we wore navy blue knickers, called bloomers, underneath our gymslips. These bloomers were held together by elastic at waist and knee; but Daphne's (for she tended to be unaware of such trivia, living as she did in her own dream-world) sometimes came loose and tumbled below the hem of her dress. So when John came across her essay describing laburnum flowers as 'falling cataracts of bloom' he immediately shouted with laughter and read it aloud as falling cataracts of bloomers. Poor Daphne snatched the exercise book from him telling him to, 'Shut up you beast!' So of course I hid my novel from him. But I did show it to Dr Pat. He read it through seriously. It didn't take him long. He made no comment but asked instead if I was writing another book.

'I'm writing a Joke Book now,' I said.

'That's a grand idea!' he said. 'A grand idea! And I've a good one for you.' So he told me the story of "Johnson's at the Door".'

'There was a grand lady who lived in a big house, and had a butler called Parsons,' he began; and I wrote it down. 'She liked giving grand dinner parties to the gentry. But she had one misfortune, and it was this: whenever she'd had a glass of wine and was enjoying the party a drop began to form on the end of her nose. She didn't always notice it because she was so interested in the dinner-table talk, you see.' He gave me time to catch up on his dictation. 'So one evening, when there was to be a special dinner party, she said to her butler: "Parsons, I want you to do something for me tonight. When you see the drop on the end of my nose, just come up behind me and tell me that Johnson's at the door. Then I'll know; and I'll be able to use my handkerchief."

'Almost as soon as the guests were seated Parsons stood behind her, and bending over her he spoke confidentially: "Johnson's at the door, Madam."

'But forgetting her own instructions, she said, "Tell him to wait, Parsons. I can't see him now."

'A few minutes later, when there was a lull in the conversation, she called her butler to her side. "What was all that about a man at the door, Parsons?"

' "It's too late now, Madam," said Parsons. "Johnson's in the soup." '

There were a lot of jokes in my book by the end of that year, but the only one I remember now is the one about Johnson's being at the door.

On Saturday afternoon Dr Pat went to Wimbledon College to watch my brother Pat playing rugby. When the time came for our uncle to return to his hometown of Tulloh in County Carlow we were all sorry to see him go.

'Will you come and visit me in Ireland, Noree?' he asked me before he went. 'And I'll teach you how to catch a salmon.'

'A salmon is a very big fish...' I said doubtfully.

'Terrible big,' he agreed. 'Why, I saw one once, under the water, 'twas as big as a cow. You could stand on its back.'

I couldn't help reflecting, even then, that his fishing stories were not subjected to the rigours of his philosophy of modtheration in all things.

It was at about this time that John converted me to Pacifism. He lent me Norman Angell's book, *The Great Illusion*, in which the author tried to prove that in modern warfare all participants are losers, and there is no longer such a thing as victory in war. We all read it, and it provoked many arguments in the barracks.

'How can you stop men fighting if they want to fight?' asked Pat.

'The League of Nations will be a forum to which they can bring their grievances and get them sorted out,' was John's reply

In spite of the League of Nations, Hitler's grievances were gathering adherents in Germany, which was where Mary went as soon as she'd obtained her degree. In Stuttgart, where she taught English in a Gymnasium for girls, she met Georg, a handsome romantic student at Heidelberg University, and before long she wrote home to tell us she was engaged.

In those early days of Hitler's politicking, women were not encouraged into the newly emerging Nazi party, but on one occasion, when he held a rally in Heidelberg, Georg and his fellow students smuggled her into the hall, and there in the middle of the crowd, being a small girl, she went unnoticed. Hitler stood on a raised platform, so she could both see and hear this little man with the harsh unpleasant voice. He looked to her like a small boy working himself into a tantrum, so she was astonished at the effect he had on the young men around her. She listened carefully to this new would-be leader they were so excited about, and thought most of what he said was excessively silly, but everybody else in the room seemed to be entranced by his oratory. They were all cheering and stamping their feet, their eyes ablaze with hope and happiness in the belief that Hitler had discovered the elixir to dispel all Germany's troubles, including the 'decadence' that was said to be infecting Berlin. Whether due to Georg's politics, or to his sentimental vision of a married life in which Mary would bring him his warmed-at-the-fire slippers every evening when he came home from work, and was quite the last thing Mary dreamed of doing, the engagement soon came to an end.

One of Daddy's enterprises to try to increase his income was to import from India light straw 'Panama' hats in bright colours, and sell them on to be blocked into fashionable shapes and decorated in this country. As he was unable to leave the house himself, Mummy had to travel to London as his saleswoman with samples of the goods; and one Easter holidays I went with her to help carry the suitcases. I was wearing a biscuit-coloured jersey dress cut down from one of her own by Lulu, with a scarlet belt and a new red hat in the cloche style that was all the vogue. I suppose I must have looked older than my years. Rylands Wholesale Warehouse was a tall building with many floors, and we had to find the floor that dealt in hats. The place was sparsely furnished and uncarpeted so that our heels resounded on the bare boards as we crossed them towards the lift. It was a primitive lift consisting of a series of open sentry-like boxes in perpetual motion. You had to jump into an ascending box as it rose, and jump out with all your gear when it reached the right landing. I would have liked to travel on it, jumping on and off simply for the fun of it; but Mummy found it difficult to manoeuvre herself and her baggage into the small space in time, and one of her suitcases nearly fell out when we tried to dismount. I caught a cheeky assistant eyeing us with amusement. When she disappeared into a cubicle with her samples he spoke to me, leering and jerking his head towards the lift:

'Like to step in and ride up with me?' And when I shook my head he laughed.

'Scared, are we?' I still made no reply, so he added, 'What's she like—the old girl?'

I blushed violently. The 'old girl' was my mother, and I was not her employee. Confused and humiliated, I had to stand enduring his mockery till Mummy emerged from the office.

A few hats were sold, but the business was not profitable and was soon dropped. However my father's insurance agency was successful, and by 1928 was earning him as much money as his pension. Moreover his expenses were less, since both John and Mary were off his hands, John earning a livelihood, though still living at home, and Mary now teaching in a school in North London, where she was renting her own bedsit during the week, and only coming home for weekends. At about the same time his five-year lease of No 11 Ridgway Place was coming to an end, so he was able to consider buying a house.

In the autumn of 1928 we left Wimbledon and moved to East Molesey, near Hampton Court and the Thames. The move seemed sudden to me, and unwelcome too. It meant travelling daily by train to school, we would no longer be near enough to our friends to drop in and out of their homes, and I was sorry to lose this easy companionship. But as soon as I saw the new house I was enchanted. The parents had bought for £1,500 an airy, sunny house built at the beginning of the twentieth century. It had a garden big enough to provide a tennis lawn, a small orchard, a rough area where Daphne later kept hens, and a rockery with ornamental pool, around which, in Spring, tulips of various colours bloomed. At the front of the house, bushes of old-fashioned roses scented the path in June.

Lulu immediately set to work on the rockery, planting it with miniature plants with the help and advice of our neighbour Mr Rosenheim, a stockbroker with a Swiss wife, a garden filled with well-tended rockeries and a passion for alpines. These precious plants were sometimes a cause for gentle complaint when Daphne's hens escaped over the fence to make a meal of them.

Lulu had broken off her engagement with Cyril Echlin. 'He told me a dirty story,' she explained to us. 'I couldn't take his smut any longer. I don't mind him being around,' she added, 'so long as he's not too near me.' So he continued to spend his Sundays at our house, smoking and talking with Daddy, playing tennis with the boys, and making us all laugh. Lulu took little notice of him till one Sunday he brought his brother Frank with him. Frank was older, though shorter than Cyril. He was home on leave from India, and had hired a car in which he took Lulu out to dinner in town. Lulu had to get special permission from Daddy for this, as he usually locked the doors at nine-thirty p.m., when he went to bed. Frank took her out punting on the river too. Perhaps he gave her chocolates, or a bouquet of flowers when his leave ended and he returned to India. If she was disappointed she didn't show it.

'Oh! it's only for two years,' she said. 'We have an understanding. He'll be back.'

And he did come back; but this time it was Daphne he pursued with pleasantries and took out in his hired car; and Lulu hovered silently in the background. At the end of this holiday, Cyril went with him to India to work in what my mother, with a drop in her tone of voice denoting self-mockery of her own snobbism, called 'trade'. In Hindu terminology they were *box-wallahs*. We never saw either of the brothers again.

The parents bought some new furniture, new, that is, to us, but it was old stuff picked up at an auction, possibly what might now be called 'antiques'. There was a gigantic satinwood wardrobe with matching chest-of-drawers, in one of which Joanie and I found a little Swiss chalet carved in wood that the auctioneer forgot. When you lifted the roof to peep at the velvet-lined box underneath it began to play a merry tune.

Mummy decided to redecorate the house. It was suddenly very exciting to have new bedrooms of our own and to be able to choose our own wallpapers, the most memorable of which was Mary's, which was black, and terribly smart. Through its night tripped Geisha with parasols, cherries somehow blossomed in the dark, and boats with gold lanterns floated on its inky sea.

Lulu, who had chosen a tangle of wild roses for her wallpaper, received from the auction an oak bed and wardrobe, carved with leaves and flowers intertwined with grotesque heads so that entering her bedroom was like walking into a Grimm's fairy tale.

It wasn't only the new wallpapers that we liked; there was an agreeable new atmosphere of space and relaxation. The drawing room was a large L-shaped room with a French window facing south and opening on to the tennis lawn. The big crimson Indian carpet lay on the floor, on either side of the window the haughty carved camels stood, ready now to accept tennis balls and even Daphne's hens' eggs on their brass backs. An open fire warmed one end of the long room; the piano and a wireless, boxed in a polished wood case with a window for the loudspeaker, stood in the short arm of the L. Here Joanie and I were allowed to listen to Henry Hall's Dance Band broadcasting from five to six p.m. every evening before we began our homework.

Our first Christmas in East Molesey was not a happy one. I

became ill with a bad sore throat and fever. When the doctor visited the house he took a swab from my throat which grew diphtheria. He then took swabs from other members of the family, and Joanie, Daphne and Pat were all found to be carriers of the germ, though not at all ill. On Christmas Eve that year we were all bundled into an isolation hospital. Instead of the usual Christmas feast we were given jelly to eat. This made Pat so indignant that he discharged himself within a week against medical advice. Daphne and Joanie remained in the hospital for a month before their throat swabs became negative, but mine continued to harbour the diphtheria bacillus for three months in those tonsils that the Belgian doctor had wanted to 'cut out'. It was a boring period, though I made friends with the nurses, who lent me romantic novellas to read. There was in the ward a tinny little gramophone on which I played over and over again the only record there: 'The March of the Toreadors' from *Carmen*. But someone from home brought me a French grammar, and I was able to learn by heart all the French irregular verbs, which was a great help in exams later in that year.

It was wonderful to be released, to be free to go out again. In Spring, when all the gardens in Spencer Road began to flower, when golden Forsythia gleamed suddenly on a corner, and pink almond blossom leaned over a fence, it was a joy to walk to the station to catch the train for school.

We acquired a dog, Mickey, a henna-haired mongrel whom we all adored. We used to take him shopping with us when we went into Kingston on the bus. He was allowed to travel on the upper deck, where we sat, the three of us, Daphne, Joan and I, with Mickey stretched across our knees in sensual abandon. The bus conductor, as he punched our tickets, gazed enviously at Mickey and sighed, 'Wish I was a dawg!'

At home there was no more singing in parts round the piano on Sunday evenings; but Mummy, finding there was only an

175

organist but no choir at the local Catholic church, decided to make one. We were all soon enrolled in it and learning to sing simple masses. We also had to sing for Benediction on Sunday evenings, accompanied by the organist, an admirer of all things German, including this new leader Hitler, whom my mother thought of as a vulgar little show-off, though my father did say, 'Now Mabe, whatever you think, you must admit he has reduced unemployment in his country by using the unemployed to build good new roads.' The organist insisted on playing the tune of 'Deutschland Über Alles' for the Tantum Ergo, at Benediction, much to Mummy's annoyance. It amused us to watch the battle of wills between them. He was in her opinion not only a common chap with foolish opinions but a 'wretchedly low' taste for sentimental music. He also had an inordinate love for 'polyphony'. He seemed to be addicted to the very word. 'Ah! Polyphony! That's what we want. Polyphonic masses. Plenty of polyphony!' I can see my mother's face, now, tightening up in her efforts to control her irritation. She wanted to introduce the austere and much more difficult Plain Chant, which of course he hated. I can't help wondering as I look back over this long stretch of years whether the Plain Chant wasn't my mother's subconscious attempt to rid herself of the organist. No musical accompaniment is needed by Plain Chanters other than a tuning fork.

That was the only instrument we had, that and my mother's hand conducting us, when we went carol singing before Christmas. How happy I was walking through the frosty darkness from house to house under a moon across whose face wisps of torn cloud-veils passed in quick succession while Robin Tollast, our new schoolboy bass walked beside me talking of Shelley in jerky excited sentences, waving his torch in the air as he recited:

'O art thou pale with weariness of climbing heaven
'And gazing on the earth

'Wandering companionless among the stars
'That have a different birth?'

We sang traditional carols, the much loved 'Silent Night', and 'Venite Adoremus', but also 'The Holly and the Ivy', evergreen reminders of Yule, an older pagan festival celebrating the winter solstice and the hope of a new spring to come after it. And best of all, my favourite, comic and mysterious in its mix-up of English and dog-Latin from the Middle Ages, from the time of unquestioning faith: *'In dulce jubilo-o-o, Let us our homage sho-o-ow...'* There cradled in straw among farmyard animals lay the world's joy. *'There are angels singing.... There the bells are ringing....'* And then the long ripple down of notes spilling over in a triumphant carillon *'Ubi sunt gaudia? Where-e-ere? If that they be not there?...'*, to settle at last in a declaration of the amazing paradox: God in a helpless infant. *'Alpha es et O – O! Alpha es et O!'*

The sharp weather improved our voices, or perhaps we sang well simply because we were young and glad. At any rate strangers seemed to like our singing, and we were sometimes invited into a house to sing again in the hall, and afterwards rewarded with sherry and biscuits as well as a donation. I forget what charity we collected for, probably the church building fund, as the parish priest of the day was always scrounging about here, there, and everywhere, and throughout far too many sermons, to squeeze money out of the congregation for the building of a new church, to the detriment I believe of preaching the Word. Foxes had holes, if I remember rightly, but the son of Man had nowhere to lay his head, but that didn't stop his preaching his message.

There were now two maids, both redheads. Susan, a Presbyterian Scot, cooked, and Anastasia, a very pretty Irish girl, who was a wonderful dancer, cleaned the house. Once or twice we persuaded her to climb up on the kitchen table and dance an Irish jig, while we all sat round clapping out a steady rhythm, to which she moved her elaborate and tricky but never faltering steps. Besides being a dancer she had the good manners natural to a gentle kindly person, and a happy disposition to go with them, so we all loved her. And Susan too, became her loyal friend. There were times when the kitchen became a social centre with a trace of the old Barracks about it.

Once Pat brought to the kitchen an Ouija Board marked with the letters of the alphabet, and placed it on the table with an upturned glass in the centre. We all sat in a circle with our hands across the board, our fingers touching the glass. Solemnly he turned off the light. We were going to summon the spirits of the dead to answer our questions.

'Silence please!' he ordered, as someone squawked:

'Oo! It's scary!' There was a lot of giggling, but eventually we sat quiet and still.

The questions asked didn't get much response from the spirits till Joanie asked whom she would marry. Then the glass began to move quite rapidly, spelling out the letters E U G E N E. Good heavens! Who was Eugene? I knew Pat was cheating because I was sitting beside him and could feel his fingers pushing.

'Oh no! Not him!' cried Joanie.

Eugene Esmonde had been a friend of Pat's since Wimbledon College days, and was now learning to fly aeroplanes. In a few years' time he would be piloting an Imperial Airways Flight from England to Australia. Eugene nurtured a faithful love for Joanie that lasted from the time he was a schoolboy till he was killed during World War II. He joined the Fleet Air Arm, and commanded the squadron of Swordfish torpedo planes that were launched from the *Victorious* to attack the German battleship *Bismarck*. They were relatively slow old-fashioned biplanes, but nevertheless got through the fire from the battleship and hit her steering mechanism. The circling British warships were then able to close in and fire on her in her rudderless state. For this action

Eugene was awarded the DSO; but nine months later (on 12th Feb 1942) while leading six Swordfish to attack two German cruisers in the Dover Straits his plane received a direct hit. He continued the run-in to his target, but burst into flames and crashed into the sea. For this action he was awarded a posthumous VC. He was a very brave man, but Joanie never loved him.

Pat was repaid in full for his cheating when the calendar moved on to 14th February. Then Joanie and I went into Kingston and bought a Valentine card. It had a number of tiny coloured ribbon bows stuck to it. Beneath each was written a rhyme: If of me you often think / Send me back my bow of pink. If to me you will be true / Send me back my bow of blue. And so on. This card we put inside an envelope which we addressed to Pat in capital letters and posted in Kingston. He was quite excited when it arrived for him on Valentine's Day. We saw him open the envelope, we watched him as he sat down at the dining-room table, and pondering the matter, slowly detached the little bows and sent them off, each one to a different girl.

In the new house there was no place for the Barracks. We met and ate and did our homework in the dining room where a slow-burning 'Esse' Anthracite stove gave warmth, but the old intimacy and arguments were no more. We were all growing up and going our own ways, Daphne as a student at the Royal College of Art in Kensington, Pat as an engineering student at King's College in the Strand, to which he'd won a scholarship. John spent his weekends with Constance Lovell in North London, or in making furniture for use when they eventually married. He was a gifted carpenter. Among the pieces he made was a handsome dressing table of geometric Art Deco design in mahogany, with cubes containing drawers on either side of a large circular mirror. Mary was falling in love with a tenor. He was, she told us, older than herself, had lost an arm when fighting in the trenches, but sang 'Oh! So well!' She sighed. Mary was teaching French and German in a county secondary school for girls, but was disenchanted with the teaching profession and longed for a more glamorous life. She was having singing lessons, and it was through these that she was given the part of the Mustard Seed Fairy in an open-air performance in Regent's Park of *A Midsummer Night's Dream.* She used to mime the scenes for us in the garden at home, including scurrying off the greensward stage to a dressing room behind bushes to adjust hair blown out of place by the prevailing wind, and wiping off greasepaint streaked by showers of rain. Perhaps it was in Regent's Park that she met her singer, whose name I have forgotten, so I shall call him Nevil. Inclement weather did not, it seems, dampen their romance. We never met him because she never brought him home. For a long time she kept the affair secret from the parents.

I too was in love, not with a singer of songs but with the bright ring of words. I was entering upon that period of emotional turbulence, of fierce feelings and sudden changes of mood we call puberty, when the outward person is convulsed from deep down in the subconscious by something like a volcanic eruption of hot lava. In my case the flood of sex hormones had thrown me into the embrace of Poetry.

At school we were 'doing' Shakespeare's *Richard II,* acting it with relish, arguing with each other about the relative merits of the protagonists. Of course I loved the young king best because of his inevitable demise, and his memorable lines:

> For God's sake let us sit upon the ground
> And tell sad stories of the death of kings,
> How some have been deposed, some slain in war, ...
> Some poisoned by their wives, some sleeping killed,
> All murdered, for within the hollow crown
> That rounds the mortal temples of a king
> Keeps Death his court...

And then I stumbled upon Keats, and learned how much words could express. In the onomatopoeia of *'the murmurous haunt of flies on summer eves'* I could hear the buzzing of insects, and feel the heat. I read about his tragic youth, and incurable illness, I could feel his longing for sensual joy in his lines: *'O for a beaker full of the warm South...With beaded bubbles winking at the brim / And purple-stained mouth...'* I learned of his adoration of Beauty, which he declared to be one and the same thing as Truth. And then came Coleridge whose subtle interweaving of sounds and rhythms enchant the ear, and at last Wordsworth. 'Intimations of Immortality' trailed such clouds of glory through my soul that once when travelling home from school alone in a carriage, and watching through the window a beautiful winter sunset, I was seized by an ecstasy that made me stand up in the rocking train and recite the poem at the top of my voice from beginning to end. God in a sunset blaze, His face in an almond flower, Divinity in a grain of sand, and Wordsworth the Forerunner.

It must have been about this time that I borrowed from Pat and read a book on popular astronomy, James Jeans' *The Mysterious Universe*. It had a profound effect on my thinking. It made my imagination stagger to consider the vastness of space, the distances between the sun and its planets, the possibility of other suns and other planetary systems existing out there beyond the telescopic vision of man, and the infinitude of time, not the four thousand years of biblical interpretation but four billion years from the Big Bang. I understood then how small a thing the human species was, how infinitesimal a speck of dust I was, and how arrogant and self-centred, how absurd it was to expect or even hope for immortality. Why should the Creator of all this immensity, with so many other more important things on His Mind, bother to think of me at all? I began to think that personal immortality was extremely improbable. At the same time I still believed in it. I did this by wrapping up the inconvenient criticism of faith and stowing it away on a shelf remote in the library of memory.

Scott Fitzgerald is quoted as saying that the creative mind is capable of holding two contradictory views and still functioning; but there comes a time to all of us while growing up when new concepts crowd in upon childish ones. Then we all learn to think double with equanimity. You don't have to be an artist to achieve this balancing act; it is something we all have to do in order to survive with any sort of sanity. No system of philosophy can be a perfectly logical whole.

We can't explain the world, and perhaps never shall; all cultures are tangles of irreconcilable attitudes, and we all believe a lot of myths mixed up with incontrovertible facts.

I must have mentioned James Jeans and the doubts he had aroused in my mind to my English teacher, Mother Theresa Neylan. She was interested in my development and in my reading, and was always very kind to me. It was said among the girls that she had taken the veil when her fiancé was killed in the trenches. Her comment when I voiced my doubts surprised me. 'How much more disturbing doubts are,' she said, 'when one has given up everything for the Faith.' Could it be that her faith sometimes faltered, that she even sometimes regretted becoming a nun?

She disapproved of some of the books I read, especially of *All Quiet on the Western Front*, by the German writer Erich Maria Remarque, which was being widely read and talked about. It makes war look not only terribly sad, but dirty, wasteful and in the end futile. I don't think she ever read it herself, but she took the view that it was an immoral and indeed a filthy book. I remember wondering even then whether in order to accept the loss of her lover she had to believe that he died nobly defending a noble cause.

Another nun who suffered from 'doubts' was Mother Gonzaga. She was a gentle, soft-spoken woman with a sallow skin and a sad expression, inevitably nicknamed Gorgonzola, Gonzie or simply Cheese-Face. She was unable to keep order; during her classes I am sorry to say we rioted; but she was a wonderful teacher one-to-one. I was alone in learning German (my father had visions of my studying languages one day in a bilingual university city such as Strasbourg), and it was she who taught me German. She was in fact Danish. In summer we sometimes sat together in the garden for this lesson; and it was then she drew my attention to robins and other birds she loved. I think she was obsessed by the awareness of the suffering that every living thing, including innocent birds, have to suffer. She consoled herself by remembering the words of Jesus about God watching the fall of a sparrow. But it was sad, wasn't it, that so many had to fall? The dogma of hell must have been to her an unacceptable horror. 'We have to believe in hell,' she once said to me, 'but we don't have to believe that anyone goes there. God in His mercy can forgive us all.'

I also experienced a surge of religious emotion during adolescence. I used to go to early mass and take communion daily. It meant rising at six-thirty a.m. in order to attend Mass at the Catholic church, ten minutes walk away, and get back in time for breakfast before catching the eight-twenty a.m. train from Hampton Court station. A near neighbour, a retired major with military shoulders and a splendid moustache, who was also a daily attender, used to walk back with me after the service. One day he invited me to tea to meet his son Roger. The boy proved to be only twelve years old, quite embarrassingly childish for a fifteen-year-old like me, but we played ping-pong, watched by his father, and had tea prepared by his mother. I was glad when at last I was able to leave the house. The major walked with me to the gate where he suddenly seized hold of me and implanted a very rough kiss, not on my mouth, as I turned quickly away, but on my cheek. As I struggled out of his grasp I looked back and caught sight of Roger standing in the porch. I can still see his face. It haunts me with guilt, though I was not guilty. I ran all the way home and up to my bedroom to look at myself in the mirror. I could still feel a burning sensation on my cheek where that moustache had pricked me, and was surprised there was no fiery red spot to be seen. It was the first time I'd ever been kissed by a man other than a relative. I managed to escape any repetition of teatime games with Roger, no doubt to his relief as well as mine, though I never divulged to Mummy my reasons for avoiding him.

The heightened religious emotions of adolescence were fanned into intense heat by a Retreat given at the convent for senior girls by a Dominican monk, Father Valentine, a handsome man and a fine orator, who today would be dubbed a charismatic preacher. For those who don't know what a Retreat is I should explain that it requires taking part in three days of intense introspection and prayer, interspersed with three sermons a day in chapel. Meals were eaten in the refectory in silence, silent walks in the garden were allowed. The intensity of feelings that can be aroused in such circumstances is marvellously described by James Joyce in his *Portrait of the Artist as a Young Man*. In that case the retreat was given for a group of adolescent males terrified into fears of hellfire by guilty secrets of masturbation; in our case Father Valentine was talking to girls, and he chose to make his theme the decay and death that is our common lot: youth is brief, beauty is ephemeral, all worldly things are but toys, all is vanity unless we pursue God. This life is but a dream; we see as in a glass darkly; only after death do we wake to the ultimate reality. Then we see God face to face. I had been stumbling towards thoughts such as these myself, and had written a poem about them that was printed in the school magazine. Father Valentine had read it, and when he interviewed me he talked about it. Did I know I was touching on *Cartholic* Metaphysics? No, of course not;

but I was flattered by being spoken to as if I was adult by this priest who seemed to understand my innermost thoughts better even than my best friend, Biddy Kelly, who also wrote verses. We used to exchange these effusions, and write letters to each other about our secret thoughts and feelings. I was certainly in love with her at that time. No doubt fearing a lesbian relationship Father Valentine told me to distance myself from this love. The separation his influence enforced made me weep for a day, but it was in fact no more than a damping down of ardour, and did not destroy our friendship, which lasted till she died at seventy. The impression Father Valentine made on me, as on most of us, was profound. I suppose it was an experience akin to psychoanalysis.

When Mary announced her engagement to Nevil she added calmly that he was divorced. There was a stunned silence, broken by Mummy's saying, 'You can't marry him if he's divorced.'

'Well, I'm going to,' said Mary.

'But you can't be married in church!'

'No. It'll have to be a Registry Office.'

'I don't know what your father will say.'

'I do. But it won't make any difference.'

And then the row began. My father took to his bed. Mummy, unaware of the emotional blackmail she was being subjected to, dutifully took his blood pressure at regular intervals. Mary was brought to his bedroom. Voices at first only hostile grew loud and angry: marriage is a sacrament uniting two persons before God till death do them part. / But these persons are not united. They've lived apart for several years, have no love whatever for each other, and are unsuited in every way. / Are there any children of the marriage? / No, no children. / Well, that's one mercy. Divorce isn't only a sin; it's a social disgrace. / That is something

Mary is willing to face. And she's now old enough to manage her own life. / If she takes this step she will be disinherited because of her wickedness, she would no longer be allowed to come home, and her father would no longer acknowledge such an obstinate, ungrateful, hard-hearted girl as his daughter... . So Mary walked into her black-walled room, packed up her clothes and whatever other possessions of hers remained there, and left the house.

We were tearful and frightened when we kissed her goodbye. I took a bowl from the kitchen and went out into the raspberry patch. There, staring at the rows of canes I spoke aloud fiercely: 'I hate him! I hate him!' Then, as I began to pick the ripe fruit the repetitive soothing movement calmed my rage, and I saw what a moral quandary I'd stumbled into. The fourth commandment bade me honour my father and my mother. How could I honour him? And what did 'honour' mean anyway? It was a conundrum not easily solved, but at least I had a full bowl of lovely juicy berries for the rest of us to share at teatime.

The row rumbled on for some time, as Daddy took whatever opportunity he could to lecture us on Mary's faults, on how she was throwing away her education and all the other opportunities in life he'd given her, and how she was running into all sorts of unseen and unimaginable dangers. Somehow, in spite of her wickedness we were all on her side. He must have known he faced a wall of intransigence. Meanwhile Mummy had thought of a way in which they might get round the difficulties. She remembered that Mary had said Nevil's first wife was a Catholic. She remembered her name: Beryl. It occurred to her that if Beryl had married Nevil in a Registry Office, or even in an Anglican church, the marriage, because it was not a true Catholic sacrament, might be considered null and void. She discovered Beryl's address, and she travelled up to London to visit her. I can only imagine their meeting. No doubt Beryl thought her crazy. In any event it turned out that Beryl had married Nevil in a Catholic church, and that the marriage was therefore indissoluble. There was no way out. Mary remained in London, estranged, and probably, my mother feared, living in sin with Nevil. Her room at home remained empty. Mummy began to call it 'the spare room'.

The boys had their own method of dealing with rows. They avoided them, chiefly to spare Mummy the distress they caused. But complete obedience to my father's wishes was not part of their plans. They shared the room above the backdoor. It was above the kitchen and below the maids' attic. The garage stood parallel with the door, at the top of a slight slope, so it was possible to let the car run out freewheel and in reverse, and only crank up the engine when it reached the road. John and Pat were always inside the house by nine-thirty p.m., but Pat sometimes left later to drive to a party in town with his student friends, a meeting (no doubt followed by a drinking session in a pub) of the King's College Engineering Union, of which he had been elected president, or perhaps a Faculty dance. He climbed out of the window and into Daddy's car, and so to town. On the way home he was able to turn off the engine some twenty or thirty yards from the gate and freewheel into it. There was enough momentum in the car to get it back into the garage without being heard by the parents asleep on the other side of the house. Pat climbed in and out of his bedroom window like a cat burglar.

Similarly when John, who had to catch a very early train in order to get to the City by nine a.m., overslept, Pat used to drive him to the station and arrive back in time for breakfast. John then had to wash and shave in the toilet cabin of a rocking train. They were never found out, though I suspect the maids knew what was going on.

In old age, Pat once remarked that these escapades were a good training for the escapes he had to plan, and the one he himself succeeded in making from Colditz Castle, where he was imprisoned during the War.[2]

Mummy possessed a very strong sense of smell, an occasionally inconvenient gift I have inherited. She could detect even faint odours, though she was not always correct in diagnosing their origin. One evening when John was sitting at the kitchen table enjoying a quick drag with the maids to whom he'd given cigarettes, she ran into the kitchen crying out in alarm: 'I can smell brown paper burning!'

'How do you know it's brown?' he asked.

And Mummy, waving her hands through the smoke and telling them to open the window, retired laughing. In those days, before doctors had learned what a slow poisoner tobacco is, nearly everybody smoked; it was an expression of friendship, like breaking bread together, or the giving of salt.

On her afternoon off, Anastasia went into Kingston by bus to meet her Irish boyfriend, and I guess she was sometimes back after nine-thirty p.m., when no doubt she had a pact with John to unlock the door for her. But one night she didn't come back at all. My mother was naturally alarmed to find her missing in the morning.

'She'll be back, Ma'am,' Susan Callaghan reassured her. 'I daresay she missed the last bus.'

'But good heavens! Where would she stay all night?'

'They would have given her a bed in the pub where Paddy works behind the bar,' said Susan. 'She's safe enough. Don't you worry.'

But that was just what Mummy feared. Sex was surely teeming behind that bar, rampant and raising its many ugly heads! And her fears proved to be well grounded. Anastasia didn't come back to work for us, nor even to claim her wages. She returned to visit us six months later to tell us she'd just been married. She was very, very pregnant. My mother of course disapproved of a baby conceived out of wedlock, but was pleased that Anastasia was now married. She paid her arrears of wages, adding a few extra pounds as a wedding gift; and I gave her a pair of rhinestone earrings someone had given me for my birthday. Anastasia was a blithe spirit; and we were all sorry when she went away.

One evening Daddy received an anonymous phone call to tell him that his son Patrick had been kidnapped. The message was softened by the information that he was being held hostage by University College students till the King's students released 'Fergus' whom they'd captured. All this amused my father. He wasn't angry but curious to know the full story when Pat returned twenty-four hours later looking decidedly the worse for wear and showing a few bruises. In fact it was an alibi cooked up by Pat in order to take part in the London University Colleges annual Rag, and stay overnight to enjoy the junketings afterwards. The King's College engineering students used to try to capture University College's mascot, Fergus, a dummy highlander in full kilted regalia, and University College aimed to get hold of the King's College mascot, a lion with a red cloth skin. Considerable quantities of beer were drunk by all concerned, there was a certain amount of fighting and vandalism, and the police intervened. Certainly that Rag got out of control, and in the excitement a War Memorial was tarred and feathered. ('Half a dozen feathers', according to Pat's confession decades after the event.) Pat, as leader of the engineers, was in the thick of the trouble; but we heard nothing about all this till one afternoon in late June, when on returning from school I was met by Daddy with a long face and a voice tolling like a funeral bell: 'Pat has been expelled!' Daddy seemed more shocked than angry. Pat had never caused trouble at home. His behaviour was exemplary. He mowed and rolled the lawn willingly before marking out the court with white lines, he kept the car in working order and washed it regularly, and was always agreeable. What had he done to deserve such punishment? Daddy had received a letter containing the report of the Disciplinary Tribunal on the affair to say that Pat had been suspended from King's College for two terms for riotous behaviour and damage to a public building.

Pat didn't come home that night, but sent a telegram: GONE TO MEDITERRANEAN FOR SUMMER AS COOK ON PRIVATE YACHT. I felt sorry for the victims of his cooking. I don't believe he could cook an egg. By the time he did come home in September Daddy's initial anger had been mollified into curiosity about his travels. As it turned out the whole affair was a blessing in disguise. Pat went to work in a factory during those two terms when he was suspended from college; and when in the early Thirties, at a time of severe unemployment, he obtained his degree, and was looking for work, this experience of practical mechanical engineering helped him greatly to get a job.

*References — Chapter Eight*

---

1  St Vitus' Dance
2  My brother Pat was P R Reid, Escape Officer at Colditz and the author of *The Colditz Story.*

# 9

It was while Pat was enjoying a summer sailing in the Mediterranean that my father suddenly asked me what I wanted to do when I grew up.

'I want to be a writer,' I said.

'Fleet Street's no place for a woman,' was his response. And sitting down penniless to write a novel was simply out of the question. 'The only careers really open to you are teaching or medicine.'

Teaching was something Mary was doing; and I knew she hated it. So I chose Medicine. I had no idea what Medicine was, what demands it made of its acolytes and whether I'd be able to fulfil them, nor how it would change my whole way of living and thinking. On such an ignorant whim was my future decided.

There were no science classes held at the Convent, but my father discovered that the Wimbledon High School held a First MB Course for prospective medical students. It was planned that I take my matriculation from the Convent, and then go to the High School for a course in Physics, Chemistry and Biology.

It all seemed far away in the future as my adolescent 'puppy-fat' fell off me together with my excessive enthusiasms, and I moved into a flirtatious phase that included going with Joanie to the Kingston Roller Skating Rink to meet the Boys on Saturday afternoons, and inviting our favourites to tea and tennis at home on Sundays. Much time was spent in preparation for social life, in trying to clear my skin of acne, and curling my hair. This was done with hot iron tongs (the Marcel wave) or by damping the hair and rolling it up into curlers the night before.

We were even allowed to give an 'evening party'. The drawing-room carpet was rolled up, Fuller's Earth was sprinkled over the floorboards to make them more slippery, and we danced to the gramophone. Lulu made me an elegant dress of lavender-coloured taffeta, and on its full short skirt she painted pink and purple tulips that bloomed briefly for the occasion.

Both my brothers were good dancers, but most of the other boys we knew had very little idea how to move to music. I soon discovered that the few who could do a natty foxtrot had nothing to say, and that the talkers couldn't keep time, and frequently trod on your toes. A witty male with nimble feet was a rare bird indeed.

One of the boys invited me to go to the pictures with him. Mummy gave me permission to go on condition that Daphne went with me. Such a suggestion was of course ludicrous, but Daphne and I agreed to it. Privately, we arranged to travel together by bus and then part immediately till the show was over. It was a lame-duck film whose title I've forgotten. The Boy held my hand decorously in the dark, and told me I was a peach. His name was Cecil.

The parents made the mistake of suspecting and fearing boys who were far too timid to kiss us, let alone attempt anything more daring and dangerous, but trusting their daughters to the care of older men of status and respectability.

I was not quite seventeen when a charming elderly man, an old friend of my parents, asked their permission to take me to London and show me the sights, give me dinner in a restaurant, and since we would be too late to get back to East Molesey that night, to put me up in his hotel, a very respectable one, he assured them. I met him at Waterloo and we climbed into a taxi, in which he tickled my knee to test me, so he told me, to see if I was a good rider. If I laughed when I was tickled it would prove that I wasn't any good in the saddle. I was very ticklish, and I laughed. We drove into the Strand and then into Trafalgar Square, where I had to crane my neck in order to see Nelson on his high column, then down Whitehall and round the outskirts of Buckingham Palace before turning towards the Houses of Parliament, all of which he pointed out to me from the windows of our taxi.

I noticed, when we entered the restaurant, several very sophisticated women in long evening gowns. I was wearing my best summer dress, a pretty red cotton voile printed with a scattering of daisies and closed at the neck by a prim white collar. I must have looked a mere child among the other diners, but I was happy and confident as we sat down at our little table in a corner of the room. It was all a great thrill for me. We had a very pleasant meal during which, as he filled my glass with white wine, he made jokes about not allowing me to drink too much. It was when young ladies drank too much of the stuff that they did delightfully wicked things, he told me. I looked like a perfect little plaster saint, he said, but he suspected there might be a bit of a devil hidden somewhere underneath. And he laughed. I suppose the trend of his conversation must have given me some inkling of his possible intentions because when I went to bed, in a room next door to his own, I kept my dressing-gown wrapped tightly round me. All the same it was a great surprise to see him coming into my room by way of the communicating balcony I had hardly noticed before. Without any preliminaries he climbed into my bed and lay on top of me. He was wearing pyjamas. I lay absolutely rigid, saying nothing. I wasn't afraid, but I was too surprised to speak. What was happening was unimaginable.

Why…! He was as old as my father! After a little fumbling he suddenly said, 'You're not a very sentimental gel, are you?' And in my firmest school-prefect tones I replied, 'No. Not at all.' Upon which he slid off me and took himself out of my room by the way he'd entered it.

Next morning I dressed as soon as I woke. I had been invited to take breakfast in his room; but he seemed disappointed when he saw me.

'Oh Nora, you shouldn't have dressed,' he said. 'It's so much nicer when one is *deshabillé*.'

The situation is even more comic in retrospect when I remember that at the time of his attempted seduction I was a Sunday School Marm. I was what is now called 'Supply', temporarily taking the place of the regular teacher, who was no doubt better equipped than I to cope with the questions, direct and logical, of small boys in the class. When I showed them a picture, in an illustrated catechism, of God sitting in glory above the clouds, and hell below, full of devils with long forks pushing naked souls into the flames they were of course fascinated.

'Where's hell then, Miss?'

'Well, it's not really a place, like Surbiton, Billy. It's a sort of… . It's a state of mind.'

'Must be underground, Miss.'

'Well, I don't know, Jimmy…'

'Stands to reason, Miss. Heaven's up in the sky. We're on the floor. Hell must be under our feet, Miss.'

'Cor!' escaped in collective exhalation from the class, and one little girl quickly lifted her boots to make sure they weren't getting singed.

I asked Daphne what her experiences had been when she'd been taken up to town by the same gentleman a couple of years before. He had not been so forward with her. He had shown her a copy of Radclyffe Hall's novel *The Well of Loneliness*, which had

194

been banned as immoral and obscene because it dealt with a lesbian love affair. He'd talked about it with evident relish in what we might now call 'soft-porn talk', and asked her what she thought. She had been more mystified than shocked. Neither of us told the parents anything about our experiences, and they remained in contented ignorance of what their old friend was up to.

Following my matriculation, I spent the next two terms studying the basic sciences at Wimbledon High School in the mornings, and in the afternoons attending classes at the Convent. With Mother Theresa we studied *Hamlet*. Was he really mad, or only pretending? With Mother Augustine we did French classical drama, not Racine, who might have proved risky, but Corneille's *Horace*: an honourable stiff. She also taught us Latin. She was popular with the girls because, earthy Belgian that she was, she laughed often, finding life, and even Ovid's *Metamorphoses* funny, though sometimes she would say, 'We'll pass over the next two lines.' It was always these two lines, of course, that we pored over longest later in our efforts to translate.

It was a wonderfully happy time. No exams were as yet looming; and I was finding my introduction to science inexhaustibly interesting, particularly physics.

At the High School I had to carry the banner and uphold the honour of a different tribe, but I was so enthralled by what I was learning, and the marvellous teaching of it, so armoured, too, in my own faith, that I didn't in the least mind being alone.

I made no new friends there apart from Celia Coleman-Young, who travelled with me by train from Hampton Court, and who, it turned out, actually lived at the end of Spencer Road in Greene Arden, a house whose garden bordered the bank of the River Mole, where a gigantic willow hung its green tresses over the muddy waters. Celia had contracted poliomyelitis when she was nine years old, and as a result was partially paralysed in one leg. She limped when she walked, but this did not deter her from dancing, which she loved, partly perhaps because the long evening dresses worn at the time hid her deformity. She was also a good tennis player, and had developed a strong backhand. She was in the sixth form, studying arts subjects.

Science was for me a road to Damascus, certainly a revelation of the order and balance that existed behind our seen world. Physics consisted of Heat, Light and Sound, and was taught by a woman who wore dowdy clothes, and pinned her greenish-blonde plaits of hair into coils like earphones round her ears in a fashion already long out of date. She was certainly eccentric, but she was a gifted teacher. I well remember one demonstration she made to prove to us that sound moved in waves: the long box full of sand with two wires stretched tightly over it. When she plucked the fine wire its rapid vibration produced a high-pitched sound and a quick wriggle in the sand below, when she struck the thick wire she produced a bass note and a wide slow undulation like the passage of a snake.

The laws of physics filled me with the joy of a revelation, showing how the Creator holds the universe in His hand, and chaos at bay. Biology gave a different message that crept into my mind gradually and insidiously as I began to understand the concept of evolution. The evidence seemed incontrovertible that life, beginning in one-celled creatures, in slime from the seas, had gradually developed through vast eons (remarkably paralleled by the six days of creation in the bible) into complex organisms, and finally into human beings. Our embryo life recapitulates the history of our ancestors, showing how from blobs of undifferentiated cells we grow through various phases of evolution, through a fish-stage complete with gills for breathing instead of lungs, to the foetal mammal form with lungs as yet unused. That all this had happened, is still happening, through a ruthless struggle for food and mates, in which only the fittest could survive, did mean that the weak and ill-adapted must fall out and be lost. The process of evolution is undoubtedly cruel. Reproduction in its excess and waste is harsh. Of every eight robins hatched in summer only two survive the winter. In nature more than half of what is born is very soon attacked by sudden death or disease, for pathological bacteria and viruses also have their right to struggle for survival and reproduction in the savage battle. Nature is red in tooth and claw. Does God look on and let it be?

And then there were the revelations of Gregor Mendel, Abbot of Brunn in Silesia, and his two dissimilar peas. He was a gardener-botanist interested in the hybridisation of plants. He worked quietly and perseveringly in his monastery garden, pollinating a pea with round, smooth-skinned seed, with another that had an angular wrinkled seed, and carefully recorded his results over generations of pea-multiplication. In 1865 he published a paper among the reports of a local natural history society, *Experiments in Plant Hybridisation*, showing that the offspring of this cross-fertilising produced these characteristics in a regular pattern of three to one. Three quarters were smooth and round, and these he called dominant, one quarter was wrinkled, and these he called recessive. Of the dominant three-quarters the next generation produced the same ratio of dominant to recessive. In other words he had made what was, at a time long before there was any knowledge of chromosomes or genes, a revolutionary discovery: that some inherited factor was passed down the generations of peas programming them to develop in a certain fixed way. His paper lay unread by the larger world for thirty years until at last this startling fact was rediscovered. Further experiments were made in cross-fertilising other plants, and in birds and mammals, to confirm his findings; their meaning began to be understood by biologists, evolutionists, philosophers, and eventually ignorant students like myself. Although I was excited by all this new information its philosophical implications did not as yet challenge my beliefs, but inevitably it was to work in my mind, like a worm in the bud, nagging for an answer to the question: how much are human beings, like other animals, subject to the laws of heredity? What is Free Will? How programmed, and in fact how free are we? I had a lot to think about.

I left both my schools before the summer term, as my mother wanted me to spend a few months at home learning 'how to run a house'. It was not a very arduous job. The real work was done by the cook and the char (a casual worker in more ways than one), who had replaced the two red-haired maids. I also learned to drive a car, my father beside me, shouting incoherently when I stalled the engine of his Singer at a busy crossroads on the way to Bushey Park. We had to get out and try to crank the engine into life while behind us a growing queue of impatient drivers honked horns and shouted encouragement or derision according to their temperaments.

May Foster, whom I had loved so much when I was six years old, was now dead. Her sons, Anthony and Francis who had just left Downside School, and her daughter Joan, whom I knew in Eekloo days, spent the summer holidays with us. Another young man from Downside, Richard Powers, used to join them on Sunday afternoons. He spent his lunchtime in a pub whose garden adjoined ours, and when it closed at three p.m., he used to climb over the intervening fence and enter our house via the French windows. He was the funniest man I ever knew, and also, at that time, the best read. He added greatly to the inventiveness in games we played and the conversation we enjoyed on those lively Sunday afternoons.

I was supposed to produce supper for them all. I'm afraid it was basic to say the least, consisting of soup made from Oxo cubes, followed by cold meat left over from the Sunday lunchtime roast joint, with sliced beetroot soused in vinegar, and bread and butter. It was all eaten up, and nobody complained till one evening, finding a pot of brown liquid on the stove beside my Oxo soup, I poured the two together. Pat was suffering from toothache at the time, and this brown liquid was half a pint of Guinness that he was warming to comfort his jaw. It did not add to the quality of the soup, and at suppertime there was some grumbling about the cook.

It was that summer that Aunt Fanny came to stay. She slept in the black bedroom. It must have been a great pleasure for the sisters to meet again and talk after so many years of separation. Fanny was fourteen years senior to Mummy, certainly over seventy. We all expected to see someone extremely aged, so we were surprised to meet this spry and very pretty old lady. When Joanie took up the breakfast tray I'd prepared, and saw her sitting up in bed, supposedly frail but with a pink skin, a halo of white hair brilliant against the black wallpaper, her neck wrapped in the white lace collar of her nightdress and her shoulders in a pretty pink bed-jacket, Joanie was dumbfounded. She must have revealed her surprise, because Aunt Fanny said, 'I do believe one should try to grow old gracefully, you know.'

'But she's so beautiful!' Joanie reported to me downstairs. 'If you can look like that at seventy—well, I wouldn't mind so much being old.'

To Joanie, beauty was of prime importance. She had learned in childhood the power her own beauty conferred, in her early teens she was already being noticed and pursued by men. On more than one occasion I was asked by an admirer to act as a go-between. Lieut Commander Fogarty was one such lover who needed help. He was a grisled retired naval officer, a bachelor who lived with his mother in a Grace and Favour house at Hampton Court. It happened that he also attended our church. Joanie was not quite fifteen at the time. He didn't approach her directly but invited us both for a day out in Portsmouth. He gave us lunch in a posh hotel full of naval uniforms, all so quietly but solemnly aware of what England expects that when I accidentally clattered a spoon on a plate it sounded mutinous. He took us to see Nelson's ship, *Victory*, hauled up in dock and awaiting rescue from decay. She looked pretty battered. I was able to pick a splinter from one of her decks as a souvenir. Not long afterwards, Fogarty approached me after Sunday Mass. 'Sound her out for me—could you?' was how he put his request. Perhaps he knew he was destined to be a no-hoper. For Joanie, who dreamed of nothing less than a film star with the good looks of Ramon Navarro's Ben Hur, or Ronald Colman, poor Fogarty wouldn't do at all. 'Good Heavens! That old Fogey!' was what she said. And I was the fool in the middle having to obtain and deliver this uncompromising message.

A red post-box stood at one end of Spencer Road. More than once when I took a letter to drop into it I came across a young man who was doing the same thing. We eyed each other furtively till at last he spoke to me. 'You must be Celia's friend,' he said. He was, he said, a sort of cousin of hers, and lived at Greene Arden with his Aunt Elsie. He knew my name, and quite a lot about me. He told me his: Egbert, and apologised for it. Great unifier of Saxon England though the original Egbert was, the name sounded outlandish in my ignorant ears, and I couldn't bring myself to call him that, nor did I like 'Bert', so I decided to call him B, just B. He seemed to like that, and soon we were meeting less by accident than by design. It was not long before I was introduced to the complicated web of relationships, covering four generations, that hung in Greene Arden.

Mary came home one weekend unexpectedly to announce that she and Nevil had parted company. The parents were delighted to see her, recriminations were forgotten, and she reclaimed her black bedroom. She also lent me a pretty evening dress, as I had as yet none of my own, to wear at an important *Conversazione* to be held in London, when my new friend Egbert was to receive his AMICE, or membership of the Association of Civil Engineers. His aunt had invited me as her guest.

Auntie Elsie had reached the magisterial stage of womanhood, but still turned heads as she walked across the crowded room, wearing a billowing dress of deep blue silk, her head of copper-coloured hair held high. She was always charming to me, and it was many months before I saw the cool organising brain behind her smiling blue eyes. On the evening of the *Conversazione* she led the way up a great curved staircase to shake hands with the President of the Association who stood at the top. It was for me a very thrilling occasion filled with possibilities of awakening love, of this being the Real Thing. I had felt brief romantic crushes before, but never with a man five years older than myself, and a good deal more sophisticated. I was aware of his admiration as his eyes rested on me and my borrowed dress, whose skirt of ivory voile, printed with sweet-pea flowers of many colours, fell in layer upon layer of flounces from hips to ankle.

When the boring speeches were ended at last he took my hand and squeezed it as he led me to the supper room. Here delicious canapés were served, and champagne toasts were drunk to British Civil Engineering, to their Association, and to the new members of it. Here I raised my glass to B, and our eyes met in a long ardent look. I don't think Auntie Elsie intercepted it.

At the end of the evening, when I thanked her, she expressed the hope that I would come often to visit them at Greene Arden. She encouraged me to play with her little boy, David, who was just four at the time, and even once let me bathe him and put him to bed. She had been a married woman when she took lessons in singing at the Wimbledon Conservatoire, and had fallen in love with its director, Coleman-Young, a widower with a small daughter, my friend Celia. Elsie had been his mistress when David was conceived. Divorce proceedings in those days were difficult and slow, and unfortunately he died before they were completed.

Elsie took care of Celia, who was in fact David's half-sister. She also gave house-room to her nephews Egbert and his two engineer brothers, Paul and Ross. When War broke out these two joined the RAF; and in later years Paul rose to the rank of Air Marshal.

Auntie Elsie was expecting a fortune from her own Uncle Taylor, who adored her, and in whose house they were all living. He, too, in youth had been a civil engineer, and partner in a famous firm. He was a music-lover, and a keen Wagner fan, and had once visited Bayreuth to hear the operas. He was keen, too, to tell you about it if you were unlucky enough to sit next to him at afternoon tea. 'Ah! The Ring! Wagner! Have you seen it? It takes four days to hear it all.' And then he would start all over again: 'Ah! Wagner! The Ring! It takes four days you know.' He repeated this endlessly. The poor old man was losing his wits.

As soon as Auntie Elsie heard Mary sing she wanted her to perform at her summer musical garden party; but Mary was elusive, working in London, and seldom at home. She had now met and fallen in love with a handsome soldier, an officer in the Royal Signals, Norman de la Poer Tate. She was soon engaged to be married. But when it was learned in Spencer Road that she intended being married in St Margaret's Westminster, a fashionable Anglican church, there was consternation in the house. The parents would have nothing to do with it. Mary was adamant; she refused to alter her decision, she refused to come home to discuss it. Her mother-in-law, Rene, eventually gave the wedding reception, which we were all forbidden to attend, though later when I visited Mary's London flat I heard the interesting details and saw photographs. She was not married in white; she wore a blue diaphanous dress and a large blue 'picture' hat. Her engagement ring displayed a large sapphire surrounded by diamonds, and Rene gave her a bracelet to match.

The parents never acknowledged her marriage. It was the final breach between them.

*1   Painting of his house in Chowringhee, Calcutta, by William Prinsep, 1820s, but later sold to meet his creditors when he was declared bankrupt.*

*2 Fanny Louise Prinsep leaning on the shoulder of her sister Amelia, 1850s.*

*3 Clarmont Daniell ICS married Fanny Louise in 1860.*

*4 Catherine Murphy on her marriage to John Reid Senr in Carlow, Ireland, 1872.*

*5 John Reid Jnr, ICS, CIE, as a young man in Dublin 1896.*

*6 Pat Reid aged four and Nora Reid aged six months, in Patna, India, January 1915.*

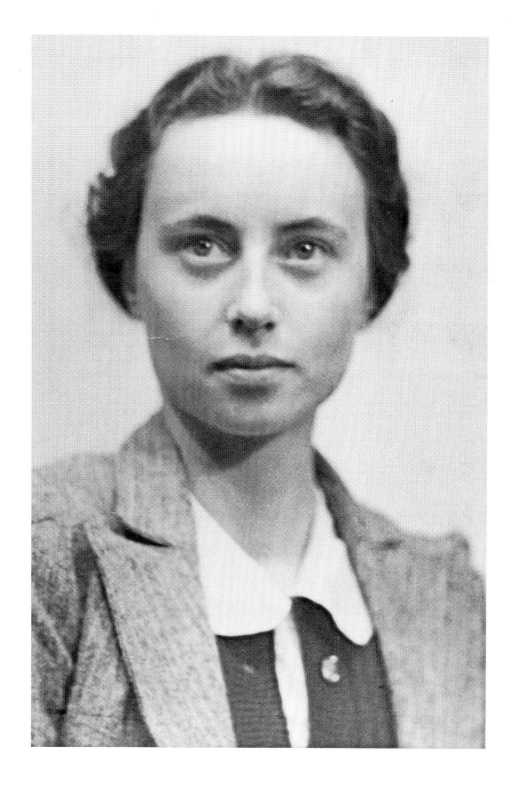

*7 Nora Reid, just qualified MBBS 1938.*

Norman was a very taciturn man, and a lazy man too, but a brave soldier, and Mary loved him dearly. She was so voluble and amusing herself that perhaps she didn't notice his silences; perhaps she didn't give him a chance to speak. During the War he was taken prisoner in Singapore by the Japanese and made to work on the Burma Railway. He was one of the few who survived that experience. It was one of he things he didn't talk about; but once many years later he told me, 'You could be dying of starvation or dysentery, and the Japs wouldn't care.'

I waited while he smoked his seemingly endless chain of cigarettes.

'But if you got a skin disease they'd notice it.'

It happened that he'd developed a large diphtheritic ulcer on his leg, and the Commandant of the camp, seeing it, sent him into a hospital. 'And, do you know, he sent me half a dozen eggs while I was there!' Long pause. 'Queer coves, the Japs. Not like us at all.'

When in old age Mary and Norman were staying in my house, and they'd both swallowed their 'sundowner' gin-and-tonics, she used to like to talk about the past. She was suffering from a brain tumour, and would soon die, but she hadn't made her peace with her father, who'd been dead for forty years. 'I hate him, Nora,' she said to me more than once. 'I hate him still!'

They had recently attended the cremation of a friend; and Mary had been horrified by the banal canned music played during the ceremony. She expressed a preference for cremation to burial, but she asked Norman to see to the music himself, should she die before him, and ordered that a record of Myra Hess playing Bach's *Jesu, Joy of Man's Desiring* should be heard.

B's first job after qualifying was to build a reservoir in Midhurst, Sussex; and I began my real medical studies at King's College in the Strand. It was for me a very satisfactory arrangement. I was able to concentrate on my studies during the week without being distracted by the problems of young love, and could enjoy having a 'steady' boyfriend in tow at the weekends, when he met me in his old car and took me for a spin in the country, a walk, and tea in some village teashop. Our affair consisted chiefly of kisses and arguments about religion.

One Saturday he took me to Croydon aerodrome for a 'Five-Shilling Flip'. We climbed into a small biplane and sat behind the pilot in a cockpit that seemed open to the elements. As soon as we took off and began to climb, the speed of our flying set up such a wind that my hair was torn out of its demure bun on the back of my neck, and all my hairpins were scattered. It was a thrilling experience that made us both laugh wildly and cling together in the sky.

With the approach of winter and the difficulties of driving on snow-covered or icy roads he spent some of his Saturdays alone in his digs in Midhurst writing me long letters of argument. Catholicism was to him a clamping of minds into many irrational notions, as well as a number of uncomfortable prohibitions: No divorce. No choice of religion for the children of a mixed marriage, who must all be brought up as Catholics. No birth control, which meant having a large family, and perhaps relative poverty because of it. I was not too worried by these things because I was still in a state of 'faith'.

Pat had joined the territorial Army 'for a free camping holiday', as he described it, before starting to earn his living in earnest. This meant that as soon as war broke out he was immediately drafted into the British Expeditionary Force and despatched across the Channel. In 1932 he left King's just as I began to study there, but he asked a student friend of his to keep an eye on me, which the young man duly did, dancing with me at Freshers' Tea Dances, introducing me to a few people, and then leaving me to my own devices.

I often saw my cousin Brenda at these Tea Dances. She was, like me, a Fresher; but she was studying for an Honours degree in French and German. She was the daughter of my uncle Tom Reid, who had recently retired from the Ceylon Civil Service and was hoping to enter Parliament, which he did as a Labour MP after the War. Brenda was a marvellous dancer, and had found in Pat Steptoe, a medical student, the perfect dancing partner. They were a joy to watch. Pat Steptoe was one of those few men who have brains in their feet as well as in their heads. He was in his last year at King's, and soon left to pursue his clinical studies. He became famous years later when he helped to produce and deliver the first baby fertilised *in vitro*. Brenda remained at King's to sit her exams. During the War she married Jorge Diaz-Nielsen, and left England for Argentina.

I found the atmosphere at King's not too different from school, but being in a mixed-sex establishment was a bit more fun, though we didn't waste much time on flirtations. We had six years hard work ahead of us before we could qualify as doctors; we were fifteen girls to sixty or so men, and we knew that if we failed our exams we would lose our places on the course.

Julian Huxley was Professor of Zoology. I once had the pleasure of going up in the lift with him, which gave me a thrill, not only because he was famous, but because he was the brother of Aldous, whose novel *Brave New World* I'd read with admiration mingled with horror at the materialistic, unfeeling society he prophesied, and which in some respects has come to pass. Julian didn't teach the medical students. Our zoology course was run by an excellent lady lecturer, who taught me so well that at the end of the year, and rather to my surprise, I won the Hare Prize in Zoology. Physics teaching was poor, and the afternoon 'practicals' were nothing but chaos: fooling about and horse-play, students filling large thermometer cases with water to explode them over the heads of other students, and once, accidentally over the head of the professor.

When it came to my First MB Physics exam I was not so lucky. The examiner paused over my practical demonstration and said, 'I can't understand, Miss Reid, why you are so good at Heat, Light and Sound, and so bad at Electricity and Magnetism.' It was only years later that hindsight told me the reason. I had been taught about Heat, Light and Sound by the dowdy physics mistress at Wimbledon High School; Electricity and Magnetism was what she taught during that third term that I'd missed, and so I had no grounding in these subjects. The Professor of Physics at King's, though no doubt very clever, was a poor teacher, quite unable to enlighten me. However, I did pass my exams, and went on to the Second MB course: Anatomy, which meant learning the names of all the different parts of the body and how they fit together, and Physiology, or the study of how the body works.

I was joined at King's by an old convent school friend, Margaret McLaughlin, who'd passed her First MB through a South London Technical College. We became partners in Anatomy, and dissected together. The first thing that hit us when we were ushered into the dissecting room was the smell of formaldehyde in which the bodies were preserved; it was almost overpowering till we got used to it. We were silent and solemn in the presence of so many corpses laid out on deal tables. Most of us had never seen a dead body before, but there was no fainting as we were assigned our tables and told by the Anatomy Demonstrator what instruments we needed, and what textbooks to buy. Margaret and I began on 'Arm'. We used Buchanan's *Anatomy*, an old-fashioned book that used Latin names. So began two years of tedious memorising of the three-dimensional geography of human muscles, bones, joints, nerves and blood vessels, as well as more complex organs, and last and most difficult of all, head and neck. Some students possessed their own 'bones', or skeletons, which helped greatly in learning the proper placing of muscles, etc. A skeleton came in its own black box, and cost three guineas, too expensive for me.

We women students were a serious-minded bunch, very conscious of being a privileged minority, although of course not the true pioneers of two generations earlier. It was our duty to succeed in order to prove to society that 'women could do it'. We kept to ourselves; we didn't waste time on men. Our hair had to be short and neat, our fingernails short and unvarnished, and our white drill coats buttoned up. In the Anatomy Lab we were effectively neutered, though there was one among us, Thelma, whose femininity couldn't be repressed by the prevailing ethos and cover-all uniforms. Even as we sat, earnest fingers probing and cutting, intent eyes reading relevant texts, Thelma was demanding the Demonstrator's attention. He was known to be a woman-hater, so her efforts there were wasted. Instead, she drifted up and down the aisles between the tables, searching for forceps she'd left somewhere, or pencil she had to borrow, and as she drifted she trailed from one pocket of her coat a chiffon scarf that gave a mysterious signal. It was like the lure in a glow-worm's tail. Somehow her sexual pheromones overcame the scent of formaldehyde that her fingers and her scarf must have reeked of; and in her passage through the lab she usually had one or two males in tow.

I didn't have to borrow a dress for John's wedding to Constance, because I was one of her bridesmaids. It was a winter wedding, so we wore velvet dresses with long sleeves. The bride in white carried a bouquet of trailing white, heavily scented stephanotis flowers considered very exotic in those days. After the wedding, John left home to live in his own house in Winchmore Hill, north London, till the outbreak of World War II, when, during the Battle of Britain, the Blitz and fear of Invasion, he had to sleep in the vaults of the Bank of England. He was put in charge of the gold bullion that had been loaded on to vans, and slept beside them. He was prepared, had the order come, to drive the bullion to a secret destination out of London and out of reach of Nazi hands.

Connie was a Nonconformist, but love and mutual tolerance bridged the religious divide between her and John. She was a sunny person, skilled in the domestic arts, with a gently mocking sense of humour that chimed with his. There was nothing of Freud's Penis Envy about her; she was happily female, safe in her own domain of home, which was well run, pleasantly orderly and comfortable, her husband and two children much loved, well fed and well content. Unhappily for them all, she died rather suddenly in middle-life. John married again, this time to an old friend of Wimbledon days, Mary McKechnie. When he retired from the Bank he became Hon Treasurer of the Mother Theresa Committee, managing all donations to her work. A decade later, as he grew older, he restricted himself to looking after the Wills and Bequests made to her charity. When he died she wrote to his wife thanking her 'for lending John to me'.

At 25 Spencer Road family and friends were leaving to pursue independent lives. Joan Foster, who had been studying languages at University College London, left England suddenly and travelled to Spain. She had fallen in love with Spain and all things Spanish on a visit to her sister Cicely, an accomplished pianist and a pupil of Da Falla; and Joan wanted to live there. She achieved her wish when she married a Spanish artist, Ramis, and lived with him in Mallorca, moving to Morocco during the Spanish Civil War.

Francis became in due course a Dominican monk, and Anthony, after falling in love with Daphne and pursuing her unsuccessfully for a time, was apprenticed to the sculptor Eric Gill.

One afternoon in 1934 while sitting in the dining room at tea Daddy placed a hand across his chest. He didn't complain of pain, but he looked pale. He rose from the table and sat in an armchair by the fire, where he vomited a little fluid into his handkerchief. Mummy knew he was ill, and called Dr Humble, who lived in Spencer Road. He was a Quaker, soft-spoken and modest, and entirely bald from birth; he was also a very good doctor. He examined Daddy carefully, and announced his verdict: a heart attack. Daddy must be kept in bed for several weeks without exertion of any kind, without work or worry. Complete prolonged rest was the only therapy available then.

Mummy nursed him entirely herself, but we were allowed to visit him in his bedroom. During this period I noticed a mellowing of his mood and temper. He seemed eager to hear about our doings, and was interested by my tales of the Anatomy Lab at King's. 'Where do the bodies come from?' he asked. As far as I knew they were imported from Eastern Europe, and were the corpses of paupers who had no relatives to claim or bury them. Once, to my surprise, he remarked, 'I think perhaps I may have made mistakes with my children.' And I, embarrassed, stood silent beside his bed.

After three or four weeks he was allowed to get up and walk about the room, and soon after that he came downstairs for lunch. His bedroom was then moved to his study on the ground floor to save him the exertion of climbing stairs. He began to walk about the garden. It was a time of great unemployment in Britain. Some of the unemployed took to the road as tramps, moving from place to place in search of work. If any tramp came to our backdoor asking for work, or a cup of tea, Daddy invited him into the kitchen and saw that he was given a good meal of bacon and eggs and sausages. He sat at the table while the tramp ate, and persuaded him to talk about his life. The days were passing slowly for Daddy.

Within six months he suffered a second heart attack. Mummy called me out of bed in the middle of the night. I suppose she called me because she thought of me as 'medical', though as yet I had not entered a hospital precinct, and the only dead people I'd seen were anonymous corpses in the dissecting room.

'I think your father's dead,' she said.

I put on a dressing-gown and slippers. They were mules with loose heels, and the noise they made on the stairs as I went down seemed irreverently loud in the nocturnal silence of the house.

My father lay quite still. He seemed to me unchanged, but he wasn't breathing. Neither Mummy nor I knew quite what to do next, but while I roused the others she phoned Dr Humble, who arrived very quickly to find the whole family (apart from Mary and John) gathered round Daddy's bed. He held Mummy's hand briefly, and said a few comforting words; and his kind eyes were wet. I think he was rather shocked to see that not one of us, not even my mother, shed a single tear. I believe she was too exhausted by the long-drawn-out anxiety of nursing him, and too stunned finally by his loss to feel anything for several months. The prescribed rituals of mourning, black clothes, the funeral, prayers for the dead in his passage through Purgatory, and implementing her husband's Will, all these things pushed her along.

When, a few days after his death, I saw him laid out in his coffin I was surprised at how beautiful he was. The white skin stretched taut over the bones of his skull made the high prominent nose and noble forehead appear as if carved in marble by some antique masterhand.

His legacy of gifts to me I could not appreciate at the time of his death; their value has survived and increased like safe investments over the years. I owe him a great deal. Paradoxically, since he was a despot on the hearth, he gave me something rare for those times: confidence in my femaleness. He was a man who did not regard women as belonging to an inferior sex. His mother he always spoke of with veneration as having a powerful mind and a strong body; to his wife he gave unswerving loyalty, love and admiration. To me he gave his inquisitive mind. I owe to him my lifelong love affair with books; it was he who insisted that I had a good education, and it was he who first planted in my consciousness the moral imperative of continuing the struggle to attain justice for all.

When Daddy died Mary was in Egypt with her husband. Mummy had written to her after Daddy's first heart attack, hoping Mary would write and make her peace with him. She did write, but only after some delay, so that her letter arrived too late. He never read it, but Mummy did, and it must have been some small consolation to her in the first months of her widowhood. She had always been an independent person, and now she stood alone. She didn't ask for the support of her children, and perhaps we were too selfish, too bent on going our own ways, to give it. Religion was her refuge, and into this she dug deeper than ever. Daddy was sixty when he died; she had thirty-three years of widowhood ahead of her.

## 10

It was for me a bleak year. My father's death cast a long shadow. I had to wear a black suit for three months; and I was finding anatomy and physiology dreary subjects to study. Physiology could have been interesting if we'd had a different teacher, but Professor McDowell, whose textbook I was using, although a very distinguished academic, had no idea how to teach ignorant young men and women. He would begin his lecture clearly enough, and then in the middle of a sentence he'd suddenly think of something else, no doubt related in his own logic, but not in his listeners' minds. With great enthusiasm he would develop his subsidiary thought, and then just as suddenly take off into a third idea, so that by the end of his lecture we were often completely lost.

B and I met one Saturday afternoon and drove to some beauty spot. Perhaps it was Leith Hill, perhaps the Devil's Punch Bowl. In the sweet slanting autumn sunshine, we walked through woods, cracking underfoot the thousand and one yellow and copper-coloured fallen leaves. We held hands when we suddenly came to the edge of a cliff and stood silently looking down on a still green valley. And then we kissed slowly and tenderly.

When we got back to the car he began to talk, faster than he usually did, releasing long-held-back words.

'I still love you, Nora,' he said. 'You know that, but I've been thinking a lot—now that my job in Midhurst is completed, and

I'm looking for another…I don't think we'd make a happy marriage, you know—not with so much difference in religion between us. And anyway I'll probably leave the country for a good few years. Probably go to Palestine in the Public Works Department there.' He changed down to a lower gear as we were descending a very steep slope.

'It'll be terribly hot, and rather dangerous too,' he said, 'with all this hatred of the British Mandate—and all these Jews coming in and trying to settle in the place. I think it'd be best if we didn't meet again really. Nablus is where I'll probably be. I shall miss you, Nora. Terribly.'

We didn't talk much on the way home. He left me at No 25 Spencer Road. I didn't stand at the gate to wave him goodbye, but ran straight into the house and up the stairs to my bedroom.

The story of our affair has a twist in its tail that I came across fifty years and a whole lifetime later when I visited Celia in her retirement flat. She had always taken a great interest in our romance, enjoying a vicarious thrill by observing it. She was fond of B, and often in the old days used to tell me snippets of gossip about him as we travelled by train, she to work in a London office, I to College.

'It was Auntie Elsie who really put a spanner in the works,' she said.

I sat in her neat sitting-room and listened.

'It was she who controlled the money-bags, you know. And she didn't like Catholics much. "If you marry a Catholic," she told B, "I shall cut you out of my Will." '

I said nothing, turning this piece of information over in my mind. It was an interesting revelation, but after all these years no more than an addendum to a page long unturned in the book of memory.

'The irony of it all was,' Celia continued, 'that he did in the end marry a Catholic.'

'Really?' I murmured. How had the marriage worked out, I wondered? I didn't ask if Auntie Elsie had then actually cut him off with the proverbial shilling. I daresay she changed her mind. The War with its exigencies softened so many rigid attitudes that it was possible even hers had bent a little.

'It's all water under the bridge now,' I said.

But that night in 1934 I did cry myself to sleep. I can't honestly say that I was heartbroken, but I was certainly despondent. I'd been rejected, I had only dreary anatomy and muddled physiology to look forward to, our house was quiet, our family diminished, with only Lulu and Joanie and me still at home now that Daphne too had joined the exodus from No 25. And in the background Mummy was silent and sorrowful. Each day seemed dull when it began, and left little satisfaction behind it.

At the Royal College of Art Daphne had been learning to paint in egg tempera for Mural Decoration, as well as designing book illustrations in watercolour, and modelling a plaster bust of Joanie for her diploma. Very soon after getting her ARCA she left home to work in Eric Gill's commune, first in Ditchling, Sussex, later at Piggott's near High Wycombe. She had become interested in G K Chesterton's social theory of 'Distributism', and would have liked to walk backwards to his imaginary Merrie England, to a time of monastic sharing of work and wealth, to the Middle Ages as seen by William Morris, when every craftsman could 'do his own thing' with his own hands in a simple country environment, without becoming enslaved by the soul-killing effects of the repetitive use of industrial factory machinery. These ideals could be realised to some extent by Gill's group of artists, though she soon found that the women had to do most of the digging and hoeing necessary to grow their vegetables, as well as the domestic chores, all without help from labour-saving machines. She had withdrawn from a modern world that was money-loving, gross and unnatural, full of new Science that seemed to her dangerous, from a civilisation prophesied in Aldous Huxley's *Brave New World* that she saw as already threatening her, into an older, simpler, safer life. At Piggott's Eric and his apprentices drew, designed, carved and printed wonderful works of art.

Anthony Foster had joined him, and was carving figures in wood as well as in monumental stone, and Walter Ritchie, who after the War produced marvellous sculptures, including some elegant ironic bas-reliefs on the brick walls of churches and public buildings in Coventry and Bristol, was working with them.

Daphne admired the strength and beauty of Eric Gill's erotic drawings and sculptures, but was completely unaware of his mastery in sex over a number of the women in the commune, including his own daughters, and was shocked by the revelations, fifty years after the artist's death, of the incest that had been practised. She had lived there what she believed to be a truly Christian life, thinking Eric Gill was some kind of latter-day saint. 'I thought a halo shone round his head,' she told me after the scandal broke with the publication of Fiona MacCarthy's biography of Gill.[1] Daphne's friend Petra, Gill's youngest daughter, by this time a matriarch with a happy family of her own, had to leave England to escape the persecution of newshounds.

Daphne was gifted / cursed (according to how you look at it) with an extraordinary innocence / blindness. She had been left to board with nuns from the age of not quite four. Did this experience make her what she later was? She was probably too young to comprehend what the separation from her mother meant, nor how long it would be, but at a deeper, more instinctive level she must have felt the loss. Pat, who at seven was older when first left at boarding school in Ireland, told me of his own experience of such an event.

We were both old, divorced and living alone, when he visited me in a house I'd had rebuilt out of two derelict cottages in Gloucestershire. We had just finished eating the dinner I'd cooked for him, and were sipping coffee with the last of our wine, both of us in a remembering-our-childhood mood, when he suddenly told me. He was the youngest of the five children Mummy left that day at the Dominican Convent in Cabra, Dublin. He knew he would not see her again for three years. It seemed an eternity.

'We stood in the convent parlour,' he said. 'And when Mummy said goodbye I began to cry. Then Mummy cried. And then the Reverend Mother cried. It was the most desolating experience of my whole life.'

From across the table I watched in silence as tears rolled down his seventy-year-old face.

Daphne was markedly short-sighted, which must have cut her off from her surroundings to some extent; and this disability was neither discovered nor corrected for several years. Nor did the spectacles later provided help her much; she kept losing them; she disliked wearing them; she preferred not to look too far.

While working at Piggott's she met and married Eddie Nuttgens, who had set up his studio for making stained glass windows nearby. He was recognised by the *cognoscenti* in his field as an outstanding artist. He was also a delightful, kind, and humorous man, but he was eighteen years her senior, a widower who already had four children. She had to prove to them, as all stepmothers must, that although a stranger she was at heart a friend, while producing in quick succession another eight babies for Eddie, all strong, handsome and healthy. She had little time left for painting. Several of their children became artists, craftsmen and women, draughtsmen and potters. The eldest, Joseph, now runs the studio, producing much sought-after stained glass as well as giving training in the craft to students.

At the end of that sombre year of 1934 there was, however, one glorious weekend I spent virtually snowed up in Gloucestershire with Biddy Kelly and Pat in Rissington, where he was building hangars for an aerodrome. They were to be covered with grass, so that from the air they looked like part of the undulating countryside. Somebody, but certainly not I, was contemplating war with aerial bombardment. Biddy and I stayed in rooms Pat booked for us in a cottage near his digs. It was very cold, but this didn't cool our euphoria, nor deter us from getting around. We helped to dig his car out of a snowdrift, we pushed it, clearing snow from under its wheels, and finally got it moving. And then we drove to Stow-on-the-Wold for lunch in the Unicorn, an ancient pub where, sitting by an enormous log fire in a stone and beamed fireplace, we drank punch. I had no idea then how intoxicating punch could be, and much to the amusement of the others, I got very drunk. Pat was a bit in love with Biddy then; in fact he was in and out of love with her throughout his life, but she was always rather cool towards him. I was glad of this, because I believed Biddy had a ruthless streak in her character that might make him suffer if they married. She was an ardent Irish Republican, quite willing, at least in theory, to commit assassination or other violence for the Cause. Her father, whom she adored, was rich with inherited wealth. He was an American citizen who had actually fought against Britain during the Troubles, had been taken prisoner and held briefly in Reading Gaol. Years later his son-in-law told me that 'Pop' had never fired a shot, but in his own opinion, and in Biddy's, he was covered in glory for his patriotic deeds. His wife, who was English, refused to live with him in Ireland, where he had made his home, but Biddy decided to join him, and being at that time horse-mad and keen to ride she found work in a riding stables outside Dublin.

'On Stow-in-the-Wold the wind blows cold' is what they say there, but we spent that wonderful weekend cocooned in warmth and laughter inside a frozen world.

And there were other glowing evenings. Sometimes on a Friday, which was Beethoven Night at the Proms, I paid two shillings to promenade. I was allowed to stay late in town for the concert. There were also at King's a few evening lectures open to the public that I attended. I remember well a lecture given by Isaiah Berlin on D H Lawrence, whose *Sons and Lovers* I was devouring, trembling at some of his (at that time) 'daring', and certainly highly charged, emotional scenes. On another occasion I heard T S Eliot talk to a large audience. I have no recollection of what he said. He was an insignificant looking man compared with the tall, white-haired and white-bearded George Bernard Shaw, who attended the same lecture, and whom I followed out of the hall along the Strand, feeling a thrill at being at least near, even if not conversing with the great. I then travelled home alone on my season ticket. I was never molested in the street, but occasionally on the train some commuter hiding behind his newspaper as he sat opposite me in a crowded carriage would push a polished shoe up under my skirt.

Somehow I scrambled through the syllabus for Second MB, and managed to pass the exam. In May 1935 three of us women students, Margaret McLaughlin, Joan Webber and I passed into King's College Hospital, seven more followed six months later, which with two girls from Oxbridge made twelve women in all to be admitted that year. Thelma was not one of them. She must have taken her chiffon scarf elsewhere.

University life had been a pleasant extension of school days; the hospital was a different world. I had frequently heard life described as a Vale of Tears, but hearing facts is a very different thing from seeing and touching them yourself. Hospital existence was for many patients a Valley of Death as well, and I was brought suddenly face to face with people, mostly poor and ignorant, struggling with suffering and death.

I was the only girl on my Surgical Firm of a dozen students.

We were called Dressers, I suppose because in the past the main function of surgical assistants, chiefly in the army, was to dress wounds. Our function was to interview the patients assigned to us on the wards, and to record our findings of their pathological symptoms and signs. The Registrar who instructed us in procedures such as how to test urine and how to take blood pressures and blood samples, answered our questions and generally helped and taught us. When the Chief did his Ward Round we had to read out to him and to all the students surrounding the bed the notes we'd made. The Chief, after examining the patient to check our findings, discussed the case, the patient usually sitting up and listening meanwhile. Some Chiefs were more tactful than others. Mine was a kindly Welshman, Edward Edwards, affectionately known as Teddy.

Annie Zunz Ward was a great barn of a place, with high ceilings and big windows along each side. Below them, and ranged against the lower, green-painted portion of the walls were twenty-six 'female beds'. In No 14 my first patient was awaiting me. She was a woman of about thirty who looked like a frightened rabbit. She was thin, her movements were quick and agitated, and her eyes started out of her head. I found on counting her pulse that it was very rapid, and her blood pressure was high. I also noticed a swelling at the front of her neck. She was suffering from over-activity of the thyroid gland, or thyrotoxicosis, which was driving her body metabolism at such speed that her heart would give way under the strain unless a large piece of the gland was removed. I had to try to explain to her what was going on, to tell her that operation would be necessary, and to hold her hand and listen to her fears. And in those days fears of what might happen were a great deal more realistic than under the relatively safe conditions of surgery today. There were very few drugs available to reduce thyroid activity and blood pressure before surgery; it was known to be an operation that was especially risky.

The temperature in the operating theatre was always high, the atmosphere of tension even higher. In order to save the patient undue stress everything had to be done quickly. In order to save possible infection asepsis had to be as perfect as possible, because in those days before antibiotics sepsis following surgery was a major hazard. So you had to wear clean but very heavy rubber galoshes over your shoes, and scrub your hands and forearms under running water (lever taps had to be turned off with the elbows) before donning, with the help of a nurse, a sterilised cap, garment and mask, and lastly rubber gloves, often too large for me, always fiddly and difficult to put on over damp hands. It was a very strange world, and I was afraid of doing something wrong in it, which of course I did by seizing hold of an instrument trolley by its legs, under its sterilised covering, so contaminating my gloves. The surgeon's eagle eye was on me, and he immediately shouted, 'More sterile gloves for Miss Reid please, Sister!' I wished the floor would swallow me up, so great was my shame.

All these small anxieties and humiliations were as nothing compared with what awaited me next morning in Annie Zunz Ward. Bed No 14 had been remade with clean sheets and pillow case, its blankets turned neatly down; but it was empty. During the night my patient had died of post-operative haemorrhage. 'It does happen,' said the Ward Sister, 'especially with thyrotoxicosis, when the blood pressure begins to rise as they come out of the anaesthetic.'

My second patient was a woman in her thirties who was still nursing a small baby. She had a large hard lump in one breast. Her husband was often at her bedside, comforting and encouraging her. No glands in the armpit, nor in the neck on that side could as yet be felt. The young couple talked it all over with each other, and with me. Naturally they were both horrified and frightened by the prospect of having the breast removed, but they eventually agreed to a mastectomy.

In the operating theatre Teddy Edwards excised the breast quickly, closing the cut ends of all bleeding vessels with Spencer Wells forceps as he worked; and then he turned aside to the table on which the theatre sister had placed the solitary breast, so that I could observe what he did. He cut through the tumour. I remember well the gritty sound, and how he threw the scalpel on the floor in a rage.

'It cuts like an unripe pear,' he said. 'These lactating carcinomas are always the most malignant.'

He completed his work in silence, but as he was stitching up the skin he looked across the operating table at Sister and nodded: 'We've given her a year or two.' And Sister smiled wanly, wrinkling a face that was not old but already so criss-crossed with lines that she was known in the Medical School as Clapham Junction.

It was my job to dress my patient's wound in the ward in the days that followed. It healed perfectly after a little drain was removed. She recovered well. Her husband brought in her baby son to visit her. They were filled with hope and happiness. They had not seen the unripe pear cut through as I had. Before leaving the hospital they gave me a Fuller's iced cake, for them an expensive expression of gratitude, for me knowing what I did, a gift with a feeling of guilt attached to it.

In the Outpatient department I saw all sorts of lumps. I learned to diagnose a harmless but disfiguring sebaceous cyst that was easy to shell out, enlarged glands in the neck that might denote tuberculosis, a secondary spread of cancer, or a simple sore throat, and swellings in the abdomen that might be malignant. The patients were all poor, their clothes shabby, their teeth bad, and their talk astonishingly cheerful.

The journey to and from King's College Hospital was a good deal longer than to King's College in the Strand. I had to leave the train at Vauxhall station, a grim and grimy place, and take a tram across Vauxhall bridge. Crossing the Thames was pleasant on a fine day when you could ride on top in the open air, but it was soon apparent that the south was the poorer side of the river as the tram clanked through run-down Walworth with its battered looking shops, some boarded up, with windows above uncurtained and in need of paint, towards Camberwell Green, still wearing the shreds of old Victorian gentility. Here I got out and walked up Denmark Hill till I reached two enormous buildings, the Maudsley Hospital for Mental Disorders on the left, and on the right King's College Hospital. Further up towards Dulwich, the Salvation Army had their training college. Sometimes as I walked uphill down came their students marching to the sound of brass, the girls with chins held high under stiff straw bonnets, heavy navy skirts swinging with the energy of their movements, blue banners waving their message in bright red letters: BLOOD AND FIRE. They marched with a joyful step that I was beginning to envy.

During that first month on the surgical firm I felt so tired that all I wanted to do was sleep. I was spending three hours every day in travelling. For my first three weeks as a clinical student I wept myself to sleep each night. How much longer could I do it, I wondered? I began to think I was simply not cut out for this physically and emotionally exhausting job. What else could I do then? Perhaps become a teacher of Biology...? However, the habit of rising, dressing and travelling by train kept me going, and I struggled on. Gradually I became accustomed to this new way of living, but I learned very little surgical pathology; I believe I was too exhausted for my brain to absorb new facts.

I did learn some other important lessons. The Women's Common Room was comfortably furnished, but it was not a comfortable place to be in. The atmosphere was not relaxing. I found it stiff and tense; there were no amusing conversations going on, nor even clinical discussions to be heard. The senior women students were far from friendly; I certainly found no guide,

222

philosopher and friend among them to help a newcomer find her way. I have often wondered why this was so. Perhaps it was my fault. But later when I met other women students from the Royal Free, at that time an all-women's medical school, and found them all relaxed, friendly, confident, and eminently intelligent as well, I have wondered whether the very fact of being in a minority made the King's women too competitive, too wary and afraid to put a foot wrong, and rather disapproving of anything ever so slightly deviating from their accepted norm. It taught me to stand alone, a necessary lesson, for sooner or later there comes a time in every doctor's life when a decision has to be made, an action taken without help from anyone else.

I also gradually learned to distance myself from patients without losing sympathy with them, to listen and hear with kindness but not feel too much. It is an art essential to the doctor if he is to remain sane and to maintain good judgment. Sometimes to solve a medical dilemma, the wisdom of Solomon is called for. Had King Solomon been a relative or intimate friend of the two women quarrelling over the baby in that famous case, or felt more emotionally involved in it, he might not have been so wise.

Fortunately there was some relief at mealtimes in the refectory, when I ate with Margaret and Joan Webber, exchanging gossip and jokes with them. They were both doing their first six months on medical firms, perhaps a gentler introduction than surgery to that *Ars Longa* that needs the whole of one's *Vita Brevis* to acquire.

Many of the male students were very earnest young men we called 'brown-baggers'. They dressed in sober suits and wore unnoticeable ties; they kept their heads down and their eyes lowered; they walked to and from the hospital carrying their small brown cardboard suitcases that carried their books and stethoscopes; they worked and studied continuously and with fear because they simply could not afford to fail exams. Many of them were Jewish, a few Indian, and one or two were Caribbean.

There was an English student, John Todd, who was friendly. His father was a GP in the East End of London. How he survived in those days before the NHS, when doctors had no salary and the poor, if unemployed, and especially the women, had virtually no money to pay for his services, is difficult to imagine. John Todd was not a brown-bagger. He was a scruffy, unkempt youth, who had been hauled over the coals by his Chief and told to clean himself up. But he was intelligent and filled with curiosity, inquisitive enough indeed to lean over me as I pored over a book in the library to see what I was reading, and he was very much surprised. I had seen on the shelves a copy of Marx's *Das Kapital*, which I'd taken down to look at. I was in no way a political animal, but I wanted to have some idea what this book, so much discussed, was all about. It is not exactly an easy read. Somewhere within its dense verbiage can no doubt be found the famous slogans: 'Religion is the opiate of the people', and 'Workers of the world unite: You have only your chains to lose'. I never found them there; I never managed to read further than page three. But John Todd was amused that I was trying to read it. He was himself a Marxist, disapproving of my bourgeois background, but having spent a Saturday afternoon with me at Hampton Court exploring the palace and enjoying getting lost in the Maze, found me quite companionable.

During our King's-College-in-the-Strand days he had been a follower of Thelma's chiffon scarf, but now he was the proud possessor of a mistress, which was in those days still *avant-garde*. It was to her digs that I was invited to a party. I was aware of being a stranger in their midst, and although I knew I was despised for being an anti-Communist Catholic living in a leafy suburb, and a virgin, too, I was content to be an observer at the feast. It was after the guests had drunk several pints of beer, which I had not because I disliked beer, that they pulled the landlady's potted aspidistra to the middle of the floor. It was soon after Orwell's

*Keep The Aspidistra Flying* had been published. They began with mock homage to dance round this symbol of bourgeois taste, bowing and chanting, and even crossing themselves. I felt embarrassed then. They were all laughing ecstatically except me, because of course I was included in their mockery of the unfortunate plant, although neither I nor anybody I knew kept potted aspidistras in their windows.

In spite of these demonstrations I knew I was not really disliked, and for my part, in spite of his (at least in medical-school circles) odd-ball appearance, I liked John Todd for his warm heart, his undoubted intelligence and the fact that he did think, and even care about our common human lot.

On one occasion while I was queuing for a cup of tea at the refectory counter a tall, impeccably groomed Sinhalese student spoke to me. 'It is an honour to meet Tom Reid's niece,' he said. I looked up at him in amazement. How did he know Uncle Tom, and how that I was his niece? His name was Jayawardene, a distinguished family in Ceylon, and his father knew my uncle, who until recently had been busy drafting and introducing a Constitution for an independent Ceylon, later to be renamed Sri Lanka. For this work he was awarded the Order of St Michael and St George. Tom had been Mayor of Colombo. He had become convinced fairly early in his career in the Ceylon Civil Service that British rule and British missionaries were doing more harm than good in the country. He suspected that the many forms of Buddhism practised there might be better religions for its inhabitants than Christianity. He even dared to think that the many improvements the British had made in health, in irrigation and food production and the control of famines, might actually be doing harm. Had we not interfered with nature's birth control? We had, by reducing infant death rate and lengthening life expectancy, actually added to the great problem of the population explosion that was hitting the subcontinent.

225

It was high time, he believed, to go home and let Indians get on with ruling themselves. Perhaps, too, he'd had enough of the executions he had to witness before breakfast, which put him off his food. All this had made him resign before completing his full term of office; but to this day the tourist can see in Colombo a long tree-lined Reid Avenue dedicated to his memory.[2]

I must invite Jayawardene to that party I'm going to give at the flat, I thought.

On some afternoons while walking the length of Annie Zunz Ward to visit my patients I would be called to the phone. Richard Powers was ringing me from the City, on the other side of the river, to invite me to spend the evening with him in a very different world. He had usually had a few drinks before we met. He took me to dine at Rules off the Strand, and spun for me with his inimitable wit a vision of the late Victorian age when Oscar Wilde, reclining on the red plush benches under the *Spy* cartoons, dined here with his treacherous Bosie, and Edward Prince of Wales entertained Lily Langtry in a private room reserved for them upstairs.

Once or twice Richard took me to *Quo Vadis*, a restaurant with a pair of green bay trees growing in tubs at its entrance, and introduced me to gourmet food, including their special high-calorie but absolutely delicious dessert *Zabaglione.* It was made at your table by the chef who dribbled Marsala wine into it as his assistant beat up eggs and sugar over a spirit-flame, and as the sweet began to thicken he poured it into glasses for you to eat while it was still warm.

Best of all were our skirmishes in the East End, to the famous pub the Prospect of Whitby, with its spittoons laid on a floor of sawdust, its rickety wooden balcony overlooking the Thames, where all manner of craft, including the beautiful red-sailed and slow-moving Thames barges, stately dames of the coal trade, could be seen manoeuvring their way into the Pool of London. Then there was Charlie Brown's pub, the Blue Posts in Limehouse, near the West India Dock, where delicious chills of fear ran up and down my spine when Richard told me to stick close to him because it was rumoured to be a place used by White Slave Traffickers ready to kidnap unwary girls and transport them to South America. On the ground floor there was a space where prostitutes danced with sailors, many Americans among them. Richard pointed out to me a spot behind the bar where not many months ago a Chinese barman had been murdered as he leaned against a door. An unseen assassin with a long knife had struck him in the back through a wooden panel.

Several times we attended music-hall performances at the Queen's in Poplar, where a long bar at right angles to the stage could be visited by members of the audience throughout the show. Richard left his seat to get drinks, beer for himself, for me the East End barmaid's favourite Port and Lemon. Strangers were friendly, the whole world was full of kindness, even pianos would be 'handled like children'. This was promised by a removals firm advertising on the asbestos Safety Curtain during the interval. The audience was determined to enjoy itself, and make its neighbour do the same. Not exactly days of wine and roses, but certainly these were evenings of laughter and good cheer.

Richard's father had been a doctor, a venereologist, but had died young. Richard would have loved to go to Oxford, and spoke of its undergraduates with envy as *la jeunesse dorée*, but I guessed his widowed mother couldn't afford the cost. So he lived with her in Surbiton, and, travelling daily to the City, went straight from school at Downside into the Bank of England as a clerk, and hated it. He was a writer *manqué*. He did eventually become the editor of the Bank of England's own magazine, *The Old Lady*, for which he wrote essays and many amusing epitaphs such as one 'For a Cynic':

Here I lie quite neglected
This is what I had expected

He was reading Proust, and used to talk about his characters
as if they were his friends, so that I became familiar with them
long before I ever read *Remembrance of Things Past*. When he spoke
of Baron Charlus he snorted and chuckled at his obscenities, but
he didn't describe them to me. Nor did he lend me the book,
which I read only several decades later. That was a lucky thing
for me, for to appreciate the master naturalist of the human psyche
you need experience of life, some understanding of what we are,
and time to read him slowly, none of which I possessed when
young.

Instead he lent me Dostoevsky's *Crime and Punishment* to read,
so leading me on to Tolstoy, Turgenev, and Chekov, as well as
introducing me to his favourite poet, A E Housman. He knew
the whole of *A Shropshire Lad* by heart, and spoke lovingly of the
Shropshire countryside where he had once spent a holiday walking
from village to village. 'Clun...' he used to say, and laughed with
delight as he droned:

' "Clunton and Clunbury,
Clungerford and Clun,
Are the quietest places
Under the sun." '

We also enjoyed the cult novels of the day, reading together
Rosamund Lehmann's *Dusty Answer*. Reviewing it Alfred Noyes,
the poet, described it as the sort of novel Keats would have written
had he been a novelist. It was lush and lyrical and full of youthful
yearnings, and we wallowed in its purple-stained prose. Richard
was writing a novel of his own about a public school, and had
sent a section of it to Compton Mackenzie, a successful novelist

of the day, who had replied with a kind letter urging him to complete the book. Richard used to talk about it a lot when on Sundays during the summer we went on long walks in the country outside London, stopping at pubs for sandwiches, and he for several beers. I believed in his talent, and always encouraged him, but he never did finish that novel.

He was not a handsome man, nor an athlete, but he was a wonderful companion, full of ideas and very funny. He had mocking brown eyes and a small moustache. He looked, I thought, as if he might be French. He talked a great deal, but never about politics, nor of the Civil War that was convulsing Spain. We were never in love though we often kissed, and sometimes thought we might be, but he was a marvellous friend. The rift between us began to open up when I told him he drank too much, and he told me I was a school-marm. The revelation of this sort of truth is often a shock to the system. We see ourselves as blurred images in dusty windows till someone wipes the glass; but others see us face to face. Very soon he was telling me about a lovely girl he'd met with a name that sounded, he said, like glass: Alison. And I was thinking of the large melancholy eyes of John, a tall gangling student from Cambridge I'd bumped into on the Medical School stairs.

Dear Richard, what happened to him during and after the War? I owe him a great debt. He taught me much about European culture and literature, which acted as a counterbalance to the rational rigour and scepticism of medical thinking I was exposed to on the other side of the Thames, and the realism that was a reminder of what I'd learned as a child in India. The life of man was still almost as poor in Peckham and thereabouts, as nasty brutish and short as Hobbes had found it.

## References – Chapter Ten

1 MacCarthy, Fiona, *Eric Gill*, Faber and Faber,1990.

2 Reid Avenue, a tree-lined street dedicated to Tom Reid's memory, can still be seen in Colombo.

## 11

Joanie arrived at King's College soon after I left. She had decided
to take a short two-year course in journalism, but was somewhat
distracted from her studies not only by active participation in
the university amateur dramatic society productions but by falling
in love with an engineering student, Bill Hyne. He was a Canadian
with hair of a golden copper colour, and was tall and graceful,
and as beautiful as any film star. He visited us in East Molesey
at weekends to take Joanie swimming or punting on the Thames.
They spent most of their leisure time together. When they walked
out in the street they made such a handsome couple that people
turned to stare at them; they danced together at King's Faculty
dances, and went to the pictures to see Fred Astaire and Ginger
Rogers in *Top Hat* instead of poring over textbooks in the library;
they were, it seemed, inseparable. Unfortunately, Bill was bitterly
anti-Catholic, and told Joanie frankly he could never marry her.
When at the end of her course they parted, poor Joanie was in
a state of mourning for the loss of love.

She began to learn shorthand and typing at a secretarial school
in town, and was also writing short pieces for the gossip columns
of a small provincial paper, which demanded a certain amount
of travelling. An old school friend of ours, Biddy Kelly's sister
Nancy, was at the same time learning to cook at a *Cordon Bleu*
college in London's West End. We met one day for tea at a Lyons

Corner House, and, after talking it over, came to the conclusion that by sharing a flat we could all save travelling time. Joanie and I now had an income from the Indian Civil Service Family Pensions Fund of £135 a year each (£5,000 today) as long as we remained single, and Nancy had an allowance from her father. We found a first-floor flat in a stone-built Victorian house at 116 Belgrave Road, within easy walking distance of Vauxhall Bridge, at a rent of £96 a year. It had a splendid large living room with parquet floor, and two large windows opening on to stone-balustraded balconies, a smaller bedroom behind, and an even smaller kitchen-cum-washplace overlooking a grubby garden. The bath, with penny-in-the-slot gas geyser to provide hot water, was on the landing below. It cost 2d to enjoy a good bath.

Mummy did not oppose the idea. She helped us to furnish the flat, and even bought a beautiful grand piano on Hire-Purchase (known as the Never-Never) for the living room. It happened that our scheme fitted in with her own plans.

Daddy had during his last months asked Mummy to take special care of Lulu. Although as yet only thirty-two she had lost her youthful prettiness. She had become sharp-featured, narrow minded and sharp-tongued. Men were to her by and large an unpleasant breed, though priests were exempt from disapproval. No doubt Daddy realised that he had used up her youth, and that she was unlikely to marry. She now had no job and fewer personalities to compete with at home. Her own character seemed to expand, but Mummy found this new Lulu quarrelsome and difficult to live with. No doubt Lulu was chafing at what she regarded as restrictions on her liberty, and wanted independence and a place of her own. The Spencer Road house was in any case too big for the two of them. So after much thought, and advice from her elder son John, Mummy made up her mind to sell it and build a small modern house for Lulu in East Molesey, and later a cottage in the country for herself.

Lulu was able to add to her ICS pension by working as a secretary for an insurance firm. She settled into a frugal but busy life in her new home. She adorned her large garden with irises, and rockeries for alpine plants, she painted in water colours, and sold some of her flower paintings at local exhibitions, and she kept a dog, quarrelling from time to time with neighbours and other persons who took her fancy as sparring partners.

Mummy built her new home in Paddock Wood in Kent. Every summer hordes of penniless East Enders used to camp out in the hop fields to help with the hop-picking, so earning a spot of cash and giving themselves and their children a bit of fresh country air. Christian missions of various denominations also came here, including Franciscan monks to preach to the Catholics among the campers. My mother made it her job to house and feed the Franciscans. She also prepared their meals, so she must have taught herself to cook. Perhaps, having taken a vow of poverty, the good monks didn't mind too much if their diet was of the simplest kind. She herself joined the Franciscan Order as a lay sister, or Tertiary, and made a name for herself in her new role in church circles. Many years later the Pope awarded her a medal for her work.

We became estranged when, after marriage, I lost faith in religion and left the Church, but I owe her debts of gratitude I can never repay. Among the genetic threads I have inherited from her, not least among them her longevity, was an intuitive common sense that often made her laugh; but the greatest of all her gifts to me was her love of music.

'Rarely, rarely comest thou, Spirit of Delight' are Shelley's words quoted by Elgar as a preface to his Second Symphony when, after a long creative drought, he began to compose again. My mother taught me to listen to music, to wait for the coming of that spirit. And sometimes when at night I switch on recorded music, and into the parched silence of my room fall like sweet rain the first clear notes of some musical poem, such as the second movement of Brahms's Violin Concerto, it brushes over me; the oboe's notes in my imagination are transfigured into a vision: a bud that swells with sound, and as the violin picks up and elaborates the theme it blossoms with a hundred petals unfolding at last into the perfect rose, the fulfilment of all human desires. For these glimpses of paradise I thank my mother.

At King's College Hospital a grand new Diabetic Unit was opened by the Duchess of York. She passed through a corridor of white-coated students bestowing on us all that famous smile, kind and thoughtful, that was to endear her to a whole nation during her very long lifetime. Her face, innocent of make-up, shone with youth and happiness. She could not have known then that in only a few more months King George V would die, would be replaced by his eldest son Edward Prince of Wales, who very soon would abdicate, pushing her husband, the Duke of York, unwillingly, on to the throne, and so make her Queen of England.

When as a child standing on the flat roof of an Indian house in Patna I had caught a glimpse of Prince Edward, smiling and dapper in an open carriage, he had been in love with Freda Dudley Ward. After a long lasting affair he dropped her suddenly and rather brutally. One day she phoned him as usual on his personal line to Fort Belvedere, his private home, and was told by the weeping telephonist her orders from the Prince were not to put her through. He lacked the courage to tell Freda himself that an American lady, Thelma Furness, had taken her place in his affections. By 1936, when he became King, she too had been replaced by another American, Wallis Simpson, with whom he seemed, according to his friends and observers, absolutely besotted. He wanted to marry her, and she wanted to be his queen.

The royal family and the government of the day strongly opposed the marriage. Mrs Simpson had been already twice married and divorced, and was a commoner, and certainly not good breeding material for a future heir to the throne. Photographs of them both yachting and sunbathing in the Mediterranean had appeared in American and continental newspapers, but news of the affair did not break in England till towards the end of that year, when everybody began to talk about it. It was a wonderful, extraordinary romance; and all the world loves a lover.

Mrs Simpson was a bit of a mystery. She was no beauty, though always 'terribly smart', and no longer very young, yet here was a king willing to throw away his crown and country to marry her. What was the secret of her power over him? It was commonly believed that she had introduced him to certain arts of the bedchamber he had been ignorant of till he met her. Not only the romance of these two who, apart from their unique position in society, were ordinary and not very intelligent people, but the whole question of the monarchy and its future were discussed. Many of us were critical of Establishment diehards who seemed to be obstructing a happy ending to a real love story; most people seemed sympathetic towards the lovers. It was only later that their paltry and rather pusillanimous natures were shown up by events. There came a time when many were thankful that it was Elizabeth, formerly Duchess of York, and not Wallis Simpson who walked past rows of houses blasted and crumbling, and into streets burned and blackened by incendiary bombs, who shook hands and smiled with Londoners through the Blitz.

'The heart has its reasons which reason knows nothing of' is a quotation from Pascal from which Wallis Simpson borrowed the title of her autobiography.[1] She was the reason why Edward gave up a kingdom; and on reading her own story you can't help wondering if this shallow, frivolous and rather greedy woman with her inordinate lust for jewellery was really worth the sacrifice.[2]

Sometimes when Out Patients was finished, and I'd drunk a cup of tea and swallowed a few carbohydrate calories to renew my energies for the journey home, I could hear coming from the empty Students' Hall the sound of Jazz. I used to open the door and stand there in the diminishing light of a late winter afternoon and listen to the melancholy syncopation of the Blues. Ethiraj was playing the piano. He was a tall student who walked with a slouch. His father was Indian, and his mother, he told me, was English, and had 'beautiful red hair'. He was in today's *argot* 'laid back'. Unlike the rest of us, he was less focused on study and the passing of exams; what he cared about was Jazz. He was a very gifted pianist. He came into his own at Christmas time when students wrote, produced, and acted in a pantomime, which all the Consultants and their wives attended, chiefly to see themselves and each other lampooned and laughed at. Ethiraj provided the music with the help of a drummer, and even managed to find a saxophonist.

It was Aladdin that year. 'We like to find our Teddy Bare,' we sang lustily, hoping to make Teddy Edwards blush during the performance. Somehow, in the way of pantomimes, a teddy had lost his surgeon's gown. Somehow, too, a horse, its four legs provided by two men, had also found its way into the plot. I was the Fairy of the Lamp. It was my job not only to train a chorus of women students, all cheerful and willing if not exactly Ziegfield Folly girls, to kick their legs up in unison, but to teach the horse to dance a few simple steps. John Warwick was the hindquarters, and my John the head, neck and forelegs. Unfortunately, he had absolutely no sense of rhythm, and was unable to perform the simplest step in time to music, however hard we tried and however many times we rehearsed it. As it turned out, the effect was quite amusing, and the audience laughed as I led the horse on stage to see its hind legs do a neat quickstep while its forelegs staggered drunkenly about. It was while we waited in the wings on the evening of the dress rehearsal, the horse sitting quietly folded on its two pairs of knees, I in a ballerina's white tutu, with my long hair streaming down my back, ready to lead the animal on stage, that John spoke through the breathing-grid of its nose. 'I love you, Nora,' was what that horse said. I had no time to respond to this unexpected declaration as I heard my cue, and towing the unwilling animal by a rope I pranced towards the footlights.

John, who was a keen gardener, endeared himself to me by making window boxes, and filling them with earth and wallflower plants that later bloomed sweetly on the balconies of the Belgrave Road flat. He shared a terraced house with another student, Selwyn Taylor, who was to become a surgeon, and eventually to perform a very difficult operation to separate Siamese twins successfully. Their house was on Herne Hill, above and distanced from the hospital by small park. Here John and I took to eating our lunch during the summer. His, I remember, consisted of a pint of milk every day.

He was over six foot tall, and thin too. My mother and he did not take to each other when they met. He thought her narrow-minded, and perhaps rather stupid. She thought him *gauche* in manners, and delicate in health. In fact he was as strong as the proverbial horse. He could, and actually had recently walked forty miles in a day from Snowdon to Holy Island beyond Anglesey, getting a lift in a ferry across the Menai Straits. He was a clever, and also physically active young man, full of interesting ideas. He was much more alive to what was happening in the world than I, he was emotionally involved in the Spanish Civil War, and spoke with admiration of the International Brigade and its idealistic fighting volunteers. He was bitterly anti-Franco, whereas

I had been influenced by hearing from Margaret McLaughlin's sister, Katharine, accounts of the torture and killing of nuns by pro-Spanish-Government Communist and Anarchist supporters. She had recently hurried home from Spain, where she had been a novice in a convent.

John felt everything passionately, love and hate, contempt or admiration, and any criticism of himself; he held opinions that often seemed to me extreme; he was certainly not one of Uncle Pat's modtheration men. Needless to say he was an ardent lover, and it was not long before we were making love 'the whole way', as it was put in those days. Fornication wasn't easy, as we were living apart, but love, as is well known, will find a way. It was a joy snatched at when possible, but fraught with anxiety. I refused to use contraceptives, which I saw as the greater sin, and in order to avoid pregnancy was using the so-called Safe Period, so that I awaited every menstruation dreading its possible delay. Over and above the fear of pregnancy was the knowledge that I was in mortal sin, and in danger of losing my immortal soul. To him this concept was incomprehensible and absurd. Although his father's ancestors had been Quakers, John was not a Christian. He rejected the Christian view of sex, that it was a dangerous, unruly passion only to be permitted expression in marriage, and for procreation. He was a great admirer of the novels and views of D H Lawrence, and, like him, thought of sex as natural and good, and much to be desired and practised, perhaps even a mystical experience through which a sense of beauty beyond the material world could be attained.

In the summer he bought an old car for £5. It was a two-seater Standard with a white body and a 'dicky' to seat two at the back. He was keen to take me to Anglesey, where his mother had a holiday cottage. Here all his brothers and sisters (he was one of eight) converged for the summer holidays. In spite of needing a refill of oil every hundred miles, and leaving a thin black trail in the road behind us, the little car completed the journey bravely. We were approaching the village of Four Mile Bridge, a hamlet built on either side of an old bridge (probably Roman) between Anglesey and Holy Island, when we saw ahead of us a young man walking on the grass verge. John leaned over me as we passed him and shouted, 'Get out of the way, you bloody oaf!'

'Who was that?' I asked in surprise.

'My brother Charles,' he said.

I was shocked. The man had not been in our way at all. I had never before heard of his brother Charles, nor did I guess the strength of his hatred and jealousy of this younger sibling. Perhaps his words should have rung a warning bell in my head. But love is deaf as well as blind, and I was in love.

I had very little time to think about it because we immediately pulled up outside the cottage, and I was thrust into a crowd of new strong personalities, all dressed in old clothes such as Robinson Crusoe might have worn before he took to goat-skins, all talking and laughing volubly, except John's father, the Professor, who was quiet and remote. He used to take himself off for long walks along the seashore, while the others went sailing in a fleet of seaworthy but far from spick-and-span boats. Sometimes, when time and tides were right for the expedition, they went out to sea by way of the winding channel between the two islands; more often they sailed in what they called the 'lake'. This was actually a stretch of sea water deposited by the incoming tide as it rushed through the bridge at Four Mile Bridge and the railway bridge a couple of miles away to the north-east.

Meanwhile John's mother busied herself over primus stoves in a back-kitchen, cooking gargantuan stews and stacks of potatoes for the sailors' return. Dr Lucy was a large lady with untidy hair, big hands, and a wonderful laugh. When she gave way to laughter she literally collapsed under it. She was one of the

Royal Free Hospital pioneers, and had been taught medicine by Elizabeth Garrett Anderson herself, the first English woman doctor.

At the time of my first visit to her cottage there was no electricity, no drainage, but an Elsan lavatory at the bottom of the garden, and no hot water. Baths were taken by swimming in the sea. This place was for John his happy-childhood paradise, inhabited then by a great variety of birds whose habits he knew, where they nested, the number and colour of their eggs, the sound of their calls. We went sailing and walking in search of them: the Arctic terns swooping like white swallows over the sea and their nests on a tiny island at the edge of the 'lake', the stonechat sitting on top of a gorse-bush and uttering a call like the chip of one stone hitting another, and the raven spreading his six-foot black wingspan above a lonely nest high up on a cliff at Rhoscolyn. There, where we trod on wild gardens of pink thrift and pale yellow Burnet roses, it was a kind of Eden. John felt real grief when he had to return to London and the hospital.

There were two Chiefs in Midwifery and Gynaecology, and they couldn't have been more different. Mr Palmer had been a rugby player in his youth. He liked the rugger-playing boys, but he didn't like women. Perhaps he'd seen too much of the lower end of them. I kept out of his way as much as possible, and never suffered from his bullying, but Margot Halliday, who was an even smaller person than I was, attracted his attention as a suitable object to tease during his Out-Patient Clinics. He would ask her to examine a patient's abdomen and tell us what she'd found.

'Now what is your opinion, Miss Halibut?' he would enquire, smiling sardonically around at the rugger-playing boys, who all but encircled him.

'Halliday, Sir.'

'No but, only day, today, Miss Halibut?' he grinned, and the boys close around him grinned too. They were like a rugger-scrum facing her, and she the oval ball they were all trying to catch hold of. But Margot, whose father, small in stature like herself, was a Major-General, did not flinch. Not for nothing was she a soldier's daughter. She stood her ground.

'Halliday, if you please, Sir.'

This exchange was repeated week after week till even Mr Palmer got tired of it.

Mr Gilliatt was quite another kettle of fish, though such a vulgar metaphor was hardly appropriate for him. He was an *acoucheur* to royalty, had an extensive Harley Street practice, a lofty head of black hair, and impeccable manners. He treated the old ducks of Camberwell as if they were duchesses, and of course they loved it, and worshipped him.

'There's something wrong with me love-box, doctor,' said one of them, as he approached the examination couch. Magnificent even in a uniform white coat he bent his courtly head to reassure her before probing her with white-gloved hand.

'Letter-box I think,' he said, drawing out a somewhat dishevelled condom to show the assembled students. There would have been rude guffaws in Mr Palmer's Outpatients; in Mr Gilliatt's it was only permissible to suppress a smile.

'What, do you suppose, is the commonest foreign body found in the vagina?' he asked.

There was a short silence. Then a fresh-faced young man called Garrett, who looked like a schoolboy replied:

'The penis, Sir.'

This time it was impossible not to laugh. The poor young man was ever afterwards known as Penis Garrett.

Finals were approaching. Naturally all the girls were praying they didn't get Mr Palmer in the Mids and Gynae Orals. There were two ways you could qualify as a doctor. You could take Finals through the Conjoint Board of the Royal Colleges or through the London MB, BS exam. It was usual to try the Conjoint exams first, because these you could take in parts, which, if you failed, you could take again after further study. They were regarded as a form of rehearsal for the MB, BS, which you had to sit for throughout a whole week or more, being tested over the whole syllabus in written and in oral exams.

I decided to have a go at the Conjoint Surgery as well as Midwifery and Gynaecology. Unfortunately my monthly period was eight days late when the time came to sit the Mids and Gynae paper. I had been frantic with anxiety. On the morning of the written exam I began to feel very unpleasant pains. I was forced to stagger to my desk under the influence not only of violent dysmenorrhoea but of the aspirin I'd taken to control it. Though it was a relief to know I wasn't pregnant, and a blessing that I didn't have to face Mr Palmer in the Orals, it was hardly surprising that I failed that exam. I later learned that I'd failed in Surgery as well, so I certainly wasn't ready to qualify.

Joanie met Sir Seymour Hicks at a cocktail party given for the theatrical profession and the Press in the autumn of 1937. He had been knighted for his services to the Stage. He was well over sixty by the time he was acting in, and also producing the comedy *It's You I Want* at the Cambridge Theatre, but was still very spry and youthful looking. While extracting a few words from him for her gossip column, Joanie told him of her acting in amateur dramatics at King's, and of her longing to go on the professional stage. He was kind to her, and though no doubt he must have heard the same story from hundreds of other young girls, he scribbled down her name and address.

'I'm over the moon,' she told Nancy and me at breakfast next day. 'He's promised to try and get me a walk-on part. To give me a try, you know.'

Nancy and I were glad to see her so full of hope and happiness again.

A couple of weeks later, on a Saturday, well after midnight, when we were all in bed asleep in the flat, the phone rang. It was Seymour Hicks ringing to ask Joanie to join him at the London Casino for supper. She put on her glad rags and made up her face, rang for a taxi, and off she went. Next day she described for us the London Casino, the glamorous guests, the stage show, and Sir Seymour's charming manners. They had drunk champagne, and he'd told her there might be a walk-on part for her in his next production. She was of course thrilled by what was happening in her life.

During the next few months midnight call-ups to the London Casino became more frequent. Joanie began to look a bit bleary-eyed at breakfast, Nancy complained that the phone was spoiling her 'beauty sleep', and I was finding it not at all conducive to studying for Finals. Conversation with Joanie was minimal, and usually took place at breakfast. She was hardly ever in the flat in the evenings, which she spent dinner-dancing with one or other of her admirers, all invariably good-looking, as she would not consider any other sort. She regarded her young men as part of her pleasure activities. Seymour Hicks was an entirely different matter; he was a serious business proposition. But it never occurred to her that he might be looking for a *quid pro quo* of a non-professional sort for putting her on the stage. In spite of her outwardly sophisticated way of life, at this time she was really a very innocent, not to say sexually ignorant girl. She had of course years ago seen the nutcase exposing himself in a hedge on the Ridgway, but probably supposed this sort of thing happened only to madmen. When one of her boyfriends suddenly had an erection as she stood close to him, she noticed the movement in his trousers, and expressed concern that something, keys or wallet, had fallen out through a hole in his trousers' pocket! Sexual enlightenment dawned late for her.

In May 1938 *Money Talks* opened at the Lyceum. Seymour Hicks was producer, but there was no whisper of a walk-on part for Joanie. The play had a very short run, during which she faced a fact that she'd begun slowly to suspect, that he would not put her on the stage unless she was willing to go to bed with him.

'It's quite the expected thing to do,' she told us. '—If you want a job on the stage. But he's so old!'

She was rescued from this disappointment by a letter from Mary inviting her to spend a few months in Cairo, where, Mary assured her, she could get a job on the English language newspaper, and enjoy a holiday as well. There was a flourishing amateur dramatic society among the British in Cairo, Mary wrote, and a wonderful theatre to act in, and to sing in, as she herself had been doing. It was of course the Opera House built by the Khedive of Egypt in florid and red plush *belle époque* style to celebrate the opening of the Suez Canal. Festivities had to be postponed then, owing to the Franco-Prussian War. When the theatre did finally open it was to give the first performance of Verdi's *Aida*.

'I rang Mummy yesterday, during my lunch break,' Joanie said, 'and she's all for it. She even offered to pay my fare!'

It meant arriving in Egypt at the hottest time of the year, but Joanie didn't care. She bought some pretty dresses, light and cool, paid a goodbye visit to Mummy, now installed in her cottage in Paddock Wood, and gave in her notice to her editor. She sailed from Tilbury Docks, where Nancy and I saw her off. She was kicking the dust of London from her shoes. Hope springs eternal. She was sailing, if not to Byzantium, at least to fabulous Cairo where East meets West, to a new life and all sorts of romantic possibilities.

Nancy had nearly finished her course in *Cordon Bleu* Cuisine, so it was obvious we would have to give up the flat. Nancy was going home to Pop in Ireland, and I would have to find somewhere cheap to live and suitable for studying my textbooks.

Nancy's boyfriend, Pat Terry, was in the RAF. He arrived at the flat one evening with a bottle of champagne to celebrate Nancy's birthday, but although John and I were there, Nancy was not. Perhaps she had been delayed by putting some finishing touches to a dish at her posh school of cookery, perhaps she'd missed a bus. He decided to open the bottle anyway, and share a glass or two with us to drink her health. By the time Nancy got back the bottle was empty. However, she forgave him. She was the forgiving sort.

We gave a party before we left the flat. It was a very crowded and noisy affair. We served sausages on sticks and savoury titbits prepared by Nancy; some of the guests spilled beer over themselves and the parquet floor, and someone left a lighted cigarette on the shiny black surface of the grand piano, burning a hollow into the wood, but Ethiraj played his Jazz steadily through all the noise and smoke.

I found a bedsit in Camberwell at thirteen shillings a week. It contained a brass bedstead, a small table at the window, a gas fire, and a gas ring on which I boiled a kettle for my breakfast tea. The evenings I spent in Herne Hill at John's and Selwyn's house, where I was left in peace with my books and lecture notes to revise and learn for imminent exams, while John or Selwyn took turns to cook supper for us all.

The summer of 1938 was for me a time of intense concentration on work against a background of increasing unease about what was going on in Hitler's Germany; but John and I did enjoy a few visits to the theatre. We saw a fifteen-year-old Margot Fonteyn dance in *Façade* at Sadlers' Wells, and the not-yet-famous Laurence Olivier as Hamlet at the old Old Vic not far from Waterloo Station.

We also saw an electrifying performance of Eugene O'Neill's *Mourning Becomes Electra* at the new Westminster Theatre.

I intended qualifying by re-taking the surgical sections of the Finals of the Conjoint Board of the Royal Colleges of Physicians and Surgeons in October, followed in November by the London University MB, BS. It would be an examination marathon.

People were talking about the possibility of war. Hitler had for years been persuading Germans to sacrifice butter for guns because they were surrounded by enemies, so Germany was now armed to the teeth, whereas Britain, owing to our reluctance to fight another war, recently underlined by the so-called Peace Pledge, to which I had added a signature, was totally unprepared for a major European conflict. All this was to me background noise to which I paid little attention. I was not a political animal. I was too focused on my exams, my relationship with John, my moral problems and our quarrels over them to be fully aware of what was happening in Europe; but by September even I had to face the fact that Hitler was threatening to 'reclaim' the Sudetenland, in other words to invade Czechoslovakia and seize that part of it where a large number of people of German origin were living. This was awkward for us because we had a treaty with France to protect Czechoslovakia against aggression. I began to listen to the wireless news broadcasts. People were saying that should we be involved in war Hitler could bomb London with devastating destruction, so powerful was his airforce, so meagre were our defences. Some people were already filling sandbags and putting them around windows to protect them. Air-raid trenches were dug in Hyde Park, and children were evacuated to safer places outside the capital. I began to think about the possibility of death.

Personal annihilation might be swift, but what of eternal damnation? I was in mortal sin, and in fear of hell, and I trembled. I had very little sleep that week, which did nothing to strengthen my nerve; but I was still a thinking animal. I was no saint, that I knew for sure, but I was also aware that my intentions were good, and perhaps even rather more altruistic than those of many others around me. My sin arose out of love, not out of malice. John and I intended marrying and having a family when we both qualified. We had made our contract to each other after all, though we had not signed it before a Registrar of Births, Deaths, and Marriages, nor had it sanctified by the Catholic sacrament. Was I then reducing God to a pernickety bureaucrat who would throw me into everlasting torment simply for not possessing the correct passport to heaven? If this was to be my fate most of the ordinary people I knew would surely share it. It must be a very dour God indeed who sent the greater part of His human creation into everlasting punishment. Where then was the kind Father who sent His only-begotten Son to save us?

The absurdity of the concept struck me suddenly and with such force that I became calm; and although I realised this revelation that had removed a brick in the building of my faith would cause other dogmas in my system of belief to totter, I experienced a wonderful feeling of relief and freedom. Whatever happened now in Munich I could face with some degree of equanimity.

When Neville Chamberlain's unremarkable voice announced on the wireless on 29th September that in Munich he had made 'peace for our time', and newspaper photos showed him waving a piece of paper, the treaty, the 'Accord' signed by Hitler, euphoria seized hold of the nation. The Archbishop of Canterbury called for a day of public thanksgiving; Chamberlain appeared with the king on the balcony of Buckingham Palace to the ecstatic cheers of thousands; only the voice of Churchill growled that Britain had sustained a total defeat. In fact Chamberlain and Daladier had made a pact with Hitler, virtually giving him the go-ahead to march into Czechoslovakia, pocketing the modern Skoda Arms factory in his path, while they looked the other way. Whatever historians may now say about this pusillanimous act, Chamberlain did give the Allies another year in which to re-arm. I don't think many of us believed in that peace-paper for long. We knew that, on the contrary, there was going to be war in our time. What we didn't know was when.

In Paris, during the week of the Munich Crisis, there was panic, and thousands fled to the country fearing death from the air. Simone de Beauvoir, who was not exactly politically unconscious, on learning of the Munich paper peace, describes how 'that evening a great wave of rejoicing swept over Paris; people sang and laughed together, lovers clung together...', admitting that she 'was delighted, and felt not the slightest pang of conscience at my reaction. I felt I had escaped death, now and forever.'[3]

This reprieve did spur me through my last three weeks of revision. In mid-November I passed all my exams in company with the two other girls who had arrived at KCH at the same time as I had. When we saw our numbers were among those passed we were delirious with joy. I turned away from the wall on which hung the lists of the lucky ones, and threw my arms round anyone near enough to be embraced and kissed. The hall echoed with laughter and happy young voices congratulating each other on success.

## References – Chapter Eleven

1 Windsor, Duchess of, *The Heart has its Reasons*, Michael Joseph, 1956.

2 Lord Halifax in a letter to 'Baba', Lady Alexandra Metcalfe, née Curzon (De Courcy, Anne, *The Viceroy's Daughters*, Weidenfeld and Nicholson, 2000.

3 Horne, Alistair, *To Lose a Battle*, France 1940, Macmillan, 1969.

## 12

The Kellys had invited me to spend Christmas with them in Dalkey, just outside Dublin. Mummy was to spend it in her new home with Daphne, Pat and Lulu, my John intended staying in his mother's cottage in Four Mile Bridge, using some of the holiday to study, since his Cambridge Finals were yet to come, and some of it in wandering along the shore with a gun to shoot a rabbit or two, and perhaps a wild duck for the pot. So he waved me goodbye at Holyhead as I boarded the ferry for Dun Laoghaire.

There was to be a fancy-dress ball at Lara House Hotel on St Stephen's Night (the Irish equivalent of our Boxing Day), and Biddy had made up her mind to go dressed as a Hawaiian girl. We spent the best part of a day chasing all over Dublin in the car Pop had given her, from hardware shops to gardening emporiums, trying to buy enough raffia to make her skirt. She also hired a hideous wig of long black hair. Nancy had to make only minimal changes in her appearance with the aid of the black lace *mantilla* and fan needed by a Spanish lady, and I, tying up my hair in a pony-tail and putting on a tutu, imagined myself a Degas dancer.

Pop drove us through a rhododendron-lined driveway and the scent of peat-smoke fires to the hotel. The place was crowded and noisy with merriment, there were ample supplies of food and drink, and there were plenty of partners for us to dance with.

When dancing with an elegant eighteenth-century gent in a black velvet coat I asked him who he was. He replied, 'Lord Clonmel.' Thinking he must be some political or revolutionary figure in Irish history I asked innocently, 'Who was he?'

'Oh no,' he replied. '*I am* Lord Clonmel.' And he laughed. On which side of the fact / fantasy barrier I was standing I couldn't be sure.

Snow was falling as we drove home, and continued to fall all night. We woke next morning to a frozen world and no water in the taps. We had to take spades and buckets out to the garden to collect enough snow to fill the bath, and, as it melted, to use the water for tea and minimal washing. However, snow does not lie long in Ireland, so it was soon possible for Pop to drive me to Carlow to spend a couple of days with my Uncle Pat, which he very kindly did.

We drove in his smart yellow Chrysler, which turned heads as we sped through the village of Borris. At The Laurels Dr Pat met us on the doorstep, with Bridgie, his housekeeper, peeping over his shoulder to look at the posh car that was arousing such a lot of interest.

'Noree! It's great to see you! How you've grown! Is it a woman doctor you are now? Who'd have thought it? But I always knew you had it in you. Come in now, out of the cold. And come in, Mr Kelly, you're more than welcome.' But in spite of the greetings, the tea and sandwiches eaten and pleasantries exchanged in the parlour, the doctor's Irish hospitality had not obscured his shrewd eye. He remarked as he watched Pop drive off back to Dublin in his expensive car, 'That man's never done a day's work in his life.'

It was true. After his moment of glory as hero of the Troubles Pop worked only at being a gentleman of leisure. He handed over the management of his wealth to others, he played at learning Gaelic, he toyed with Irish history, he visited the library to exchange the learned books whose pages he might desultorily turn when he had nothing else to do. Often of a morning he drove into the city to take coffee and cakes at Bewlay's before returning home for lunch, and later a talk with the gardener. Sometimes he attended a play at the Abbey. He was a free spender, and his generosity made life easy for those around him. He was good-natured and made jokes, and children loved him; but of his precious assets of time and money he made little use.

He lived to a great age, and when he died Biddy spread an Irish flag over his bed, and for three days and nights she lay there, refusing to move. When at last she did move it was to spread the flag across his coffin. She found several men sympathetic towards, although not members of the IRA, who formed a guard of honour. They stood on either side of the grave, and fired a volley of shots over it as the body was lowered.

In Borris that evening we played cards with the girls from the Post Office, just as my brothers had done in times past. Bridgie brought in a tray of tea and ham sandwiches flavoured with finely sliced raw onions, which must have upset the doctor's guts, for that night he woke me with his groans and his voice coming across the corridor from the bedroom opposite mine: 'Noree! Did you have any of them onions?' I had. 'Well mind now, or they'll blow you up out of the bed!'

Dr Pat refused to take me to see Mount View, the old house and the family farm.

'I'd be ashamed for you to see it now,' he said. 'James has let it all go to wrack and ruin.' He blamed him for it, as had my father, who'd held him responsible, too, for the loss of three good mares he'd bought in 1917 and left in his care, hoping to breed from them when he left India. During a severe winter that followed they all died of neglect. Daddy never forgave James. That he was idle and wasted what money he had, I had heard. Was he a drinker too? I never knew.

'Remember me now to the Boys, won't you?' said Dr Pat when I said goodbye. 'And all the best for the New Year, Noree! Get yourself a good job, and don't be in too much of a hurry to get married!'

It was the last time I saw that kindest of men.

I spent the New Year sitting round the fire in Dalkey with Pop and his daughters, talking, laughing and drinking Irish whiskey that has that elusive yet inescapable whiff of peat smoke about it. We talked of the future, trying to imagine what was to come.

After the War, the sisters migrated to South Africa, Biddy to Johannesburg and a job in advertising, Nancy and Pat Terry, now married, to farmland twenty-five miles outside the city, and tried to grow peaches. They also learned about Apartheid when a neighbouring farmer branded with a red-hot iron the back of one of his labourers. The black worker had been accused of theft of his master's property; but there was no trial, and no appeal.

Nancy talked freely with the 'Boy' who worked for her in the house, so she was well aware of black rebellion brewing.

'When freedom comes will you kill me?' she asked.

His eyes widened with fright.

'Oh no! I no kill you! You nice lady. I go kill lady next door,' was his response.

Peach growing proved unsuccessful. And perhaps too many sundowners were drunk. Nancy decided she couldn't bring up children in a country with a moral climate such as she'd found. So they returned to Dublin to settle in Blackrock near Pop.

Biddy had been having a seven-year love affair with a Polish army officer, who would not marry her. He might or might not have been already married to a Polish wife, who might or might not be still alive. In all the disruption and confusion of post-war Poland it was impossible to find out; but seven years with an ambivalent lover proved enough for Biddy, so she too returned to Dublin and to Pop.

The last time I saw Biddy was when Pat and I travelled to Wexford, where she met us for the brief season of opera held there. All three of us were old and grey. We stayed in a comfortable hotel with an indoor swimming pool, a great luxury and pleasure for me; we dined on oysters with the local drink, Black Velvet: Guinness and Champagne. I preferred less of the black and more of the velvet, so I opted for champagne.

In the small theatre, built in the eighteenth century for the entertainment of officers of an occupying army, the foyer before the performance was crowded with merrymakers, all in evening dress, the ladies bejewelled and perfumed. Biddy pointed out to us the Dublin celebrities among them. As we took our seats one young woman in the row in front of us emitted such a cloud of the scent I recognised as 'Femme' that we were in no doubt as to her gender.

The works performed in Wexford are often the less well-known; that evening we saw Catalani's *La Wally*, in which the heroine had to make her way singing through veils of white muslin representing snowdrifts in the Austrian Alps. Afterwards we walked back to our hotel with hearts as soft and kind as the air of that Irish October night. Apart from the music and the heart-warming hospitality that Ireland extends to her guests, it was our three-way friendship, old and understood, its boundaries and our mutual foibles accepted, that made that meeting shine with happiness.

I had begun to speculate that Pat and Biddy might yet get married, but Biddy said, 'I like him as a friend; I don't want him as a lover.' And Pat said, 'It wouldn't work out, you know. All this English-Irish business…'

All these things were folded away in a future that could not be known. On the eve of January 1939 war loomed, vague, uncertain but menacing. Hitler would not strike till after the corn was cut and harvested, so before the bombs fell we had one more summer to look forward to. What would happen after that nobody knew.

After our turbulent two-year courtship, John and I agreed to separate for six months, he to concentrate on his Cambridge Finals, I to go to my first job far away in Egypt. One of two women doctors who ran the Lady Cromer Dispensary for Sick Children in the Boulac district of Cairo was expecting a baby; she wanted a locum to do her work during the last months and immediately after the birth. Mary had written to me to tell me of this opportunity, and I had applied for and got the job. About marriage John hesitated; he did not really want to be tied up for life, and I too realised that at this stage in our careers it would not be a sensible step to take. We agreed to regard ourselves as free and uncommitted to each other till we met again. So we parted, soberly and rather sadly, but still with hope, and I with excitement about travelling to the fabled city where East meets West. Time and events would test the strength of our love; circumstances would map the way we had to go after the War. Britain would emerge victorious but bankrupt, having sold so many of her assets to finance the fighting. We belonged to a generation that survived that struggle, holding strong beliefs in equality and justice, but our cities and factories had been shattered; there was still plenty of coal in the ground, but an impoverished nineteenth-century mining industry to dig it up. And we carried an enormous load of national debt. The great British Empire of the past would split into pieces, and the India my family had known and loved for so long would be a new independent nation.

# Bibliography

Ackroyd, Peter, *Dickens*, Sinclair Stevenson, 1990

Allen, Charles, *The Buddha and the Sahibs*, John Murray 2002

St Aubyn, Giles, *Queen Victoria: A Portrait*, Sinclair-Stevenson, 1991

Becher, Augusta, *Personal Reminiscences in India and Europe, 1830-1888*, Constable and Co, 1930

Bloch, Michael, *Wallis and Edward: Letters 1931-1937*, Weidenfeld and Nicholson, 1986

Coogan, Tim Pat, *Michael Collins: A Biography*, Arrow, 1991
de Courcy, Anne, *The Viceroy's Daughters*, Weidenfeld and Nicholson, 2000

Dalrymple, William, *White Mughals*, Flamingo, 2002.

Daniell, Alice Mabel, *Unpublished Diaries 1889-94*, and unpublished memoirs written in the 1960s

Daniell, Fanny Louise (*née* Prinsep), *Unpublished Diary 1850-80*

Dakers, Caroline, *The Holland Park Circle: Artists in Victorian Society*, Yale University Press, 1999

Davidar, David, *The House of Blue Mangoes*, Weidenfeld and Nicholson, 2002

Eden, Emily, *Up The Country: Letters Written to Her Sister from the Upper Provinces of India*, ed. Edward Thompson, Curzon P, 1978

Edwardes, Michael, *Red Year*, Sphere Books, 1975

Eliot, T S, *Collected Poems, 1909-1935*, Faber, 1958

Eraly, Abraham, *The Mughal Throne*, Penguin, India, 1997; Weidenfeld and Nicholson, 2003

Fraser, Antonia, *The Gunpowder Plot: Terror and Faith in 1605*, Weidenfeld & Nicholson, 1996.
*Marie Antoinette*, Weidenfeld & Nicholson, 2001

Gittings, Robert, *The Older Hardy*, Heinemann, 1978

Glendenning, Victoria, *Trollope*, Hutchinson, 1992

Godfrey, Rupert *(ed.), Letters from a Prince: Edward Prince of Wales to Mrs Freda Dudley Ward*, Little Brown & Co, 1998

Gordon, Lyndall, *T S Eliot: An Imperfect Life,* Vintage, 1998
*A Private Life of Henry James: Two Women and his Art*, Chatto & Windus, 1998

Hibbert, Christopher, *The Great Mutiny*, Allen Lane, 1978.

Hill, Brian, *Julia Margaret Cameron: Portrait of a Victorian Family*, Peter Owen, 1973

Holroyd, Michael, *Bernard Shaw*, Vintage, 1998

Horne, Alistair, *To Lose a Battle*, France 1940, Macmillan, 1969

James, Henry, *Portrait of a Lady*, OUP, 1947
*The Bostonians*, Amereon, 1976

Joyce, James, *Portrait of the Artist as a Young Man*, Jonathan Cape, 1968

Kajariwal, Om Prakash, *The Prinseps of India: A Personal Quest*, Indian Archives 1993, Vol XLII,
*The Asiatic Society of Bengal*, OUP, 1988

Kaye, M M, *Share of Summer*, Penguin, 1998

Lee, Hermione, *Virginia Woolf,* Vintage, 1997

du Maurier, George, *Trilby*, Osgood McIlvaine, 1895

Mayo, Katharine, *Mother India,* Jonathan Cape, 1927

McCarthy, Fiona, *William Morris*, Faber and Faber, 1995
*Eric Gill*, Faber and Faber, 1990

O'Toole, Jimmy, *Grange: The Path to the Present,* J O'Toole, 1987
*The Carlow Gentry: What Will The Neighbours Say?,* J O'Toole, 1993

Prinsep, Sir Henry Thoby, *Three Generations in India: 1880s*, unpublished memoir in India Office.

Prinsep, James, *Benares Illustrated*, originally published 1833; republished by Vishwavidyalaya Prakashan, 2002

Prinsep, Valentine C, *Glimpses of Imperial India*, 1879, Mittal, 1979

Proust, Marcel, *Remembrance of Things Past*, translated by Terence Kilmartin, Chatto and Windus, 1981

Rushdie, Salman, *The Moor's Last Sigh*, Jonathan Cape, 1995

Scott, Paul, *The Raj Quartet*, Harper Collins, 1978
   *Staying On*, Bookthrift, 1977

Trollope, Anthony, *Phineas Finn*, OUP, 1937

Watts, M S, *George Frederick Watts: The Annals of an Artist's Life*, Macmillan, 1912.

White, Antonia, *Frost in May*, Virago, 1994

Wild, Anthony, *The East India Company: Trade and Conquest from 1600*, Harper Collins Illustrated, 1999

Wilson, A N, *The Victorians*, Hutchinson, 2002

Windsor, Duchess of, *The Heart Has Its Reasons*, Michael Joseph, 1956

Windsor, Edward, Duke of: *A King's Story*, Cassells, 1951

Wise, Dorothy (*ed.*), *Diary of William Tayler, Footman, 1837*, Westminster City Archives, 1998

Woodham-Smith, Cecil, *The Great Hunger: Ireland, 1845-49*, Hamish Hamilton, 1987

Yeats-Brown, Francis, *Indian Pageant*, Eyre and Spottiswoode, 1944.

Ziegler, Philip (*ed.*), *Diaries of Lord Louis Mountbatten: Tours with the Prince of Wales 1920-1922*, Harper Collins, 1987